HALF A SECOND MORE

Half a Second More

The Meditation Guide for Brains That Won't Sit Still

by Andrew Hill, PhD

Peak Brain Press LLC
Los Angeles, California

2026

Copyright & Disclaimer

ISBN: 978-1-971402-04-8 (paperback)
eISBN: 978-1-971402-05-5 (epub)

Disclaimer: This book provides educational information about brain function, attention training, and mindfulness. It is written by a cognitive neuroscientist with clinical experience, not as a substitute for professional care. The practices described complement, but do not replace, therapy, medication, or neurofeedback. Consult qualified healthcare professionals before making changes to your care.

Stop and seek professional support if you experience: suicidal thoughts or self-harm urges; panic attacks that don't resolve; flashbacks or dissociative episodes; psychosis or loss of contact with reality; symptoms worsening across multiple sessions.

Crisis resources: **988** Suicide & Crisis Lifeline (call or text) | **911** for emergencies | **1-800-662-4357** SAMHSA | Crisis Text Line: text HOME to 741741

Phenotype names ("Grumpy Old Man," "Happy Little Kid," etc.) are affectionate clinical shorthand, not diagnoses. See Chapter 1 for the naming disclaimer. Neutral descriptors are provided throughout.

Client stories in this book are composites. Each is drawn from patterns seen repeatedly across similar cases, with details combined and changed so that no story describes an identifiable person. The brain patterns, practices, and outcomes are true to the clinical work. The people are not individuals you could find.

Dedication

For the kids who were too fast, too restless, too loud, too scattered, and never told it was wiring, not failure.

And for my parents, who gave me room to find my own way to quiet.

This is the book I would have wanted at fourteen. It is my offering to every dysregulated brain still looking for the door.

Acknowledgements

This book exists because 25,000 brains taught me what no textbook could.

To every client who handed me their brain map and their honest account of what had and hadn't worked: your patterns became the phenotypes. Your breakthroughs proved the matching works.

To the Peak Brain Institute team, for two and a half decades of clinical infrastructure. None of this is possible without you.

To the researchers whose work grounds this book: your findings gave me the authority to make clinical observations with confidence. Any errors in interpretation are mine.

To my family, for giving me room. Then, and now.

And to the readers who picked this up because meditation has already failed them at least twice: you were never bad at this. You had the wrong door.

Contents

towards a positivity bias

Sid observed that we are of types.
delusional, aversive, greedy.
never one define you. not that there is such a thing.

but we live and play with habits of want.
wanting more. wanting less. wanting solipsism.
roiling currents of craving. moving through moments
in reaction and action, shift happens.

but just have a private moment,
with that moment, for a moment.
apart from any non-moments clamoring.
they don't exist anyway.

sail as Theseus. shift happens
weather all weather, all storms of wanting.
the nots, be others, and mores.

simply have a moment, with your moment, for a moment.
or the non-moments will have you
but good news! you don't have a moment to lose.

Andrew Hill, PhD

STOP.

Do this now:

Breathe in for 4. Breathe out for 6.

Do that 10 times.

Each time your attention comes back:

Count it. That counts. That's a return, and you'll keep counting them in your Return Counter: a little more room between stimulus and snap, each time you come back.

If You're in Crisis Right Now

Panicking or heart racing? Start with the floor, not the breath. Feet flat, press down hard. Name five things you can see. If breathing helps, add it: in for 4, out for 6, three times. For some people breath focus makes panic worse, so if it does, stay with the floor and the room.

Some symptoms are not panic. New chest pain, fainting, severe shortness of breath, a racing heart that will not settle, weakness on one side, or the worst headache of your life. Do not assume those are meditation or anxiety. Call 911 or get to an emergency department.

Frozen, foggy, or can't think? Stand up. Walk ten steps. Count them. Name five things you can see. Come back when you're a little more here.

Dissociated: floaty, unreal, disconnected? Hold something cold. Feel it. Press your feet into the floor. Say your name out loud. Look around and name where you are. This usually passes with grounding. If it persists or you feel unsafe, call your provider, or call 988.

Crying, flooded, overwhelmed? Close the book. Hand on your chest. Breathe. Come back when you're ready. This book will be here.

None of the above, only here? Good. Keep reading.

The 90-Second Reset

The rest of the book names the parts. This is the move, no map required. Ninety seconds of gap-training, anywhere.

Step 1: Body (30 seconds) Both feet flat on the floor. Press down. Feel the floor: temperature, weight, pressure. Notice. That's it.

Step 2: Breath (30 seconds) In for 4. Out for 6. Three times. Don't try to feel anything. Count.

Step 3: Permission (30 seconds) Say silently: *I'm allowed to be here.* Notice what happens: softening, a skeptical eyebrow, nothing at all. All correct.

That was it. Ninety seconds.

If nothing has shifted after three rounds (about five minutes), stop and turn to the Decision Tree.

Every return widens the gap between trigger and reaction by fractions of a second. You're counting reps, not calm. That was half a second more. You built it in ninety seconds.

If something shifted, even slightly, that's a rep. If nothing shifted, the Decision Tree will find your practice.

Permission Practice

Say each phrase silently. Notice what it does in your body:

"I'm allowed to stop at any time."

"I'm allowed to do this imperfectly."

"Whatever my brain does in the next thirty seconds is fine."

That clench you just released: that was the rep.

Today's practice: ___ returns. Duration: ___ seconds.

Where to Go From Here

Ready to start? → Decision Tree (Chapter 2).

In crisis? → Chapter 16.

You came back. Log one return and you're done for today.

THE 90-SECOND RESET

Photograph this. Use it anywhere.

1. Feet on floor.

Press down. Feel the ground under you.

2. Three breaths.

In for 4 counts. Out for 6. That's it.

3. Say silently:

"I'm allowed to be here."

Do this once. If you feel worse after, see Chapter 16.

Seated or standing: if you feel floaty, sit first.

Count your returns when you're ready.

What's loudest right now?

Find this feeling. Go to that chapter. That's all you need to do.

MOVE	Frozen, can't make yourself start	→ **Ch. 4 Stabilizer**
	Impulsive, can't stop or slow down	→ **Ch. 4 Supervisor**
	Exhausted, foggy, falling asleep	→ **Ch. 5 Fog**
MOOD	Dread: "what's the point"	→ **Ch. 6 Grumpy**
	Bored, can't sustain interest	→ **Ch. 6 Happy Little Kid**
	"Don't tell me what to do"	→ **Ch. 6 Problem Child**
ORIENT	Can't close eyes, scanning the room	→ **Ch. 7 Lifeguard**
	"Am I doing this right?" loops	→ **Ch. 7 CEO**
SENSE	Body too loud, sensory overwhelm	→ **Ch. 8 Princess**
	Voices or tone feel threatening	→ **Ch. 8 Bard**
	Inner narrator won't stop	→ **Ch. 9 Interpreter**
PROCESS	Everything too fast, or too slow	→ **Ch. 10 Timekeeper**
	Multiple patterns? Start with the loudest.	→ **Ch. 11 Stacks**
	Still unsure? Start here:	**Start walking. Ch. 4.**

Your mind will wander. Come back.

DON'T KNOW WHAT TO DO? DO THIS.

Feet on floor. In for 4, out for 6. Say silently: *"I'm allowed to be here."*

WHEN YOU'RE READY FOR MORE:

1. Find your practice.

What's loudest right now? Use the Decision Tree (previous page). Still unsure? Start walking. Chapter 4.

2. Do it.

Three minutes. Twice a day.
Your mind will wander. Come back. That's the whole practice.

3. All you're doing is coming back.

Count returns if it helps, or don't. Coming back is what matters. A busy mind just means more chances to come back.

Your mind will wander. Come back. Count the return.

You're back in the practice.

How to Use This Book

Count returns, not minutes. Every practice trains one thing: more space between what happens and what you do next.

If meditation has never worked for you, this book was written for your brain. The gap and the return are the spine; everything else routes to your version of the work.

If You Feel Something Right Now

Photograph this table. Left column: what you're feeling. Right column: where to go.

If you feel...	Do this	Chapter
Can't start anything	Walk 10 mindful steps	**Ch. 4**
No energy, foggy	Eyes-open standing awareness	**Ch. 5**
Dread, "what's the point"	Vagal Toning: 4 in, 6 out, 3 min	**Ch. 6**
Scanning for threat	Grounding: "Is this now?"	**Ch. 7**
Body too loud	Sensory Sanctuary	**Ch. 8**
Narrator won't stop	Mantra Redirect	**Ch. 9**
Everything too fast	Rapid Noting	**Ch. 10**
Worse after meditating	Stop. Ground.	**Ch. 16**
Don't know where to start	Decision Tree	**Ch. 2**
Need a reset now	90-Second Reset	**STOP section**

If the table answered your question, go now.

The Words This Book Uses

If you've never been taught to meditate, a handful of terms show up in every chapter. They are plainer than they sound.

Anchor. The one thing you put your attention on, on purpose. A breath at the upper lip. The pressure of your feet on the floor. A word repeated silently. When your mind leaves, the anchor is what you come back to. Different brains do best with different anchors, which is most of what Part II sorts out.

Noting (or labeling). Naming what just happened in one word, then letting it go. The mind drifts to a worry; you note "thinking" and return to the anchor. No analysis, no story. The word is a tap on the shoulder, not a sentence.

Body scan. Moving attention slowly through the body, one region at a time, feet to head or head to feet, feeling whatever is there. Not relaxing it, not fixing it. Just feeling it and moving on.

Open monitoring. Letting attention rest on whatever arises (a sound, a sensation, a thought) without chasing it. This is the advanced setting. If it feels like too much early on, it is. Start with an anchor.

You will see each of these again, with step-by-step instructions, in the chapter that fits your brain.

If You Know Your Pattern

ADHD-heavy: Ch. 4, 5, 6, 10, 12, 14 **Anxiety-heavy:** Ch. 6, 7, 9, 12, 16 **Trauma-sensitive:** Ch. 6, 7, 8, 12, 15, 16 **Autistic/sensory:** Ch. 6, 7, 8, 12 **Anger/impulse:** Ch. 4, 6, 7, 8, 15 **Burnout/fatigue:** Ch. 4, 5, 6, 13, 15

Never-Read Mode

You don't have to read this book front to back. The practice cards are at the start of Part II.

Open to your practice card. Do the Entry Move. Count returns. Close the book.

That's the loop. The rest is optional depth.

One rule, regardless of path: Emergency Mode first. Ninety seconds. Your body gets there before your brain does.

What This Book Does (and Doesn't)

This book is for: when your brain is dysregulated: when you cannot focus, calm, or act. Seconds to minutes. Acute regulation.

This book is not for: sleep architecture, schedule design, long-term habit systems, or fine-tuning circadian timing. Those belong elsewhere.

Here's the boundary: if you need this book all day, every day, the problem is cadence, not attention.

This book handles acute dysregulation. *Action Cadence* (Peak Brain Press) handles schedule and cadence when you're crashing all day.

Where This Book Sits

Peak Brain Press has published five books sharing the same underlying anatomy: the phenotype system, the five regulation systems, and the clinical position that brains run different programs, not broken ones. *Half a Second More* is the practice book in that lineup.

What this book covers

Half a Second More is a practice manual. Its job is to take the twelve phenotypes and route each of them to the specific meditation practice matching the circuits running loudest. Chapter 2 is the routing tool. Part II is the practice library. Part III is the mechanism layer. Part IV is the program. All of this aims at one result: a working practice habit, matched to your nervous system.

The twelve phenotypes in this book are the full catalog set. The other books in the series use subsets or mappings specific to their subject.

The other books, briefly

Gifted & Tortured (Hill & McCann) covers the same twelve phenotypes as this book, but from the temperament side: what it looks like to live with a brain running hot or loud or fast when no particular trauma drives it. That book explains the phenotype. This book trains it.

Your Brain on Trauma covers nine of the twelve phenotypes, shaped by the particular way trauma configures circuits over time (the motor and timing patterns, Stabilizer, Supervisor, and Timekeeper, stay here in the practice book). It extends the borrowed-versus-built distinction, introduced in Chapter 16 of this book, into trauma-shaped regulation patterns: what it means to borrow calm through substances, relationships, or compulsive behaviors rather than build it. If the phenotype chapter you're reading lands differently than expected, and your history is clinical or traumatic, that book has the trauma-shaped version.

Borrowed Peace is the book for the things you reach for: alcohol, cannabis, stimulants, the phone, food, work, and the rest. It treats substance use and behavioral compulsion as intelligent self-medication, not moral failure: your nervous system borrowed calm, focus, sleep, or distance from pain because it had not yet built those states on its own. Its spine is the same borrowed-versus-built distinction this book introduces in Chapter 16, carried onto harder terrain and organized through a five-pattern map of what a given nervous system tends to reach for, a frame that overlaps with the twelve phenotypes without being identical to them. It is moderation-friendly and abstinence-respectful, skills before identity. If meditation keeps losing to something faster and easier that is doing the regulating for you, that book names the trade and shows what building actually costs.

Action Cadence covers chronobiology and the regulation of attention across the day, week, and sleep cycle. The two books run on one timing thesis from opposite ends of the spectrum: this book works at the fastest scale, the half-second between stimulus and response, the moment-to-moment regulation; *Action Cadence* works at the slow scales, from hours to decades, the daily and weekly arc and the long one. Chapter 13 here connects meditation to circadian rhythm at the oscillatory level; *Action Cadence* goes deeper on that territory.

A note on what this book does not engage

This book uses autonomic-state language (vagal tone, arousal, sympathetic activity), terms with measurable correlates in heart rate variability research (Kirk & Axelsen, 2020), while leaving aside the contested anatomy of polyvagal theory. The five regulation systems in Chapter 2 are based on cortical circuit mapping from QEEG work, not the ventral-dorsal-sympathetic ladder. If you want the polyvagal critique and an alternative framing, see *Your Brain on Trauma*, Chapter 15.

The borrowed-versus-built frame

The borrowed-versus-built distinction appears in Chapter 16 of this book, in the medication context. A borrowed state is what chemistry produces: fast, reliable, and temporary. A built state is what practice develops: slow, reliable, and durable. Contemplative training research suggests the built kind can persist between sessions as trait-level regulation (Lutz et al., 2008). This book is about building. Every other book in the series using this distinction is extending something originating here.

The phenotype, the cascade, and the Return Counter run through all five books because they describe how nervous systems work: distributed across partially independent circuits, as lesion studies confirm (Koenigs & Grafman, 2009). Each book finds a different use for the same map.

This one shows you how to train on it.

What I Believe

Your nervous system runs configurations it built from the conditions you were given. Those configurations are not who you are; they are patterns you can train. The training happens one return at a time. Every time your attention wanders and you bring it back, that is one rep, and the rep is the unit of practice.

Most meditation fails because it assumes the wrong brain. Yours works differently. Most do. Match the practice to your configuration. Count returns. Everything else compounds from there.

The framework does not promise transformation. It promises a wider gap between what happens and what you do about it: half a second more room to choose, accumulated over years until the room is just how you live.

The framework's last job is to make itself unnecessary.

Ch 1: The "Can't Meditate" Paradox

Let me describe a scene I've witnessed a thousand times.

Someone sits down to meditate. They've downloaded the app, read the article, maybe bought the cushion: the expensive buckwheat one, because if you're going to commit, you might as well commit. They close their eyes. They try to focus on the breath.

Within ten seconds, sometimes three, their mind has bolted. It's rehearsing a conversation from Tuesday. It's composing an email. It's replaying that thing they said at the meeting that might have been weird but probably wasn't but *what if it was*. It's doing anything except resting on the breath.

They notice the wandering, feel a flash of frustration, and haul attention back. It wanders again. And again. The timer says eight minutes left. It feels like an hour.

They open their eyes feeling worse than when they started, more agitated, more self-critical, more convinced of what they already suspected: *I can't meditate. My brain is too broken for this.*

Except everything that just happened was meditation. The wandering, the noticing, the haul back to the breath: that cycle is the practice itself. The wandering is the structure. Every time the mind bolts, it leaves another return for you to make.

It doesn't feel that way. It can feel like drowning in shallow water while someone on the shore calls out to relax. The advice from the shore isn't wrong about swimming. It just doesn't fit your nervous system.

Most meditation fails because it assumes the wrong brain. If yours works differently, and most do, the instructions misfire. The problem is the mismatch.

1.1 You weren't failing. You were training.

moving through moments
in reaction and action, shift happens.
but just have a private moment,
with that moment, for a moment.

Andrew Hill, PhD

Everything in Part I rests on one fact: the gap between stimulus and response can be trained. Each time your attention wanders and you bring it back, you have done one repetition. That moment of catching and redirecting is visible on fMRI (Hasenkamp et al., 2012), and it is the whole unit of practice.

Think of the gym. You don't go and "be strong." You go and lift something heavy. You feel weak the whole time you're there. The strength shows up later, outside the gym, when you're carrying groceries up three flights.

Meditation works the same way. The distraction is the opportunity. A busy session where you kept returning is still a real session. A calm session where you returned twice is also a real session. Your wiring is not the obstacle you thought it was.

You have been doing this for years without a number to count it by. Chapter 3 gives you the number.

Progress doesn't look like calm. It looks like a half-second pause before you answer the email. A moment when you catch your jaw clenched and let it open. A small gap where there used to be none. This book widens that gap, one return at a time.

1.2 A field manual, not a religion

I run a neurofeedback clinic. Twenty-five years, around 25,000 QEEG brain maps. Most of my clients have tried meditation by the time they walk in. Many have stopped because it wasn't working. From my side I see the cortex of someone trying and the brain map of someone who's been at it long enough for it to change. From that vantage I can

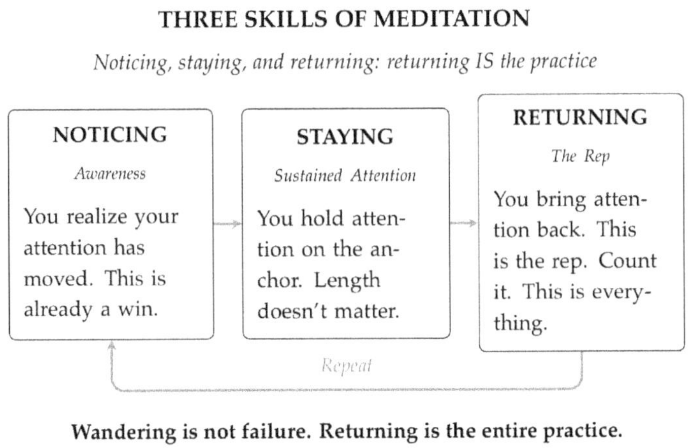

Figure 1.1: Three Skills of Meditation

tell you what tends to break, what tends to help, and which kinds of brains find which kinds of practice impossible.

I'm not a meditation teacher in the daily-practice sense. I support meditation practice in my clinic, encourage it, teach the skills. The daily return to the cushion is yours to do. My job is to point you at the practice that fits your nervous system and stay out of the way of the rest.

My working view of meditation, the one this book is built on, runs like this. Meditation is a practice of regularity, of learning to anchor your mind, slowly, on something. Guided meditation, the kind you do with an app or a recording, borrows someone else's attention to steady yours. That is a real practice, and for many brains it is the one that works. It does train something slightly different from unguided sitting, where you steer your own attention with minimal support and find it wobbling under you. The wobble is the point. The wobble is how you learn.

The other thing meditation does is anchor voluntary attention to a specific circuit. You choose what to attend to, on purpose, right now. A breath anchor works the interoceptive and respiratory circuits. A mantra anchor works the language axis. A movement anchor engages the motor system. Different anchor, different circuit, different regulation: neuroimaging meta-analyses find partially distinct network engagement across meditation styles (Fox et al., 2016). That's why phenotype-matched practice isn't a marketing frame: the anchor decides which part of you gets the practice. The practice shape is the same across all of them; the anchor determines the target.

The evidence base for meditation is real but moderate. Goyal et al.'s 2014 meta-analysis found moderate effects on anxiety, depression, and pain; the same analysis found only low-quality evidence for stress. Not miraculous, not nothing. Chapter 12 has the full evidence, including the studies that didn't find what the marketing promised. Treat the book the same way. If a tool works, keep it. If it doesn't, that's information. Adjust. If a practice makes things worse, Chapter 16 explains why and what to do.

One distinction before we go further. This book is running three separate bets, and they are worth naming apart from each other.

The first is a science bet: that matched practice produces larger or more durable regulation gains than unmatched practice for a given brain type. The trial data for that bet does not yet exist.

The second is a harm claim: that some standard practices are not merely ineffective but actively wrong for some brains, producing flooding, escalation, or dropout above the population average. That claim is supported by Lindahl et al. (2017) and Farias et al. (2020) on adverse effects, and by twenty-five years of watching brains in my clinic.

The third is an engineering claim: that routing you to a phenotype-matched practice from the start produces better subjective fit, lower dropout, and a faster path to a working habit, whether or not the twelve-month outcomes differ from a generic protocol.

The engineering claim is the one I am most confident in. The science bet is the one I am placing. The harm claim is the one that makes

Chapter 16 necessary. Know which one you're reading in any given chapter.

One caveat before we go further. The phenotype framework in this book is a clinical model based on twenty-five years of neurofeedback work and 25,000+ QEEG brain maps. It's supported by the underlying neuroscience but it has not been tested in randomized trials. Use it as a starting point for self-experiment, not as a diagnostic tool. The patterns are real. The matching of patterns to practices is well-grounded clinical judgment. The RCT evidence is still coming.

> **Already know your pattern?** Go straight to the Decision Tree (Chapter 2). It will route you to your practice. Come back here when you want to understand why.

1.3 Twelve ways your brain says "wrong practice"

Scan the list. Find yourself. Each description points to the chapter that fixes it.

If you recognize yourself immediately, skip to Chapter 2. The list will still be here.

1. "I can't make myself start." *You intend to practice. The cushion is right there. And then you just... don't.* This is the **Stabilizer**: your motor initiation circuit is misfiring. The gap between intention and action is a gearbox that won't engage first gear. *(Chapter 4)*

2. "I sit down and I'm gone in ninety seconds." *Eyes close, body settles, asleep.* This is the **Fog**: your brain defaults to low arousal the moment external stimulation drops. Sitting still with eyes closed is the wrong entry point for this brain. *(Chapter 5)*

3. "What's the point? This won't work anyway." *Before you even sit down, the dread arrives. Not anxiety, something flatter.* This is the **Grumpy Old Man**: your right frontal withdrawal circuit pre-screens every experience for probable reward, and pre-rejects anything that looks effortful. *(Chapter 6)*

4. "Am I doing this right? I can't stop checking." *You're not meditating. You're auditing the meditation.* This is the **CEO**: your anterior cingulate locked in conflict-monitoring mode, looking for errors in a process that has no errors. *(Chapter 7)*

5. "My narrator won't shut up." *You're not thinking about the meditation. You're describing it to yourself in real time.* This is the **Interpreter**: a continuous verbal loop running on the left language axis. You can't "let thoughts go" because the thought generator is the thing you're trying to let go of. *(Chapter 9)*

And seven more patterns, each with its own circuit, practice, and chapter:

What you feel	Phenotype	Chapter
Flat, no spark, nothing pulls	**Happy Little Kid**	6
"Don't tell me what to do"	**Problem Child**	6
Can't close eyes, not safe	**Lifeguard**	7
Everything too loud, body screaming	**Princess & the Pea**	8
Instructor's voice sounds angry	**Bard**	8
Everything too fast or too slow	**Timekeeper**	10
All of the above	**Custom Stacks**	11

Ready to start? Skip to Chapter 2; the Decision Tree will route you in two minutes.

1.4 The complaint is the map

Each "I can't meditate" complaint names a place where your nervous system loses the gap.

"Can't sit still" tells you the motor system closes the space before you begin. "Fall asleep" points to arousal powering down. "Everything feels threatening" means threat-scanning is consuming the space. "Narrator won't stop" means verbal churn fills the gap before you can use it.

Different circuits, different failures, different practices. You don't have a brain map yet, but you have your lived experience, and that's the translation key. Match the practice to the circuit. Part II does exactly that.

Try one breath right now: in through your nose, out through your mouth. Notice the air crossing your upper lip. That's it. You noticed something on purpose. One breath, one return. We call it the One-Breath Return, and it's the smallest practice in this book.

1.5 Vignette: The attorney who couldn't sit

Trial attorney, early thirties, someone whose entire career depended on reading a room fast and staying two moves ahead. She'd done three meditation retreats, the expensive kind. Each time she left feeling more anxious and more certain she was broken. After the third, she cried in the parking lot. The tears were defeat.

Her brain map showed three loud patterns. Her internal clock ran about 20% above average, a fast Timekeeper. She had a strong CEO locked in evaluation mode. Her right-frontal Grumpy was loud enough to pre-appraise nearly every effortful experience as probably not worth the energy.

The standard instructions she'd been given (slow down, let go, observe without judgment) were fighting all three dominant circuits simultaneously. The mismatch was the problem. Her brain was doing fine.

We started with rapid noting: quick rhythmic labeling at the speed her brain runs. *Thinking. Hearing. Feeling.* No pauses, no judgment. Her Timekeeper had something fast enough to track. Her CEO had a structured task to work. Her Grumpy didn't have the half-second it needed to appraise.

First session: ninety-two returns in three minutes. She looked up afterward and said it was the first time meditation hadn't felt like punishment. Her jaw had unclenched. Half an inch of space between her earlobes and her shoulders. Small but real. That's what matching does.

1.6 Green / Yellow / Red: your safety signals

Before you practice anything in this book, learn three signals. They appear throughout every chapter. Think of them as your nervous system's feedback language, translated into something you can use.

GREEN, Keep Going
Mind wandering, boredom, restlessness, brief body sensations that settle. Normal. This is the practice working: wandering creates returns.

YELLOW, Modify
Anxiety rising and not settling, intrusive images, feeling floaty or disconnected. Open eyes, shorten the practice, switch to a body-based anchor.

RED, Stop and Ground
Panic that won't resolve, flashbacks, dissociation, suicidal thoughts, feeling worse across sessions. Stop. Use the 90-second reset. See Chapter 16.

Safety Signals. Green = proceed. Yellow = modify. Red = stop and ground.

If your mind is racing, put your feet on the floor and take one breath. If you can't sit still, stand up and walk. That isn't quitting. It's MOVE, the first step in the cascade you'll meet in Chapter 2. Knowing your limits is part of the practice. Chapter 16 has the full safety protocol.

1.7 Practice Lab: The Permission Practice

You may have already done this in "Do This First." Do it again. Repetition is how nervous systems learn.

This is the foundational practice because for many dysregulated brains the biggest barrier to meditation isn't technique. It's the clench: the anticipatory tension that says *this is going to be hard, I'm going to fail, I have to do it perfectly or not at all.*

The Permission Practice teaches your nervous system to approach the cushion at ease.

The Permission Practice (30 seconds)

Setup: Wherever you are. Any position. Eyes open or closed, your choice. There is no wrong way to sit for this. Parked car, couch, work bathroom because it's the only quiet place, all fine.

The practice:

Say silently to yourself: *I'm allowed to stop at any time.*

Notice what happens in your body. A softening in the chest? Shoulders dropping a fraction of an inch? A skeptical voice saying "yeah right"? Nothing at all? Whatever happens, notice it. Don't evaluate it.

Now say: *I'm allowed to do this imperfectly.*

Notice again. Some people feel relief here. Some people feel grief, the sudden recognition of how much pressure they've been carrying about doing things right. Both are fine. Neither is required.

Now say: *Whatever my brain does in the next thirty seconds is fine.*

Sit with that for a few breaths. When you're ready, stop.

When your mind says "this is stupid": Notice the thought. That's probably your Problem Child, your Grumpy, or your CEO doing their jobs. Nod at them and come back to the permission statement. The thought "this is stupid" and the practice of permission can coexist. They don't need to fight.

Closing: You just released a clench. That's a half-second more in the gap. If a thought arrived and you noticed it, label it: "thinking," "judging," "planning." One word, no analysis. That label is the Meaning Lever from Chapter 3, and the same noting practice you'll see again in Chapters 9, 10, and 12.

Today's practice: ___ returns. Duration: ___ seconds.

If your brain keeps "failing" at meditation, the next question is where it breaks. Chapter 2 maps the five regulation systems and hands you a Decision Tree that answers in two minutes. Then the training starts in Chapter 3.

Ch 2: Your Brain Has a Start Sequence: You've Been Skipping Steps

The tool comes first. The explanation can wait.

Look at the Decision Tree below. Find the feeling that's loudest right now. Follow the arrow to a chapter. That chapter has your practice. That's the entire job of this book reduced to one diagram.

If the tree already answered your question, go to that chapter now. What follows is explanation for when you want to understand why it works.

The unit of practice is still the return. What follows is routing: which practice belongs to your system today.

The routing page is below. Photograph it. Tape it somewhere. You'll be back.

2.1 The Regulation Cascade

Your brain regulates in layers. No single layer runs the whole show. Regulation is distributed across five systems, each gating a different function, each capable of failing independently. That five-system split is how I carve up the territory: a working map, drawn to show you where regulation fails and what to practice.

When everything is working, you don't notice the layers. But when regulation breaks down, it breaks down somewhere specific. When an earlier layer goes offline, the ones after it tend to follow. The gap between trigger and reaction closes at the point of failure.

Damage studies make this concrete. Damage one prefrontal subregion and depressive symptoms diminish; damage a neighboring subregion and they worsen (Koenigs & Grafman, 2009). Two areas inches apart, opposite effects on the same condition. One circuit shifts, the rest hold. That's distributed architecture.

Think of five orchestra sections, each reading different sheet music, tracking different time signatures. The brass swells for danger. The strings sustain mood. The woodwinds parse sensory input. The percussion sets tempo. They overlap and influence each other, but no conductor manages the full ensemble. The problems are too different and too fast for one baton.

When the brass section blows too loud, you don't retune the strings. You walk over to the brass and bring it down. The other sections were already fine.

This is why standard meditation instructions fail so many people. "Sit still, close your eyes, follow the breath" is one instruction aimed at one assumed problem: a noisy mind. But your Stabilizer can be offline; you can't initiate the sitting. Your Lifeguard can be running hot, and closing your eyes triggers a threat scan. Your Timekeeper can be racing; the breath count feels agonizingly slow while your internal clock hammers at double speed. That's three independent failures in three independent systems, and one blanket instruction addresses none of them. It's like handing a single aspirin to someone with a broken leg, a migraine, and food poisoning. The aspirin might touch the headache. It won't set the bone.

So "meditation doesn't work for me" is almost never true. The practice didn't match the failing system. Discipline won't close that gap. Precision will: find which system is offline, give it what it needs. Address downstream problems only after upstream ones are stable; otherwise you're mopping the floor while the faucet is running. You can mop all day. The floor stays wet.

The cascade maps where each system fails: MOVE first, then MOOD, then ORIENT, then SENSE, then PROCESS. The Decision Tree routes you to the practice that matches the failure: the specific one your nervous system needs today, based on which section of the orchestra is drowning out the rest. These are strong matches. Expect some iteration.

You don't have one broken brain. You have five systems, and yours fails in one place. That place is findable. The cascade below is the seating chart. Find which section is too loud. Every time you notice where it breaks and come back, you train control to hold at that exact point a fraction of a second longer.

I call it the Regulation Cascade:

MOVE → MOOD → ORIENT → SENSE → PROCESS

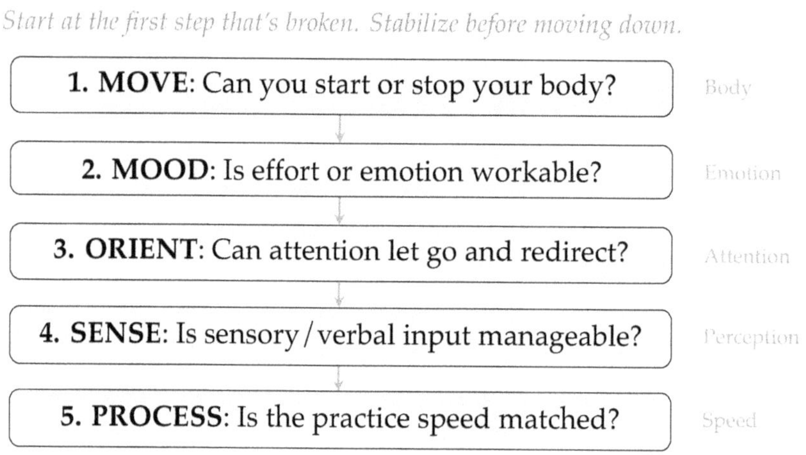

Figure 2.1: The Regulation Cascade. Stabilize from the body up: motor first, meaning last.

Those are the technical labels. What they mean:

2.1.1 The Rule

Start at the first step that's broken. The cascade tells you where your gap closes. Don't skip ahead to the thing that sounds most appealing. Find the first place where your system is failing, address it, and watch the downstream steps get easier.

If you're unsure where to start: start at MOVE. Get the body involved. Walk. Stand. Move for ninety seconds before you ask your brain to do anything subtle. It's almost never wrong.

One override: If your processing speed is sharply mismatched (everything feels like it's racing or everything feels like molasses), fix

Step	Label	Question	What blocks it
1	**MOVE**	Can you start or stop?	Can't initiate (Stabilizer) / can't inhibit (Supervisor)
2	**MOOD**	Is effort workable?	Dread (Grumpy) / flat affect (Happy Little Kid) / resistance (Problem Child)
3	**ORIENT**	Can attention let go and redirect?	Scanning threat (Lifeguard) / evaluation loop (CEO)
4	**SENSE**	Is sensory and verbal input manageable?	Sensory overload (Princess) / social tone parsing (Bard) / narrator loop (Interpreter)
5	**PROCESS**	Is the practice speed matched?	Too fast or too slow (Timekeeper)

tempo first (Chapter 10), then run the cascade from Step 1. Extreme speed mismatch makes every other step feel wrong because the *pace* is wrong, not the practice.

Within SENSE, there's an order too. SENSE holds two kinds of overload: sensory gain (the Princess and the Bard, step 4a) and the verbal loop (the Interpreter, step 4b). When both are loud, turn the sensory volume down before you try to quiet the narrator. The body has to stop shouting before the words will.

2.1.2 A note about pure phenotypes

I've done about 25,000 brain maps over the past twenty-five years. I've seen exactly zero brains that present as a single, pure phenotype. Most of you will have a top two or top three, with one loudest right now. The phenotype names are routing labels, not diagnoses. Your task is to identify which section of the orchestra is loudest today, address it, and re-route when the loudness shifts. This will shift. Tuesday's Lifeguard can be Thursday's Fog after two bad nights.

PHENOTYPE BRAIN MAP

12 patterns mapped to 10-20 EEG sites

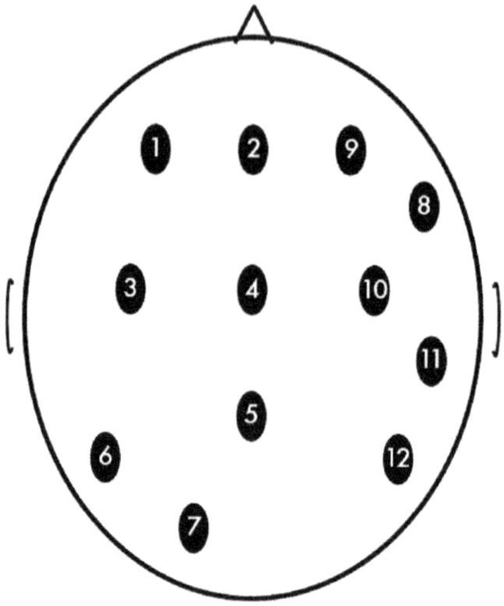

1. HAPPY LITTLE KID
   F3, Left prefrontal
2. CEO
   Fz, Midline frontal (ACC)
3. STABILIZER
   C3, Motor strip L
4. FOG
   Cz, Diffuse theta
5. LIFEGUARD
   Pz, Posterior cingulate
6. INTERPRETER
   T5, Left temporal (Wernicke)
7. TIMEKEEPER
   O1, Alpha peak
8. PROBLEM CHILD
   F8, Right lateral frontal
9. GRUMPY OLD MAN
   F4, Right prefrontal
10. SUPERVISOR
    C4, Motor strip R
11. BARD
    T4, Right temporal
12. PRINCESS
    T6, Right temporal-parietal

Figure 2.2: Phenotype Brain Map

2.2 The Quick Start Decision Tree

The phenotype framework builds on foundational work by Johnstone, Gunkelman, and Lunt (2005), who proposed that a limited set of recurring EEG profiles characterizes most of the population and could be used to guide clinical intervention. These are training profiles. They describe how your brain is running *right now*, not what you are permanently. The goal isn't to fix a phenotype. It's to notice which section is playing too loud today and bring it into balance.

What's loudest right now?

MOVE	Frozen, can't make yourself start	→ **Ch 4**
	Impulsive, can't stop or slow down	→ **Ch 4**
	Exhausted, foggy, falling asleep	→ **Ch 5**
MOOD	Dread, "what's the point"	→ **Ch 6**
	Flat affect, nothing pulls	→ **Ch 6**
	"Don't tell me what to do"	→ **Ch 6**
ORIENT	Can't close eyes, scanning room	→ **Ch 7**
	"Am I doing this right?" loops	→ **Ch 7**
SENSE	Body too loud, sensory overwhelm	→ **Ch 8**
	Voices or tones feel threatening	→ **Ch 8**
	Inner narrator won't stop	→ **Ch 9**
PROCESS	Everything too fast, or too slow	→ **Ch 10**
Multiple patterns? Loudest circuit first.		→ **Ch 11**
Still unsure? Start at MOVE. Start walking.		

The Decision Tree. Find your starting chapter based on what feels loudest right now.

Use the Decision Tree to find your starting chapter. If your top two are in different cascade steps, start with whichever is higher: MOVE before MOOD, MOOD before ORIENT, ORIENT before SENSE, SENSE before PROCESS.

Then: start with a 3-minute practice from your matched chapter. Twice daily. For 7 days. That's the whole program for now. Chapter 3 lays out the 7-Day Start Sequence in detail.

If you're still unsure: start at MOVE. Start with walking. Your body will give you more data than your analysis will.

If you know where to start, go now. The rest of this chapter will wait.

> **In a hurry?** If the Decision Tree above already pointed you somewhere, go there. Do the 3-minute entry practice from that chapter. Come back here when you want to understand the full cascade.

2.3 When the cascade isn't the whole story

The cascade covers self-regulation. Self-regulation isn't the only path to stability. There are two other modes worth naming up front.

Co-regulation. Borrowing calm from another nervous system. Sitting with someone steady. Hearing a voice that knows you. This is how mammalian nervous systems are built to work: social contact can dampen threat reactivity in the brain (Coan et al., 2006), and it's not cheating. If the cascade shows a system that's too broken to self-regulate today, you don't force it. You borrow stability from outside while the repair happens. Chapter 17 covers this in detail. The short version is on the Restart Protocol card in Part IV.

Environmental regulation. Changing the input rather than your response. Eyes-closed practice doesn't work? Try eyes open. Quiet room not happening? Try a noisy café where the noise is your anchor. Sensory overwhelm? Dim the room. This works because some failures are downstream of inputs your nervous system can't process today, and the cleanest fix is to fix the input. There's a name for the meta-version of this: the Broken Hand Problem. If you break your hand, you do not train the hand harder. You splint it, you use the other hand, and you let the tissue heal before you ask it to work again. A regulation system that is offline today gets the same treatment. Change the input, borrow from someone steady, drop the load, and come back to training when the part can carry it. Chapter 17 puts it to work in real settings.

If the cascade can't move you, one of these two can. Don't grind on self-regulation when co-regulation or environmental shift is the unblock.

2.4 A vignette: the engineer who was starting at Step 4

A software engineer. Systematic, thorough, motivated. A year of failed practice: Headspace twice, Calm, Sam Harris's app, a Zen center, a Vipassana weekend. Zero traction.

His brain map: hot Lifeguard (posterior cingulate running continuous threat scan) and sticky CEO (locked in evaluation mode). He'd been trying open monitoring, which is a Step 3 practice, while his body was tight with unprocessed activation and his Lifeguard was scanning for exits. Step 1 hadn't been addressed at all.

We moved him to MOVE. Walking meditation, eyes open, outdoors, simple counting. His shoulders softened within ninety seconds. Not dramatically, a quarter inch. Enough.

Two weeks later, he sat down for open monitoring. His CEO still evaluated. The Lifeguard wasn't screaming underneath it.

"I feel like I finally have a floor," he said. "Before, I was trying to build a house on quicksand."

Find the floor first. Everything else stacks on it.

2.5 Practice Lab: The Cascade Finder

Step 1: From the Decision Tree, your loudest current pattern: ______________

Step 2: Find it in the cascade. MOVE is Step 1 (highest). PROCESS is Step 5 (lowest). Whichever step is higher: that's where you start.

Step 3: Your starting chapter: ______________ Go there now.

You just found your starting point. Most people who think they can't meditate never get this far. You did. You now know *where* in the distributed system your gap closes. The next chapter gives you the tools to reopen it.

Today's practice: Cascade Finder. Duration: 2 minutes.

You know where you're stuck. Training that circuit is the next move: Chapter 3 lays out three skills, three levers, a scoreboard, and a seven-day plan.

Ch 3: Three Skills, Three Levers, and the Return Counter

Don't count minutes. Count returns.

That is the scoreboard, and it comes before any of the theory.

You're logging returns. Every return is one noticed moment, and the habit of noticing is how a skill gets built.

Every time your attention wanders and you bring it back, that's one return. Write the number down after every session. That number is the only thing that matters.

A session where your mind wandered a hundred times and you brought it back a hundred times is a hundred noticed moments. That's a good session.

The rest of this chapter explains why. Three skills, three levers, one seven-day plan. The scoreboard is what makes all of it stick.

The Return Counter Log *(photocopy or dog-ear this page)*

Day	Practice	Duration	Returns	Notes
1				
2				
3				
4				
5				
6				
7				

Week 1 total returns: ___ / Average per session: ___ / Trend (up / down / mixed): ___

BAD SESSION = GOOD SESSION

If your mind wandered constantly, you were annoyed and distracted, and nothing felt "meditative," look at your return count. If you returned to your anchor even twenty times in three minutes, that's twenty noticed moments. A session where you kept returning despite everything still counts, every single return.

The gym equivalent: the workout where the weights felt heavy and your form was ugly and everything was hard? You still trained that day. The return is the curl.

Count everything. Nothing is wasted.

The game is simple: count returns. The rest of this book exists to get you to a place where you can play the game.

Now: three skills that feed into that scoreboard.

3.1 What you're training

Every meditation practice in this book trains the same three core skills. Simple to name, hard to do, which is exactly why they work. You can already do one of them.

Noticing. The ability to catch what's happening in your mind or body. Observing what's there. "Oh, I'm thinking." "Oh, I drifted." "Oh, I've been composing an email for forty-five seconds." You're already doing it. The moment of "oh, I drifted" *is* noticing. You've been doing this your whole life. You didn't know it counted.

Staying. The ability to hold attention on something for a few seconds. Three seconds of feeling the air cross your upper lip. Three seconds of noticing the weight of your hands in your lap. That's staying. Dysregulated brains beat themselves up most about this one. "I can't focus for more than two seconds." Right. Two seconds is staying. Then the mind wanders, which creates the opportunity for the third skill. The trick isn't to stay longer. It's to stop punishing yourself for the natural rhythm: stay, wander, notice, return.

Returning. Noticing and staying set it up. The return is the comeback. Each time your mind wanders and you bring it back is one return: the moment your brain catches the wander and comes back (Hasenkamp et al., 2012). A calm session with two returns is two noticed opportunities. A chaotic session with eighty returns is eighty noticed opportunities. Both reflect useful practice, and a high count is not a higher dose.

The session that felt scattered, frustrated, and hard was still a real training session. You didn't have the right scoreboard.

> **Ready to practice?** You can skip ahead to the Three Levers section or go straight to the 7-Day Start Sequence at the end of this chapter. Come back for the Return Counter when you want to understand how to track your practice.

3.2 The Return Counter

The Return Counter is a philosophy shift. The session isn't about calm. It's about coming back. Calm shows up later, in the rest of your day, as a downstream effect of practice. The count is your engagement log. It is not a neural dose or an efficacy score. Eighty returns is not eighty units of brain change. It is eighty moments you noticed and came back. That is worth tracking.

Every session counts. A scattered session still counts. A calm session counts too. A dysregulated brain in three minutes might get sixty returns. A calmer brain might get fifteen. The count is not a score, and a high number is not a higher dose. Both reflect real practice.

The Return Counter is also your answer to the two loudest internal critics:

- The CEO's "am I doing this right?" → *If you returned, you're doing it right.*

- The Grumpy Old Man's "what's the point?" → *The point is forty-three returns today, up from thirty-eight yesterday. That's data.*

Why returning works (the paradox): Attention is built to move on. One example from the lab: in a spatial-orienting task, people are measurably slower to look back at a spot they just checked, a subsecond bias neuroscientists call inhibition of return (Posner & Cohen, 1984). That is one of several measures showing that attentional release is a real, observable process on a short timescale. In dysregulated brains, letting go of a stimulus is often the hard part. Attention keeps circling back to the threat, the worry, the loop. Each deliberate return practices coming back, and my clinical read is that the release gets easier with repetition. You come back so your brain can let go.

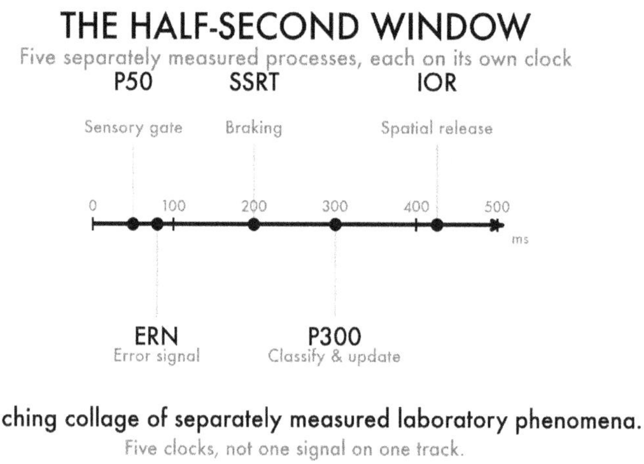

Figure 3.1: The Half-Second Window

Each of those is measured in its own laboratory task, so the diagram is a teaching collage of five separately measured processes, not one signal travelling a track. Gating, error detection, braking, classifying, and letting go all run inside roughly half a second. The moment where you noticed you were gone and came back lives in that same timescale.

How to count: Estimate after the session. "A lot / medium / a few" is enough to log. You can also use a tally counter (a clicker works well for Stabilizers and Timekeepers who like concrete feedback). If the counting becomes another thing to micromanage, stop counting. The number matters less than the habit of noticing. Feel like a failure? Count your returns. That number is your answer. Timer went off and you feel worse? If you returned at least once, you practiced. Feeling worse is separate information, and it belongs to your signals: check Green, Yellow, Red before the next session.

When you get interrupted: A kid walks in. The phone rings. The dog needs out. If your practice gets cut short, you didn't fail it. Coming back to the breath after the interruption, even if the session ends right there, is itself a return. Count it and stop. For caregivers and anyone who can't count on uninterrupted time, the interruption is not the enemy of practice. It is practice: the day handing you one more chance to return.

Today's practice: ___ returns. Duration: ___ seconds.

Every return is proof your brain can come back. You've been doing this your whole life. Now you have a scoreboard.

You can skip to the 7-Day Start Sequence now. The levers will be here when you want them.

3.3 Three Levers for Immediate Regulation

Skills widen the gap over time. Levers borrow width right now. The body lever shifts the hardware. The breath lever shifts the autonomic state. The meaning lever shifts the frame. All three widen the space between what's happening and what you do about it.

The skills are your gym work. The levers are your emergency toolkit in the car. Both are in play from day one.

3.3.1 Lever 1: Body (Bottom-Up)

Your body is the fastest on-ramp to your nervous system, faster than thoughts or breath.

Feel your feet on the floor. Not metaphorically: press them down and notice the pressure. Feel the weight of your hands in your lap. Notice the temperature of the air on your skin. Clench your fists tight for five seconds, then release them and notice what your hands feel like when they're open.

Body awareness bypasses the thinking mind. You don't have to understand anything. Feel something physical: your nervous system responds whether or not your prefrontal cortex is online. For a nervous system that's spinning or dissociating, feet on the floor is GPS data: "Oh. I'm *here*."

When to use it: When you're spinning, floating, or disconnected. When your mind is racing too fast for breath work. When closing your eyes makes things worse. The body lever is available anywhere. You're in a body even when your mind has left the building.

3.3.2 Lever 2: Breath (Bottom-Up to Bridge)

Your breath is the only autonomic function you can consciously control. Slowing it to around six breaths per minute engages the vagal brake, your nervous system's built-in decelerator. It's a hydraulic lever, not a state of mind.

The protocol: Breathe in for 4 counts through your nose. Out for 6 counts. Three to five cycles. Don't try to relax. Count. The physiology handles the rest.

Rescue breath (when counting is out of reach): Two quick inhales through the nose, one long exhale through the mouth. No counting. Three sighs, fifteen seconds (Balban et al., 2023).

When to use it: When your system is running hot. Counted breath (4:6) when you can count. Rescue breath when you can't.

3.3.3 Lever 3: Meaning (Top-Down)

The meaning lever is a cognitive reframe: a single thought or phrase that changes how you relate to what you're experiencing. Affect labeling research shows naming a state can dampen amygdala reactivity while engaging prefrontal control (Lieberman et al., 2007).

"I'm allowed to stop." "This is practice, not a test." "That thought is my Grumpy Old Man, not me." "Whatever my brain does in the next minute is fine." "Busy mind. Still here."

Each creates a micro-gap between you and your experience. Instead of *being* anxious, you're *noticing* anxiety and naming it. Instead of *being* a failure, you're *observing* a thought about failure and choosing to reframe it. That gap, half a second at most, is what this entire book trains.

When to use it: When the other two levers are at least partially online and you need to shift from reactive to intentional. Name the phenotype ("that's my CEO") to create enough distance to choose a different response.

3.3.4 The order matters: body first, breath second, meaning third

You can't think your way out of physiology. Body first: feel the floor, feel your hands. Breath second: slow, counted. Meaning third: name it, reframe it. Always in that order. The Part II chapters tell you which direction to enter from for your specific phenotype.

3.4 The Stop Signal

Before you open your phenotype chapter, one rule that applies to all of them.

You're allowed to stop. When you stop, count it as a return. The Stop Signal gets its own full chapter (Chapter 16). It is never optional.

3.5 How long?

Less than you think. For building a lasting habit, consistency beats duration (Cearns & Clark, 2023).

FOUR MEDITATION ANCHORS

Match your practice to your phenotype

1. SINGLE POINT

Absorption

Focus: One object (breath, mantra)
Trains: Sustained attention
Best for: Stabilizer, Fog

Concentration practice.
Pick one thing, stay with it.
When you wander, return.

2. PRESENT MOMENT

Observation

Focus: Watch what arises
Trains: Metacognition, flexibility
Best for: CEO, Lifeguard

Open monitoring.
Observe without chasing.
Anchor is awareness itself.

3. FEELING TONE: INTERNAL

Emotional States

Focus: Generate compassion, warmth
Trains: Amygdala regulation
Best for: Grumpy, Princess

Lovingkindness / metta.
Cultivate a feeling deliberately.
Anchor is the emotion.

4. FEELING TONE: EXTERNAL

Somatic Awareness

Focus: Body sensations
Trains: Interoception
Best for: Interpreter, Timekeeper

Body scan / somatic practice.
Attend to what the body reports.
Anchor is physical sensation.

Figure 3.2: Four Meditation Anchors

Duration	What it is
10 seconds	One conscious breath. One return. The floor. It counts.
90 seconds	The Reset Stack. Body + breath + meaning.
3 minutes	Your entry-level phenotype practice. Starting dose.
10 minutes	Standard daily practice. Most controlled trials test sessions of this length or longer (Basso et al., 2019, used 13 minutes).
20 minutes	Deeper training. The duration used in most well-powered studies.

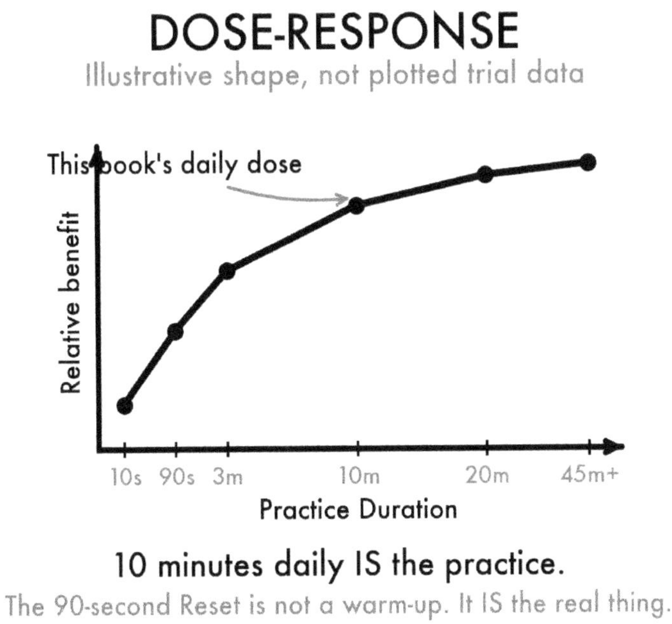

Figure 3.3: Dose-Response Curve

The honest-broker version: most controlled trials test sessions of ten minutes or longer, and nobody has established a sharp lower threshold for neural effects. Three minutes is this program's starting dose, chosen from HRV biofeedback data and brief-induction studies because it reliably builds the daily habit that makes everything else possible.

For building the *habit* and racking up returns, the circuit doesn't care whether you trained for three minutes or ten. It cares that you showed up. (Whether brief daily doses produce the same trait-level neural shifts as longer sessions is not settled; see Chapter 12.)

A three-minute daily practice repeated for months accumulates more total returns than a twenty-minute practice you do twice a week and then forget about. Whether that arithmetic applies to structural brain change the same way it applies to behavioral habit is still an open question. You can't get structural change from a practice you abandoned.

Ten minutes daily is a full practice. The 90-Second Reset is a complete practice.

Where this book aims, and where it doesn't. This book aims at the floor: the smallest daily practice that still changes your brain, because the floor is where most people fail. A fuller practice has three cadences: the daily sit, a weekly group, and the occasional retreat. The deeper two carry their own research base (Khoury et al., 2017). Chapter 18 lays out the full architecture, daily to yearly. Get the daily floor solid first. Everything else builds on it.

The progression rule, in one line: Stay at 3 minutes until it feels boring rather than hard. Move to 10 minutes when you can sit the full 3 in the Green zone, five days out of seven. Move to 20 only when 10 feels steady and you want to. Your nervous system sets the pace. Going up before the lower rung is comfortable is running before you can walk; it's how people quit. There is no "behind."

When even three minutes feels like too much: Embed one moment of noticing into something you already do. Every time you walk through one doorway today, feel your feet for one step. Every time you reach for your phone, one conscious breath first. We call this the **One-Breath Return:** one conscious breath, notice the inhale, notice the exhale, done. Zero additional time. Thirty returns.

3.6 Practice Lab: Build Your 90-Second Reset Stack

You've done this once, in "Do This First." Now make it yours. This is your customizable emergency toolkit, the practice you use when everything else feels like too much.

The 90-Second Reset Stack (customizable)

Setup: Wherever you are. Any position. No special preparation. The Reset Stack is designed to work in a parked car, in a bathroom stall, at your desk, on the subway. Three steps, thirty seconds each.

Step 1: Body lever (30 seconds). Choose one:

- Feet on floor, press down hard, feel the ground pushing back (default)
- Hands together, press palms firmly for 5 seconds, release, notice the sensation
- Stand up, stretch arms overhead, take three breaths standing
- Walk ten steps, feeling each foot contact the ground

When your mind wanders during the body lever: Notice the wandering. Come back to the physical sensation. That's a return. Count it.

Step 2: Breath lever (30 seconds). Choose one:

- 4-count in through nose, 6-count out through mouth, three cycles (default)
- Box breath: 4 in, 4 hold, 4 out, 4 hold, two cycles
- Three sighs: big inhale through nose, long exhale through mouth with an audible "ahh"

When your mind wanders during the breath lever: Notice it. Rejoin the count wherever you are. Don't restart. Count that return.

Step 3: Meaning lever (30 seconds). Choose one:

- "I'm allowed to be here." (default)
- "Whatever my brain does right now is fine."
- "This is practice, not a test."
- Label what you notice: "thinking," "tension," "quiet," "busy," "spinning"

When your mind wanders during the meaning lever: Notice the thought. Come back to the phrase. That's your best return: the one where the meaning lever applies to its own wandering.

Closing: Open your eyes if they were closed. Notice the room. You just did three regulation levers in ninety seconds. Count your returns.

Your custom Reset Stack:

Body: ______________

Breath: _______________

Meaning: _______________

Do this twice today. Before bed and when you wake up. Or before two meals. Or during two transition moments: getting in the car, arriving at work, sitting down to start a task. The trigger doesn't matter. The consistency does.

Today's practice: ___ returns. Duration: 90 seconds.

Where You'll Use This

The 90-Second Reset isn't a warm-up for "real" meditation. It IS real meditation, applied to real life. Here's where it fits:

- **Before a hard conversation:** Body lever (feet on floor), Breath lever (three breaths), Meaning lever ("I'm allowed to stop"). Ninety seconds. Then talk.
- **In traffic or on the commute:** Label ("frustration"), one breath, notice your grip on the steering wheel. Loosen it. That's a return.
- **Before sleep:** Permission Practice, 4:6 breathing, "Whatever my brain does tonight is fine." The day's last ninety seconds set the tone for the nervous system's overnight work.
- **Between tasks at work:** Stand up, three breaths, sit down. Nobody will notice. You will.

3.7 The 7-Day Start Sequence

This is Phase 1, Week 1 of your practice. It's based on the cascade step you identified in Chapter 2. If you haven't done that yet, use the 90-Second Reset as your default until you do.

The structure is simple: do one matched practice, twice daily, for seven days. That's it. Three minutes per session. Six minutes per day. Forty-two minutes for the week. Less time than a single episode of whatever you're watching right now.

Day 1: First contact. Go to your matched phenotype chapter in Part II. Find the 3-minute entry practice. Do it. Once. Count your returns. Write the number down. That's your baseline.

If it felt awkward or frustrating and you stayed Green: good. You got data. Do it again before bed. If it felt terrible, you still got data, but different data. Check your signals. Yellow or Red means: modify, shorten, or switch anchors before you try again tonight. Don't repeat the same protocol that moved you out of Green.

Day 2: Repetition. Same practice, twice: morning and evening. Don't change anything. Don't tweak the protocol. Don't add. Repeat. Notice if the return count is different from Day 1.

Day 3: Return Counter awareness. Same practice, twice. But today, pay attention to the *quality* of your returns. Are they quick snaps back? Slow drifts? Do you catch the wandering early or only after a long detour? You're not judging. You're noticing what noticing feels like. That's meta-awareness, the skill underneath all the skills.

Day 4: Add the Reset Stack. Keep your 3-minute matched practice twice daily. Add one 90-Second Reset at a transition point in your day: arriving somewhere, leaving somewhere, or between two tasks. You now have three practice touchpoints per day. Total: seven and a half minutes.

Day 5: Same plan. Notice the resistance. By Day 5, the novelty has worn off. If your Happy Little Kid is active, flatness arrives. If your Grumpy Old Man is active, effort-dread spikes. If your Problem Child is active, the mere fact that this is "scheduled" makes you want to skip it. Whatever you feel, notice it. Name the phenotype if you can. Then do the practice anyway. Or do a 10-second version: one conscious breath. That counts.

Day 6: Titrate up (optional). If 3 minutes feels stable, try the 10-minute version from your phenotype chapter. If 3 minutes still feels like a lot, stay at 3. There is no schedule to keep. There is no "behind."

Day 7: Review. Look at your Return Counter numbers for the week. Seven days of data. What do you notice? More returns early in the week (more distraction) shifting to fewer returns (more sustained attention)? Or the reverse? Either pattern is information. Neither is failure.

Weekly Review (7-Day Check)

After Day 7, answer these:

1. **Total returns this week:** ___ (add up all 7 days)
2. **Lowest day:** ___ returns on Day __: *what was different? Sleep? Stress? Didn't practice?*
3. **Highest day:** ___ returns on Day __: *what helped?*
4. **Did the practice feel matched to your brain?** Yes / Mostly / No → if No, revisit the Decision Tree
5. **One thing I noticed this week:** ________________

What to look for: Did your return count change across the week? Did you notice a wander earlier in the session than you did on Day 1? Did anything in your day (a pause before reacting, a breath you didn't plan, a moment of noticing) feel even slightly different? Any of those is progress.

Your decision: Stay at 3 minutes? Try 10 minutes? Change the practice? → ________________

What Progress Looks Like

(Illustrative composite; your numbers and timeline will differ.)

Day 1: 3 minutes. Mind wandered constantly. 22 returns. Felt pointless.

Day 7: Same 3 minutes. Caught the wander faster: 3 seconds instead of 30. Returns: 35. Almost tolerable.

Day 30: 5 minutes. Returns: 28 (fewer, because you stayed longer between wanders). Yesterday in traffic: a pause before honking. The gap was just there, without any decision.

Progress is a small gap that wasn't there before.

After Day 7: You've completed Phase 1, Week 1 of the Three-Phase Model (Chapter 15). Keep the same practice running, same twice-daily rhythm. The 10-minute practice from your phenotype chapter is available when 3 minutes feels boring.

If you fall off: Picking this book back up is a return. So is sitting on the cushion for ten seconds before giving up. Count it. You didn't fail your practice. You took a rest.

Seven days. You kept coming back.

YOUR DAY IN PRACTICE

Photograph this page. Tape it to your mirror.

Morning	90-Second Reset (body + breath + meaning)	90 sec
Midday	Your Entry Move from your Practice Card	3 min
Transitions	One-Breath Return at one doorway or trigger	10 sec each
Evening	90-Second Reset	90 sec

Total: ∼6 minutes + doorframe returns

Week 2: Swap midday for 10-min phenotype practice from your Practice Card.

My phenotype: ______________________________

My practice: ______________________________

My time: ______________________________

A shortened practice can be the right practice. So can a stopped one.

3.8 A vignette: the teacher who thought three minutes was cheating

A high school teacher came in convinced she needed forty minutes daily to make any difference. She'd read the research, internalized the gold standard, and because she could never find forty minutes, she practiced zero minutes for two years. Every day.

Her brain map: loud Grumpy Old Man (right frontal withdrawal: every effortful task pre-appraised as "not worth it"), hot Lifeguard (continuous posterior scan from thirty teenagers all day). By 4 PM, cooked. Too depleted to practice, too guilty to rest.

We started with the 90-Second Reset. Twice daily in her car. Morning: "I'm allowed to have a hard day." Afternoon: "I did enough."

"That can't be enough," she said, in exactly her Grumpy Old Man's voice.

"Count the returns," I said.

Week 1: twelve returns per 90-second session. Twenty-four per day. One hundred sixty-eight per week. In ninety-second increments.

Week 3: the gap arrived, in her case, on her timeline.

Week 6: she added three minutes of walking at lunch. She chose to because ninety seconds had made three minutes feel possible.

Three minutes wasn't cheating. Three minutes was the whole strategy. The rest was compound interest.

From clinical experience, when the practice finally matches the brain, a pause can show up before an old reflex even when the formal sitting time is short. That's not a controlled-trial finding. It's a pattern I see repeatedly. The two are different things.

Match the practice to the brain. That is the whole strategy.

3.9 The whole map on one page

1. Count returns. The Return Counter is your engagement log. Every wander and return is a noticed moment. A busy session and a calm session both count. The number is your record, not your score.

2. Practice what matches. Your phenotype chapter in Part II has your specific entry move, your 3-minute practice, your 10- and 20-minute upgrades, your troubleshooting. The Decision Tree (Chapter 2) gets you there. Go to your chapter. Do the entry practice.

3. The 90-Second Reset is real meditation. Body, breath, meaning. Ninety seconds. Real life. Applied regulation when the day won't wait.

4. You're always allowed to stop. Green/Yellow/Red tells you where you are. The Stop Signal is a feature. Chapter 16 has the full safety protocol.

The levers, the Reset Stack, the 7-Day Sequence, and the Three-Phase Model in Part IV all plug into these four.

If you're on medication (SSRIs, stimulants, or others), Chapter 16 explains how each class interacts with meditation practice. Short version: keep practicing, but some adaptations help. Medication holds the floor. Meditation builds the capacity. Both count.

What does your specific brain need? Part II matches each phenotype to its practice. Turn to your chapter from the Decision Tree and find your entry move.

Today's practice: ___ returns.

Part II: Find Your Practice

Eight chapters. Each one matched to a different brain pattern.

Find yourself in the Decision Tree below, then go to that chapter.

What's loudest right now?

MOVE	Frozen, can't make yourself start	→ **Ch. 4 Stabilizer**
	Impulsive, can't stop or slow down	→ **Ch. 4 Supervisor**
	Exhausted, foggy, falling asleep	→ **Ch. 5 Fog**
MOOD	Dread: "what's the point"	→ **Ch. 6 Grumpy**
	Bored, can't sustain interest	→ **Ch. 6 Happy Little Kid**
	"Don't tell me what to do"	→ **Ch. 6 Problem Child**
ORIENT	Can't close eyes, scanning the room	→ **Ch. 7 Lifeguard**
	"Am I doing this right?" loops	→ **Ch. 7 CEO**
SENSE	Body too loud, sensory overwhelm	→ **Ch. 8 Princess**
	Voices or tone feel threatening	→ **Ch. 8 Bard**
	Inner narrator won't stop	→ **Ch. 9 Interpreter**
PROCESS	Everything too fast, or too slow	→ **Ch. 10 Timekeeper**
	Multiple patterns? Start with the loudest.	→ **Ch. 11 Stacks**
	Still unsure? Start walking.	→ **Ch. 4**

After you practice: did you come back at least once? That's a return. If you feel worse afterward, check your signals.

Practice Cards

Twelve phenotypes. Each has an entry move in the cards below.

Use the Decision Tree to find your loudest pattern. Go to that card. **Do the Entry Move. Count returns. Start with 3 minutes.** The 10- and 20-minute variants, *On Track / Too Much* signals, and stack notes live in each phenotype's chapter.

> **If any card feels too hard:** Do the 3-minute version only. That counts.

MOVE

THE STABILIZER | MOVE | Ch. 4

The cushion is right there. Your body won't cross the room to it.

Entry move: Walk for 3 minutes before you sit.

3-min practice: Walk slowly. Count 1-2-3-4, 1-2-3-4. When the mind wanders, restart from 1. Feel each foot.

If too hard: One conscious step. That counts. *Returns:* ____ *Min:* ____

THE SUPERVISOR | MOVE | Ch. 4

The urge to move arrives before the thought to move does.

Entry move: Sit. Watch impulses without acting.

3-min practice: Notice every urge to move: scratch, shift, check. Don't act. Name it (*itch, adjust, check*). Each noticing is one return.

If too hard: 60 seconds of watching one urge. *Returns:* ____ *Min:* ____

THE FOG | MOVE | Ch. 5

Eyes close, and the lights in the room go with them.

Entry move: Stand up. Eyes open. Lights up.

3-min practice: Stand, soft gaze at a point in the middle distance. Breathe normally. When a thought pulls you inward, return to what you can see.

If too hard: Walk briskly for 60 seconds. *Returns:* ____ *Min:* ____

MOOD

THE GRUMPY OLD MAN | MOOD | Ch. 6

Before you sit, a flat voice has already filed this under not worth it.

Entry move: In for 4, out for 6. Two minutes first.

3-min practice: Sit. In for 4, out for 6. Don't try to relax. Count. When the mind lists reasons this won't work, note *doubting* and return.

If too hard: Three slow exhales. That counts. *Returns:* ____ *Min:* ____

THE HAPPY LITTLE KID | MOOD | Ch. 6

The practice was fascinating yesterday. Today it's wallpaper.

Entry move: Change what you're doing today.

3-min practice: Get curious about whatever arises: *interesting, a memory; interesting, a body sensation.* Each arising is a specimen. Treat it as data.

If too hard: Switch practices mid-session. Authorized. *Returns:* ____ *Min:* ____

THE PROBLEM CHILD | MOOD | Ch. 6

The moment it's assigned, something in you digs in.

Entry move: You choose the practice and when it starts.

3-min practice: No prescribed anchor. Notice whatever is loudest. Name it if you like. Move attention wherever you want. Stay present for 3 minutes.

If too hard: Refusing to practice is the practice. *Returns:* ____ *Min:* ____

ORIENT

THE CEO | ORIENT | Ch. 7

You're not meditating. You're grading the meditation.

Entry move: Count breaths 1 to 10. Start structured. Fade the structure.

3-min practice: Count breaths: 1 to 10. Reach 10, restart. Lose count, restart from 1. When you notice yourself evaluating, that noticing *is* the return.

If too hard: Count to 3, restart. Three only. *Returns:* ____ *Min:* ___

THE LIFEGUARD | ORIENT | Ch. 7

Closing your eyes feels like turning your back on the room.

Entry move: Eyes open. Soft gaze.

3-min practice: Eyes open. When the threat-scanner activates, ask: *Is this threat present right now, in this room?* Usually no. Return to breath.

If too hard: Feet on floor, name 5 things visible. *Returns:* ____ *Min:* ___

SENSE

THE PRINCESS & THE PEA | SENSE | Ch. 8

The tag in your collar is louder than your breath.

Entry move: Reduce sensory input first: lights dim, room quiet.

3-min practice: Check: sound, light, temperature tolerable? Then 3 min of body awareness starting with one small neutral area (hands or feet only).

If too hard: Hands only. 60 seconds. *Returns:* ____ *Min:* ___

THE BARD | SENSE | Ch. 8

The instructor's calm voice sounds, to you, vaguely annoyed.

Entry move: No human voices. Music or silence only.

3-min practice: Eyes open, soft focus on one point: candle, wall spot, plant. Return when attention wanders. Pure visual attention. Count returns.

If too hard: White noise or silence. 60 seconds. *Returns:* ____ *Min:* ___

THE INTERPRETER | SENSE | Ch. 9

You can't drop the thought. The thought is narrating the dropping.

Entry move: Give the narrator a mantra.

3-min practice: Repeat silently, continuously: *here, now. here, now.* When the narrator layers on top, use the mantra as the redirect.

If too hard: One conscious breath. Out of language, into body. *Returns:* ____ *Min:* ___

PROCESS

THE TIMEKEEPER | PROCESS | Ch. 10

The breath count crawls while your clock sprints.

Entry move: Match the practice to your speed. Don't fight it.

3-min (fast): Note whatever arises as fast as it arises: *thinking, hearing, feeling, planning.* No pauses. Each note is a return.

3-min (slow): One breath at a time. Count to 5 on the inhale, 5 on the exhale. Your pace. *Returns:* ____ *Min:* ___

QUICK REFERENCE: All 12

Phenotype	Cascade	Entry Move	Ch.
Stabilizer	**MOVE**	Walk 3 min before you sit	4
Supervisor	**MOVE**	Sit. Watch impulses without acting.	4
Fog	**MOVE**	Stand up. Eyes open. Light on.	5
Grumpy Old Man	**MOOD**	In 4, out 6 for 2 min first	6
Happy Little Kid	**MOOD**	Change the practice today	6
Problem Child	**MOOD**	You choose the anchor and when it starts	6
CEO	**ORIENT**	Count 1–10. Start structured, fade structure.	7
Lifeguard	**ORIENT**	Eyes open. Don't fight the need to see the room.	7
Princess & the Pea	**SENSE**	Reduce sensory input before you start	8
Bard	**SENSE**	No human voices. Music or silence.	8
Interpreter	**SENSE**	Give the narrator a mantra	9
Timekeeper	**PROCESS**	Match the speed. Don't fight it.	10

When your mind wanders, come back. Each return counts.

Ch 4: Can't Start / Can't Stop: The Motor Axis

The Stabilizer (task initiation) and The Supervisor (impulse gating)

Quick Check: Can't start? Stabilizer. Can't stop? Supervisor.

Three apps. Two books. A candle. A dedicated corner. Three weeks of sitting on the couch *near* the cushion, then it was 8:15 and she needed to start work.

"I'm the laziest person alive," she said.

Her brain map said: strong left precentral underactivation. The network that bridges intention and action was idling. Not laziness. A clutch that wouldn't engage.

We started with ten steps. Ten mindful steps from bed to bathroom every morning, counting feet. Fifteen seconds.

By Week 3: two minutes in the hallway. Day 22: she sat on the cushion. Three minutes. Eleven returns. She texted: "I sat down and meditated. It only took me ten steps."

The circuit just needed a smaller door. The practices below give you that door.

4.1 Choose your adventure

- **Can't get started:** you intend to practice, you want to practice, and then you don't. The gap between deciding and doing feels like a canyon. Read the **Stabilizer** section below.
- **Can't stop or slow down:** impulsive, rushing, scratching the itch before you consciously notice it. Or the opposite: perfectionism that won't let you release. Skip ahead to the **Supervisor** section.

- **If any practice triggers panic, dissociation, or persistent worsening,** go to Chapter 16.

If both apply, you're in the right chapter for both. Start with whichever one is louder right now.

A note before either section: **a quick word about novelty-seeking.** If your "can't start" looks more like "I start everything and finish nothing because the next shiny thing pulls me away," that's a Supervisor problem (the brake won't hold) or a CEO problem (anchoring captured by novelty), not a Stabilizer problem. Stabilizer is the cold-start failure. Distractibility-by-novelty is a different circuit. Read the Supervisor section below. If it doesn't fit, see Chapter 7.

4.2 What it feels like

If you're the Stabilizer: You know exactly what you should be doing. The cushion is right there. The app is open. The intention is crystal clear. And then nothing. You check your phone. You remember something that "needs" doing first. You stare at the wall because the space between wanting and doing has this strange, heavy friction, like trying to push a shopping cart with a seized wheel.

The wanting is real, and the doing just doesn't follow. Then the guilt arrives, which is its own torture. You've now failed at something you weren't even trying to do yet.

Other people just start. Sit down, close their eyes, begin. You watch them and wonder what gear they have that you're missing. Motivation isn't the problem. You have plenty of motivation. The transmission between motivation and action drops the signal.

What the Brain Map Shows: In the maps I review, a Stabilizer's left precentral gyrus typically shows reduced beta activation on EEG, the initiation network running quiet. Clinical observation within the qEEG phenotype framework (Johnstone et al., 2005), not a tested prediction.

If you're the Supervisor: You start fine. You sit down, close your eyes, and three seconds later you've scratched your nose, adjusted your posture, checked the timer, and opened one eye to see if the cat is looking at you. Your body generates impulses like a popcorn machine, and each one gets acted on before you even notice it was an impulse. Or the opposite: you sit down and the perfectionism kicks in. You can't find the "right" posture. The breath doesn't feel "right." The meditation doesn't feel "done." You hold on too tight to everything, and the session becomes a white-knuckle exercise in control rather than attention.

The brake is miscalibrated, in one of two directions. Too loose, everything leaks. Too tight, nothing releases.

What the Brain Map Shows: A Supervisor's map typically shows weak right precentral inhibitory tone: the brake reads soft. The inhibition network isn't generating enough sensorimotor rhythm to hold.

4.3 Why the motor axis struggles with meditation

In the model I use, the left and right precentral regions act as gas pedal and brake. The **Stabilizer** maps to GO: bridging the gap between "I should" and "I do." The **Supervisor** maps to STOP: inhibiting action, sustaining effort, knowing when enough is enough. Both work the half-second gap at the body. The Stabilizer when the response never starts. The Supervisor when every impulse fires before awareness arrives.

In practice, standard meditation assumes you can sit down and begin. For the Stabilizer, that gap is the problem itself: a circuit that won't fire. When left precentral activation runs low, starting anything tends to cost more energy than it should. So you don't start. Guilt adds effort-dread. Tomorrow gets harder. The Stabilizer closes that gap with intensity, and a quiet cushion gives it nothing to push against.

You have felt this already. You can drive a car for an hour without drifting into the bushes, because the road supplies enough intensity to hold the gap closed. Put the same brain in a boring boardroom or a dull history class and the circuit has nothing to fire on, so it drifts. The cushion is the boardroom; walking is the road. Every mindful step you take turns the motor system on and trains initiation to hold.

The Supervisor is the mirror image. When right precentral tone is low, impulses tend to run unchecked before you've chosen. When overactive, perfectionism locks in: you can't end because it doesn't feel done.

4.4 The dysregulation cascade

The cascade maps how trouble stacks, and the number that still matters is on your Return Counter.

Stabilizer Cascade: Motor offline → can't initiate → guilt → avoidance → Grumpy Old Man amplifies → deeper paralysis

- Typical first slip: motor activation failure, the gap between intention and action.
- Entry strategy: bottom-up. Movement first. Walk before you sit. MOVE.
- Downstream: when the motor system comes online, guilt decreases, avoidance loosens, and the Grumpy Old Man's effort-dread has less material to work with.

Supervisor Cascade: Weak braking → impulse leakage → scattered attention → incomplete actions → frustration → shame. *Or:* Overactive braking → rigidity → perfectionism → can't release → exhaustion.

- Typical first slip: impulse gating failure, can't sustain or can't release. The brain's motor brake (measured by how quickly you can cancel a response once it's started) takes roughly 200–250 milliseconds in a typical brain. In ADHD, that brake is consistently slower (Lipszyc & Schachar, 2010). Higher trait mindfulness predicts a faster brake (Logemann-Molnár et al., 2024).
- Each impulse you notice without acting on is one rep for this circuit.

- Entry strategy: Insight / Open Monitoring. Watch impulses arise without acting on them. Or practice deliberate releasing if the brake is too tight. - Downstream: when the brake calibrates, sustained attention improves, perfectionism loosens, and the CEO's evaluation loops have less to evaluate.

The Stabilizer and Supervisor come from QEEG observation. Treat them as starting points for self-experiment.

PRACTICE CARD: The Stabilizer *(task initiation / motor activation loop)* **Cascade:** MOVE: Step 1 | **Chapter:** 4

Entry Move: Walk before you sit. Three minutes of intentional walking turns the motor system on.

3 min: Walking Meditation: count steps 1-2-3-4, restart at wander **10 min:** Walking Meditation with verbal noting (lifting / moving / placing) **20 min:** Walk (10 min) → Stand (2 min) → Sit (8 min) with breath anchor

On Track: You started, even if reluctantly ✓ **Too Much:** Guilt about "only" 3 minutes → *That was the practice. 3 minutes counts.*

Return Counter: ___ returns ___ min

PRACTICE CARD: The Supervisor *(impulse gating / quality control loop)* **Cascade:** MOVE: Step 1 | **Chapter:** 4

Entry Move: Sit and watch impulses arise; let them pass. The noticing is the practice.

3 min: Impulse Watching: name each urge (itch, adjust, check) without acting **10 min:** Stillness + Deliberate Release: every 2-3 min, consciously release one held tension **20 min:** Open Monitoring: watch everything arise and pass without grabbing

On Track: Noticed an impulse before acting on it, even once ✓ **Too Much:** White-knuckling to hold still → *Release deliberately.*

Return Counter: ___ returns ___ min

4.5 The Stabilizer: practices that work

4.5.1 Your entry move

Start with Walking Meditation. Move your body *before* you ask it to be still. Three minutes of intentional walking is your on-ramp.

Meditation while walking is a complete practice. The tradition that says "real meditation = sitting still with eyes closed" was designed for brains that can initiate sitting still. Your brain can't, yet. So we start where you are: in motion. You already know how to walk. Now you're going to pay attention while you do it.

4.5.2 Practice 1: Walking Meditation

Walking Meditation (3-minute version)

Setup: Stand up. You need about ten feet of space: a hallway, a room, a stretch of sidewalk. Indoors or outdoors. No shoes if possible (feeling the floor gives the Stabilizer more sensory data to lock onto). Eyes open, gaze soft and slightly downward, about six feet ahead.

The practice: Walk slowly, about half your normal pace: slow enough that balance becomes noticeable but not so slow that you wobble or feel self-conscious. Feel each foot as it lifts from the ground, moves forward through space, and contacts the ground again. Heel, ball, toes. That's your anchor: the sensation of each step.

You don't need to think about the walking. You need to feel it. The pressure of the floor against your heel. The subtle wobble of balance as weight shifts. The moment of contact when the next foot lands. Each step is one anchor point.

When your mind wanders (and it will, because that's the training), silently note "thinking" and return to the next step. Count it.

When mind wanders: The Stabilizer's mind doesn't race like the Timekeeper's or loop like the CEO's; it *drifts*. Quietly. Like a boat slipping away from a dock. You don't notice it's gone until it's already twenty yards out. When you catch the drift, don't yank yourself back. Gently rejoin the next step. Back to the foot. No urgency. No self-criticism. The next step.

Closing: After three minutes, stand still. Both feet on the ground. Feel the stillness after the movement. Let the contrast land, then take one deliberate breath. Done.

You started. Your motor system walked itself into a session. That's the rep.

10-minute version: Same practice, slower pace. Add verbal noting: "lifting, moving, placing" silently with each step. The verbal component gives the Stabilizer an additional target to lock onto. Language engages frontal circuits, which builds a bridge to the motor system underneath. Some people find this version easier than the silent one, because the noting occupies the mind enough to prevent the quiet drift.

20-minute version: Walk for ten minutes with noting. Then transition: stop walking, stand still for two minutes. Feel the residual motion settle. Notice the shift from movement to stillness: the body recalibrating, the attention finding a new anchor. Then sit for eight minutes with breath focus. The walking got your motor system online. The standing is the bridge between motion and stillness. Now you can sit, because the gearbox is engaged. The walk→stand→sit sequence respects the Stabilizer's need for graduated transitions rather than abrupt shifts.

The Stabilizer Practice Ladder

Level 1: 10 conscious steps. Anywhere. 30 seconds. *(Start here.)* **Level 2:** 3-minute Walking Meditation with noting. **Level 3:** 10-minute Walking Meditation, slower pace, verbal noting. **Level 4:** 20-minute Walk-to-Sit: walk 10 min, stand 2 min, sit 8 min.

Move up when the current level feels manageable. Stay at any level as long as you need.

Reframe: If walking never leads to sitting (if you walk for ten years and never progress to a seated practice), that's not a failure. Meditation while walking is a complete practice in its own right. The attention training is identical: notice, stay, return. The regulation is equivalent.

For some brains, especially those that are fidgety, impulsive, or ADHD-wired, movement-based practice may always be the better fit; ADHD mindfulness programs often adapt seated practice with walking meditation for exactly this reason (Zylowska et al., 2008). The best meditation is the one you do. Chapter 17 expands this into yoga, tai chi, and other overlearned-movement practices that use the same principle: the body moves automatically, the mind practices returning.

4.5.3 Practice 2: Micro-Session Activation

Micro-Session Activation (60 seconds)

The Stabilizer's biggest enemy is the space between "I should practice" and "I'm practicing." This practice eliminates the gap by making the practice absurdly, insultingly brief. Sixty seconds.

Setup: You're wherever you are. No special preparation. No cushion, no app, no quiet room.

The practice: Set a timer for 60 seconds (or estimate; it doesn't need to be precise). Stand up. Take three conscious breaths: in through the nose, out through the mouth, feeling each one. Sit back down. Done.

Sixty seconds is the full session.

When mind wanders: In sixty seconds, you might get one or two returns. That's enough. The goal is initiation training. You're teaching your motor system that the cost of starting is approximately zero. Once starting feels easy, duration follows naturally. The gearbox warms up.

Closing: Notice: you just started something. That's the micro-win. That's the circuit learning.

The attachment protocol: Do this three times per day, attached to something you already do. Before your first sip of coffee. Before you start the car. Before you open your laptop. The trigger is the bridge across the gap. The trigger is non-negotiable, and the practice is tiny.

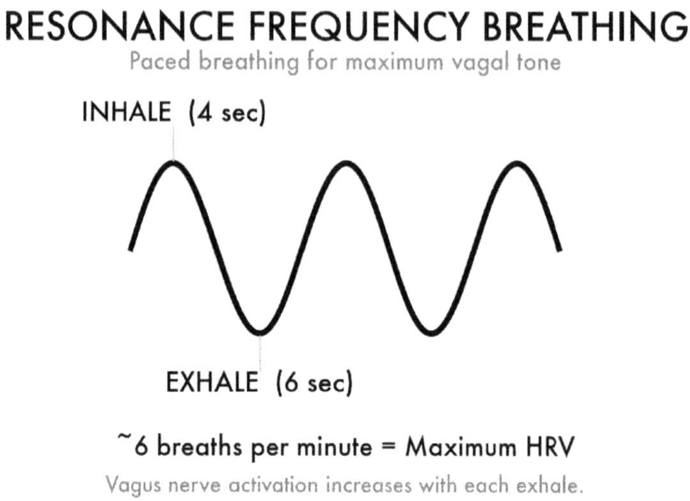

Figure 4.1: HRV Resonance Breathing

This is how you train initiation by pairing it with what you already do.

4.6 The Supervisor: practices that work

4.6.1 Your entry move

Start with Insight / Nonreactive Attention. Three minutes of noticing the urge to move without moving. This is brake training. Circuit training.

4.6.2 Practice 1: Insight / Nonreactive Attention

Insight / Nonreactive Attention (3-minute version)

Setup: Sit comfortably. Eyes open or closed (though closed tends to amplify impulses, which is good for this practice; more impulses, more training opportunities). Hands resting in your lap or on your knees. Set a timer.

The practice: Notice whatever arises. A thought. An itch. An impulse to check your phone. An urge to adjust your posture. A sound you want to identify. Label it silently: "urge," "itch," "restless," "planning," "checking."

Before you practice not-moving, know what you never sit through. Pain, numbness, a limb going dead, trouble breathing, dizziness, a joint that feels unstable, or a trauma signal. Those are not urges to observe. Notice the signal and move deliberately, because moving to protect your body is itself a clean rep. This practice trains the brake on impulse, not on your body's warnings.

Don't act on it. Notice it, label it, and wait. Watch it change. Notice how an itch intensifies, peaks, and then, if you don't scratch it, fades. Notice how an urge to move builds pressure, holds, and then releases if you don't follow it. The impulse is an invitation. You can decline.

When mind wanders: The Supervisor's mind doesn't wander the way other phenotypes' minds do. It *acts*. It scratches the itch before you notice the itch existed. It checks the phone before you decided to check the phone. The practice is catching the impulse *before* the action. If you catch yourself mid-act (hand already moving toward the itch), freeze. That freeze is the rep. Note "impulse" and return to stillness.

Closing: After three minutes, move deliberately. Stretch one muscle group, slowly, intentionally. Roll your shoulders. Flex your fingers. This is intentional action, the opposite of impulse. Notice how deliberate movement feels different from reactive movement.

10-minute version: Same practice. Add an urge counter: each time you notice an impulse and don't act on it, count it silently. Those are brake reps. A ten-minute session might generate twenty to fifty brake reps. That's twenty to fifty reps for the inhibition network.

20-minute version: Alternate five minutes of focused breath counting (GO system: concentration training) with five minutes of open monitoring and impulse watching (STOP system: brake training). Repeat twice. This is Balance Calibration: training the gas and brake to work in concert.

4.6.3 Practice 2: The "Good Enough" Release

The "Good Enough" Release (any duration)

This is specifically for the overactive Supervisor, the perfectionist who can't end the meditation because it doesn't feel "done."

Setup: Set a timer for your intended duration. Any duration. The timer is non-negotiable.

The practice: Meditate normally, whatever practice you're currently doing. When the timer goes off, stop. Immediately. Even if it doesn't feel complete. Even if you were just settling in. Even if every fiber of your perfectionism is screaming "five more minutes."

End the meditation *before* it feels done. On purpose.

When your mind says "but we're not finished": That's the Supervisor. Notice the pull. Label it: "holding." And stop anyway. The stopping IS the practice.

Closing: Stand up or change position immediately. Don't linger. Don't evaluate. Don't rate the session. Move on with your day. The evaluation impulse is the Supervisor trying to reassert control. Let it go.

Why this works: You're training the release. The overactive Supervisor holds on too tight to posture, to process, to quality standards, to the session itself. Releasing early, deliberately, before it feels "enough," trains the circuit that "good enough" *is* enough. Over time, this loosens the perfectionism that makes meditation feel like a performance instead of a practice.

4.6.4 Practice 3: Balance Calibration

Balance Calibration (10 minutes)

For when you've built some stability with the basics and want to train the Stabilizer and Supervisor together, this is the advanced motor axis practice.

Setup: Sit comfortably. Timer set. Eyes closed or open. This practice has distinct phases, so set an interval timer if you have one (2 minutes per interval), or estimate.

The practice:

Phase 1 (2 minutes): Concentration. Count breaths. 1 on the inhale, 2 on the exhale, up to 10. Start over. This is GO training: sustained, directed focus. Lock on.

Phase 2 (2 minutes): Open monitoring. Release the count. Don't direct your attention anywhere. Notice whatever arises: thoughts, sounds, sensations, impulses. Don't follow any of them. This is STOP training: the brake holding while stimuli flow past.

Phase 3 (2 minutes): Concentration. Back to counting. Notice the shift, from open to focused. The transition is effortful. That effort *is* the calibration.

Phase 4 (2 minutes): Open monitoring. Release again. Notice if it's easier or harder the second time.

Phase 5 (2 minutes): Freestyle. Choose whichever mode feels right. This is autonomy: the motor axis deciding for itself when to GO and when to STOP.

When mind wanders: During concentration phases, return to the count. During open monitoring phases, the "wandering" is the practice; don't act on what arises. During freestyle, trust your impulse about which mode to use. That trust is the training.

Closing: Take one deliberate breath. Notice: you just shifted between GO and STOP five times in ten minutes. That's motor-axis calibration in ten minutes.

4.7 Practice signals: Stabilizer

Signs you're on track:

- Practice is happening. You're starting, even if it's only sixty seconds.
- The gap between "I should" and "I did" is shrinking, even slightly.
- You started today and skipped the negotiation with yourself first.

By Week 4, you don't negotiate before starting. You walk.

Signs you're overtraining:

- Practice itself has become another item on the guilt list.
- You're forcing longer sessions before the initiation habit is solid.
- Skipping a day triggers shame spiraling instead of a simple "I'll do it tomorrow."

What to do: Scale back to Micro-Session Activation. Sixty seconds, three times a day. Rebuild the initiation habit before adding duration. The Stabilizer responds to frequency, not intensity.

4.8 Practice signals: Supervisor

Signs you're on track:

- You catch impulses before acting on them, even once per session.
- The space between urge and action is widening, even a fraction of a second.
- You can end a session when the timer goes off and stop there.

Signs you're overtraining:

- Stillness practice is triggering rigidity or tension, not flexibility.
- You're white-knuckling through sessions, muscles clenched.
- "Not acting on impulses" has become a new form of control: you're using the brake to punish yourself.

What to do: Drop to the 3-minute version. Add deliberate movement between stillness blocks. Try the "Good Enough" Release. The goal is flexible braking, not lockdown.

4.9 A vignette: the surgeon who couldn't stop

An orthopedic surgeon, early fifties, hands like someone who'd spent three decades making precise cuts and then undoing the precision everywhere else. He sat in my office the way surgeons sit: forward, ready to move. His phone was already in his hand when he walked in. He hadn't decided to check it. The hand decided first.

Precise in the OR, catastrophic everywhere else: interrupting mid-sentence, phone checked between bites at dinner, the car started before the destination was chosen. He'd committed to meditation four times and abandoned it four times. Every mental wander became an action before he'd noticed it. "I'm not impulsive in surgery," he said. "Only in the rest of my life." The brake worked beautifully when a scalpel was involved. Everywhere else, it was soft.

Brain map: strong motor drive, weak right prefrontal inhibitory gating.

We started with three minutes of Insight practice: notice each urge, label it, don't act on it. "This is miserable," he said after Day 3. Fourteen urges. He'd counted them with surgical precision.

"Fourteen reps," I said.

By Week 4, the urge count was the same, but the gap between urge and action had widened to two seconds. With his wife, two seconds was the whole conversation.

4.10 Troubleshooting

1. "I cannot make myself walk for three minutes." Start with ten steps (or three if ten feels like a lot). Attach them to something you already do: car to door, bed to bathroom. The number doesn't matter. What matters is that you start.

2. "My mind doesn't wander; it goes blank." That's Fog, not Stabilizer. Your brain may need activating practices rather than motor-initiation practices. Turn to Chapter 5. You can come back here once your arousal system is more online.

3. "I can't tell if I'm impulsive or perfectionistic. Both seem true." They coexist often. Start with Balance Calibration. It trains both modes. If one dominates, lean into that mode's specific practice.

Naming both patterns is noticing in action, the same muscle as a return.

4. "I keep starting things and getting pulled away by the next interesting thing." That's the novelty-capture problem. It's a Supervisor brake issue (impulses leak before you can hold) sometimes layered with a CEO anchoring problem (attention captured by patterns and novelty rather than the chosen target). Run the Insight / Nonreactive Attention practice above, and read Chapter 7 for the CEO side.

4.11 "If you're also ___"

- If you're also a **Fog** (energy crashes, falling asleep), see Chapter 5. Stabilizer and Fog are co-first in the cascade. Try alternating practices: Walking Meditation one day, Eyes-Open Standing Awareness (Chapter 5) the next. Both target the motor-arousal axis. Chapter 11 shows you how to merge them into a single session.
- If you're also a **Grumpy Old Man** (effort-dread amplifying initiation failure), see Chapter 6. The guilt-avoidance cycle often involves Grumpy making the Stabilizer's paralysis feel worse than it is. Start with Walking Meditation to get the motor system firing, then add Vagal Toning (Chapter 6) as your second daily session once you can initiate consistently. Chapter 11 has the full stacking protocol.
- If you're also a **Timekeeper** (everything too fast or too slow), see Chapter 10. Speed mismatch can masquerade as initiation failure: you're not stuck, you're mismatched. If speed mismatch is the louder problem, start with Rapid Noting or Self-Paced Concentration (Chapter 10) first, then add Walking Meditation once tempo stabilizes.

Meta Questions (Optional Nerd Corner)

What would change if you stopped treating "can't start" as a character flaw and started treating it as a circuit that needs warming up, the same way a car needs warming up on a cold morning?

When you notice the urge to move during stillness practice, what happens if you wait and let it pass? What does the urge feel like before you act on it? Does it have a shape? A location?

All you're doing is coming back. The Return Counter is the closing beat: ___ returns, ___ min (or skip the tally: coming back still counts). Whether you walk, stand, or sit, the shape of the session doesn't change what you're measuring.

Come back tomorrow. You started today.

When you're ready: If this is your primary match, practice the entry move daily for one week (the 7-Day Start Sequence in Chapter 3). If you recognized a second phenotype, go to that chapter next. When you're ready to combine practices, Chapter 11 shows you how to build a custom stack.

Ch 5: Brain Won't Activate: The Fog

The Fog: energy cycling and cognitive fatigue

A client sat across from me in the middle of the morning (not late afternoon when this is common, but 10 AM on a Tuesday) and fell asleep mid-sentence. Gone. He snapped back embarrassed, the way people do when they realize it happened, and said: "I've been trying to meditate for three months and I don't think my brain works right."

His brain worked exactly right. It just ran a different power schedule. His QEEG showed elevated theta across the frontal and central regions during a task that should have recruited faster activity. The arousal system was idling when the situation called for firing. This wasn't tiredness. He'd slept eight hours. It was a mismatch in his arousal clock. A brain running on a brownout.

The meditation he'd been trying sat him down, had him close his eyes, and told him to slow his breathing. He'd been practicing unconsciousness.

Quick Check: Energy right now (1–5): ___. Below 3? Start standing.

PRACTICE CARD: The Fog *(energy cycling / cognitive fatigue loop)* **Cascade:** MOVE: Step 1 | **Chapter:** 5

Entry Move: Stand up. Eyes open. Light on or face toward a window. Seated eyes-closed practice is a pipeline to unconsciousness for this brain.

3 min: Standing Eyes-Open Awareness: soft gaze at middle distance, return attention to what you can see **10 min:** Walking with Counting: brisk walk, count steps in groups of 4 **20 min:** Tide

Practice: 5 min standing, 10 min sitting (eyes half-open), 5 min standing

On Track: You stayed awake ✓ **Too Much:** Repeatedly falling asleep despite eyes-open → *More walking, brighter room, shorter sit.*

Return Counter: ___ returns ___ min

The Fog is a pattern I read on brain maps. No controlled trial handed it down. Use it to start experimenting.

5.1 What it feels like

It's not exactly tired. Tired implies you did something tiring. This is a grayness that arrives on its own schedule, sometimes mid-morning, sometimes by 2 PM, sometimes the moment you sit down for anything that requires sustained thought. The lights are on. Nobody's quite home.

You know what sharp feels like. You've had sharp hours, maybe even sharp days. The fog rolls in without warning and takes the color out of everything. Conversations feel like they're happening underwater. You read the same paragraph three times. You start a sentence and forget where it was going by the middle.

It isn't sadness. Sadness would at least be a feeling. This is flatter, the absence of feeling: gray, like someone turned your cognitive brightness to 40 percent.

Then someone says "just meditate." You sit down. You're unconscious in ninety seconds. Not because you can't meditate; because the practice was designed for brains with electricity to spare. Yours is running on a brownout.

Other people seem to have a steady power supply. Yours surges and dips: the arousal system and the cognitive demand system are out of phase, one running hot when the other needs cool, one offline when the other needs fuel. You've learned to sprint during the surges and survive the dips. Nobody has taught you how to *train* during the dips, because most training protocols assume steady power. Yours isn't steady. It's tidal.

Your brain is on its own clock.

On an EEG, this often shows up as elevated theta during tasks that should recruit faster activity. Theta isn't "sleep waves." Theta rises whenever the brain softens inhibitory control over a resource: in sleep, yes, but also during insight (the "aha" moment), creative incubation, and loss of focused attention (the "squirrel" moment). What makes it a Fog marker is theta showing up *when the task demands beta*: the control system releasing its grip at exactly the wrong time. Clinicians call it a high theta/beta ratio (TBR), a marker that multiple studies associate with arousal-cognition mismatch, though its specificity is still debated. This isn't tiredness. Tiredness resolves with rest. This is a chronic mismatch between when your arousal system delivers power and when your cognitive system needs it. Sleep deprivation looks different on an EEG. Depression-related fatigue looks different. The Fog is its own animal: a brain whose arousal oscillates when it should be steady, dipping when demands are high, surging when demands are low. (For the full picture of how theta, alpha, gamma, and other frequency bands interact to support awareness and regulation, see Chapter 13.)

What the Brain Map Shows: A Fog brain map looks like a brownout. Elevated slow-wave activity, theta and delta, in regions that should be running faster, and a theta/beta ratio that says the arousal system and the cognitive system are out of sync. The power is on; the voltage is low.

5.2 Why the Fog struggles with meditation

Standard meditation instructions are a recipe for unconsciousness if your brain defaults to low arousal. Dim the lights. Close your eyes. Sit still. Breathe slowly. Each step removes a source of cortical activation. You're being given a sedative and told to stay awake.

Closing your eyes eliminates your highest-bandwidth sensory channel. Sitting down takes the motor system offline. Breathing slowly down-regulates the autonomic lever that keeps you alert. Standard practice shuts off every circuit that keeps the lights on, then asks you to stay present. Of course you fell asleep.

The Fog collapses the gap by starving the cortex of the power to notice. You can't catch the moment between trigger and reaction at 40 percent brightness.

More effort isn't the fix. Reverse the inputs: eyes open, body upright, movement engaged, sensory channels active. Keep the lights on while you train.

Your arousal system drops below the threshold where attention can work. Every time you catch the brownout and activate, you train the system to hold power.

This recommendation draws on EEG arousal data and ultradian rhythm research, plus ADHD arousal models and thousands of clinical brain maps. It hasn't been validated in controlled trials.

What emerging evidence supports: a systematic review of 56 EEG studies found meditation most often associated with higher alpha and theta power than eyes-closed rest, though the finding was not uniform across studies (Lomas, Ivtzan, & Fu, 2015). For a Fog brain that cuts both ways. Alpha and theta are the rhythms of relaxed alertness, and they are also the rhythms of drifting off. Which one you get depends on whether arousal is holding.

5.3 But first: the Sleep-First Diagnostic

Before we go further, I need you to be honest about one thing: are you sleeping enough?

There are three reasons you might be falling asleep during meditation, and only one of them is the Fog.

1. Sleep debt. You're under-slept. Chronically, probably. If you're averaging fewer than seven hours of actual sleep (not time in bed, actual sleep), fix that first. No meditation practice in the world will outperform sleep deprivation. Address the sleep debt before continuing.

2. Fog phenotype. You're adequately rested (seven-plus hours most nights) and your brain still drops into low-arousal states. This is a circuit pattern, not a sleep problem. The EEG signature is often elevated theta and low alpha during waking tasks, meaning the brain is releasing inhibitory control when it should be tightening it. You need activating practices. Keep reading.

3. Practice mismatch. You're well-rested and your brain doesn't normally fog, but you're doing a sedating practice at the wrong time of day. The fix is easy: switch to eyes-open, standing, or walking practice. Problem solved.

5.4 The dysregulation cascade

Fog Cascade: Energy collapse → attention dissolves → emotional flatness → executive paralysis → withdrawal

- **First domino:** Arousal failure: the brain's power system cycles to low.
- **Entry strategy:** Bottom-up (activating) plus environmental (scheduling around energy cycles).
- **What resolves downstream:** When energy stabilizes, attention comes back online, emotional range returns, and executive function has fuel to work with. You can't run software on a dead battery. Charge the battery first.

5.5 Your entry move

Start with eyes-open, standing or walking practices only. Do not close your eyes. Do not sit down. Do not remove sensory input. Keep the lights on, in every sense.

5.6 Practices that work for the Fog

5.6.1 Practice 1: Eyes-Open Standing Awareness

Eyes-Open Standing Awareness (3-minute version)

Setup: Stand up. Feet hip-width. Eyes wide open: soft gaze, taking in the full width of your visual field. You can do this anywhere: your kitchen, your office, a hallway, outside. No special equipment. No special room. Stay vertical and awake.

The practice: Notice five things you can see. Name each one silently as you find it. Don't analyze them. Just label and move on.

Now notice three things you can hear. Name them: *fan, traffic, breathing.* Near sounds and far sounds. The naming keeps the language circuit engaged, which keeps the cortex active.

Now notice one thing you can feel on your body: temperature on your skin, the weight of your shirt, air moving across the back of your hand. Name it.

Return to visual. Cycle through: see, hear, feel, see, hear, feel. Each cycle is a lap. Each lap keeps three sensory channels active simultaneously. The Fog brain can't afford to lose channels. Keep them all running.

When mind fogs: The Fog brain doesn't wander actively like the CEO or the Timekeeper. It *dims*. The experience isn't "I was thinking about something else." It's "I was nowhere." You come back and can't tell how long you were gone. That noticing, the moment of "oh, I dimmed," is the return. It's Skill 1 at its most essential.

If you notice you've gone blank, stamp your foot once. Gently but firmly. The motor input sends a jolt of sensory data to your cortex and reboots the attention circuit. Then resume the see-hear-feel cycle.

Closing: Shake your hands for five seconds, quick and loose, like flicking water off. Take one sharp breath in through the nose, a quick exhale through the mouth. Notice whether your jaw has softened. You're standing. You're awake. That's the practice.

If staying awake was a battle the whole time, you just did the harder version of the practice. The harder version still counts.

10-minute version: Add slow walking between standing cycles. Walk for a minute (feel each step, count if needed), stand for a minute (see-hear-feel cycle). Alternate. The transitions maintain arousal by changing the motor demand. When you stand still, walking feels different enough to prevent the brain from habituating and dimming.

20-minute version: Walking meditation (Chapter 4 protocol) for ten minutes, then standing awareness for ten. Add a breath-counting component during the standing phase: count exhales from one to ten, reset. If you lose the count, if you arrive at some number and don't know how you got there, you fogged. Note "fogged," restart at one. The lost count is data, not failure.

The Fog Practice Ladder

Level 1: Standing, eyes open. See-hear-feel cycle. 3 min. *(Start here.)* **Level 2:** Walking with counting. Eyes open. Natural pace. 3 min. **Level 3:** Alternating walk/stand cycles. 10 min. **Level 4:** Walking (10 min) then standing awareness with breath counting (10 min). Eyes open throughout.

Move up when you can maintain awareness for most of the session without fogging. If eyes-closed or seated practice causes dimming, stay at standing/walking levels.

5.6.2 Practice 2: Walking with Counting

Walking with Counting (3 minutes)

Setup: Find a stretch of space: a hallway, a sidewalk, a path around your living room. Eyes open. Natural pace. Don't slow down artificially. The Fog brain needs speed, not slowness.

The practice: Walk at your normal pace. Count your steps silently. When you reach ten, reset to one. One, two, three… ten, then repeat the sequence: one, two, three to ten. If you lose count (and you will), note "fogged" and restart at one.

Each lost count is a fog event. Each restart is a return. Count both. The lost counts tell you how often your brain dims. The restarts tell you how often you bring it back. Both numbers are useful. Over days and weeks, you'll see the fog events decrease and the continuous counting stretches lengthen. That's your brain learning to sustain power.

When mind fogs: You'll know it when you "wake up" at step seventeen: you were counting to ten, and somehow seventeen happened. Or you're walking and realize you've stopped counting entirely. No judgment. Restart at one. That restart is the rep.

Closing: Stop walking. Stand still. Notice the contrast between movement and stillness. Take one breath. Done.

Variation (backward counting): Count steps backward from ten to one. Ten, nine, eight... one, then continue the pattern: ten, nine, eight to one. The extra cognitive load of counting backward maintains cortical engagement because the brain can't automate it. If counting forward becomes too easy (good sign), switch to backward.

10-minute version: Walk for ten minutes with counting. Track how many times you restart. That's your fog frequency. A good session for a Fog brain might have eight to twelve restarts. Fewer restarts than last week means the fog is lifting.

5.6.3 Practice 3: Tide-Honoring Micro-Sessions

Your energy cycles. It rises and falls, sometimes on a rough schedule, sometimes unpredictably. Most practice advice tells you to "establish a consistent practice time." That advice works for brains with consistent energy. Yours is tidal.

If you fight the tide, it's exhausting and pointless. Honor the tide instead; that's strategy.

Setup (the energy audit, do this first, for one week): Three times a day (morning, midday, evening), rate your energy on a 1-5 scale. Write it down. One means "I can barely form sentences." Five means "I could write a novel and run a meeting simultaneously." After seven days, you'll see your pattern. Everyone has one, even if it feels random. There's a rhythm in the fog.

The practice: Identify your two highest-energy windows each day, even if they're only fifteen minutes long, even if the "high" is only a 3 out of 5. Practice *during those windows*. Eyes-open, standing, or walking only. Three minutes per session. Two sessions per day, timed to your energy peaks.

Don't waste your energy windows on practices designed for brains with fuel to spare. Your high-energy window is premium real estate. Use it for attention training.

In low-energy windows, rest. Not screens (those add stimulation without adding regulation). Actual rest: dim light, quiet, horizontal if possible. Save calming or seated practices for the other phenotype layers in your constellation (if you have them), and schedule those during transitional periods, not troughs.

Why this works (clinical hypothesis): You're not fighting your biology. You're surfing it. The Fog brain doesn't have a broken power supply. It has an *oscillating* one, desynchronized from the demands placed on it. From clinical experience, Tide-Honoring functions as synchrony training: teaching the arousal system and the cognitive system to meet at the same time. You stop treating the oscillation as the enemy and start using it as the training schedule.

Ultradian rhythms cycle roughly every 90 minutes: 60-70 minutes of higher alertness followed by 15-20 minutes of slowing. Tide-Honoring maps practice to those peaks instead of fighting the dips.

Applied Lane: Burnout Energy Crash

You burned out. You know it. Your body says rest, and the couch has a permanent impression of your shape. The intuition says: rest *more*. Cancel things. Do less. Lie down until it passes.

For Fog-pattern burnout, that intuition is partially right and partially backward. Rest is necessary, but more rest, beyond a certain point, deepens the crash. The arousal system needs gentle activation, not indefinite input removal. Three weeks on the couch doesn't recharge the battery. It teaches the battery to hold less charge.

Practice Rx: Tide-Honoring Micro-Sessions. Identify your two highest-energy windows (even if "high" means a 2 out of 5). Practice then: eyes-open, standing or walking only. Three minutes per session. Two sessions per day. That's it. Don't add duration until the energy windows widen on their own. The widening is the signal that your arousal system is recalibrating. Don't force it. Surf it.

5.7 A vignette: the project manager and the afternoon wall

A project manager at a tech company, mid-thirties, the kind of person who ran standups and sprint reviews with the energy of someone directing air traffic. Sharp in the mornings, tracked everything, shipped on time. Every afternoon at 1:30, his brain disappeared. He described it as "the lights dimming": his eyes stayed open but his processing went to standby. He'd tried Headspace at lunch, guided meditations in the break room with his noise-canceling headphones on. Fell asleep in his desk chair three days running. His team started scheduling nothing after 2 PM, which he didn't know they were doing until someone told him.

Brain map: excess theta, tidal arousal cycle. The 1:30 wall wasn't discipline failure. It was his brain's schedule.

We surfed it. Each morning, three minutes of standing awareness at his standing desk, before the first meeting. Afternoon: at 1:15, before the fog hit, sixty seconds of walking to the water cooler and back. Enough activation to push the dip back twenty minutes. "That's it?" he said. "That's it. Work with your timing."

Three weeks later, the wall didn't disappear. It softened. He could feel it coming and intervene before it arrived.

"I used to hit the wall face-first. Now I see it coming and I have a door."

You stop fighting the weather and learn to read it.

5.8 Practice signals: Fog

Signs you're on track:

- You're staying awake during practice, even if barely, even if it's a continuous battle.
- You can feel the difference between foggy and clear moments. Noticing the fog is progress. It means your awareness is coming online.
- Energy windows are becoming more predictable, or your fog events per session are decreasing.

Signs you're overtraining:

- Practice is happening during energy troughs and making the fog worse, not better.
- You're adding duration before stability is established, longer sessions during low windows.
- Post-practice crash is deeper or longer than pre-practice fog.

What to do: Shorten sessions. Move them to your peak energy window. If standing practice is still triggering fog, walk faster. Add arm movements: swing them, clap softly, touch your shoulders alternately. Increase the motor demand until arousal stabilizes. If nothing works during an energy trough, rest. Don't practice during the bottom of the tide. Wait for the water to rise.

5.9 Troubleshooting

1. "I fall asleep standing up." That's sleep debt, not Fog. See the Sleep-First Diagnostic above. If you're sleeping seven-plus hours and still falling asleep while vertical, talk to your doctor. Sleep apnea, thyroid dysfunction, anemia, and several medications can cause excessive daytime sleepiness. Rule those out first. No meditation practice will fix a medical cause.

2. "I have energy in the morning but I'm gone by 2 PM." That's classic Fog cycling, and it's good news: it means you have a predictable energy window. Practice in the morning. Don't fight the afternoon trough. Use it for environmental regulation: dim lights, quiet space, no screens, horizontal rest if possible. The afternoon is for recovery. The morning is for training. Save your reps for when you have the fuel.

3. "Everyone says meditation should be calming. Activating practices feel wrong." They're not wrong, for you. Meditation is training, not sedation. In the Fog pattern, clinical experience (not a dedicated RCT of phenotype-matched formats) points toward activating practices: movement, eyes open, rhythmic counting, multi-sensory engagement. Walking with counting at a brisk pace is your meditation. Own it.

5.10 In the wild

When you're in a meeting and the fog rolls in, when words become noise and eyes glaze and you're reading the same slide for the third time, press your feet hard into the floor. If you can stand, stand. Count five things you can see. The activation is the practice. You're not being rude. You're keeping your brain online.

When the afternoon crash hits, usually between 1 and 3 PM, worse after lunch, don't fight it with caffeine and willpower. Step outside for two minutes. Bright light. Movement. Even a walk to the end of the hallway counts. The Fog responds to light and movement faster than to any seated practice.

When you sit down to work and nothing loads, when the screen is on and you're at the desk but your brain hasn't arrived, start with your hands. Type one sentence. Write one word. Move one thing on the desk. Motor activation wakes the arousal system. The Fog lifts from the body up.

5.11 "If you're also ___"

- If you're also a **Stabilizer** (can't initiate on top of low energy), see Chapter 4. Walking Meditation works for both: it activates the motor system AND keeps the Fog brain awake. Alternate Walking Meditation (Chapter 4) one day with Eyes-Open Standing Awareness the next. Both serve the motor-arousal axis. Chapter 11 shows you how to build a combined stack.
- If you're also a **Grumpy Old Man** (effort-dread layered on fatigue), see Chapter 6. Classic burnout constellation: address the Fog first (get power online), then tackle the Grumpy. Get your energy online with Eyes-Open Standing Awareness or Walking with Counting first, then add Vagal Toning (Chapter 6) as a second session once the fog lifts enough to sustain it. Chapter 11 has the full stacking protocol.
- If you're also a **Timekeeper slow** (processing speed dragging), see Chapter 10. Fog is a power problem; Timekeeper is a speed problem. If activating practices help, it's Fog. Address the Fog first with activating practices. If processing speed improves when energy is up, the Timekeeper layer may resolve on its own. If it persists, add Self-Paced Concentration (Chapter 10) as your second session. Chapter 11 maps the sequence.

In my clinic, SMR neurofeedback (training 12-15 Hz over sensorimotor cortex) stabilizes vigilance through the same thalamocortical circuits that keep the Fog brain's lights on. Meditation trains the system from above; neurofeedback trains it from below. If activating practices plateau after months of consistent work, that's the next rung on the clinical ladder.

A note on timing and scheduling: This chapter addresses what to practice and how to work with your energy cycles during a session. If the deeper problem is *when* to practice (how to schedule around your ultradian rhythm, use light exposure strategically, or structure your day so the Fog doesn't eat the morning), that's the territory of *Action Cadence* (Peak Brain Press). The Fog phenotype is one of Cadence's central cases. This book gives you the practice. *Action Cadence* gives you the calendar architecture.

The lights came on, even briefly. Tomorrow, again. ___ returns (or don't count; coming back is what matters).

If you fogged the whole session, the lights still came on, especially then. They'll flicker. Turn them back on tomorrow.

Meta Questions (Optional Nerd Corner)

The fog isn't laziness. It's a power-management system doing exactly what it was built to do under the conditions you've handed it.

Then ask the practical question: what would training look like if you scheduled it around the tide instead of against it?

When you're ready: Practice daily for one week, inside your energy windows. What if the problem isn't energy but the flat conviction that nothing is worth the effort? That's Chapter 6, the mood axis, and it's often the Fog's traveling companion.

Ch 6: Dread, Flatness, Resistance: The Mood Axis

The Grumpy Old Man (effort-dread), the Happy Little Kid (flat approach), and the Problem Child (oppositional resistance)

> **Quick Check:** Loudest voice right now: Dread → Grumpy. Flat → Kid. Resisting → Problem Child.

Three people sit down to meditate. The first feels a flat voice arrive before the cushion does: not worth it, won't work, why bother. The second feels nothing at all, no pull toward the practice and none away from it, just gray. The third feels a hot refusal the instant the recording says now close your eyes, a no that fires before any reason for it.

Same instruction. Same five minutes. Three different walls.

All three walls are built in the same place, the front of the brain, where motivation gets its charge. The cards below are your entry points. The chapter explains why each wall stands where it does.

> **PRACTICE CARD: The Grumpy Old Man** *(effort-dread / catastrophizing loop)* **Cascade:** MOOD: Step 2 | **Chapter:** 6
>
> **Entry Move:** Vagal toning first. In 4, out 6, for 2 minutes. Reduce activation cost before asking the approach system to engage.
>
> **Micro:** One deliberate sigh. Long exhale, audible if possible. Resets the vagal brake in 3 seconds. **3 min:** Vagal Toning: 4-count in / 6-count out, return at each wander **10 min:** Loving-Kindness (minimum dose): "May I be comfortable. May I be at ease." **20 min:** Vagal (5 min) → LKM (10 min) → Open Monitoring (5 min)

On Track: Dread softened even slightly ✓ You noticed a moment of "okay, this is fine" ✓ **Too Much:** LKM producing more dread → *Switch to vagal only.*

Return Counter: ___ returns ___ min

PRACTICE CARD: The Happy Little Kid *(flat approach / approach-offline loop)* **Cascade:** MOOD: Step 2 | **Chapter:** 6

Entry Move: Borrow approach. Practice in the same room as a calm, engaged person, or use Curiosity Meditation to nudge the dormant approach circuit awake.

Micro: Notice one new thing in the room right now. Color, texture, sound. That noticing is the approach circuit firing for two seconds. Count it. **3 min:** Curiosity Meditation: explore one sense as if for the first time **10 min:** Curiosity Meditation expanded across two senses, three minutes each, plus a one-minute reflection **20 min:** Co-Practice: sit with a calm person; alternate notice-and-share aloud, drawing approach activation from the other nervous system

On Track: A moment of genuine interest, even small ✓ You wanted something, however briefly ✓ **Too Much:** Forcing engagement makes the flatness deeper → *Borrow approach instead. Co-practice or rest.*

Return Counter: ___ returns ___ min

PRACTICE CARD: Problem Child *(oppositional resistance / anti-coercion loop)* **Cascade:** MOOD: Step 2 | **Chapter:** 6

Entry Move: You choose the practice, the anchor, and when it starts. No one is telling you to do this.

3 min: Freestyle Noting: no prescribed anchor, notice whatever is loudest, stay present **10 min:** Autonomous Practice Design: pick your anchor, change it if you want **20 min:** Self-Designed Sequence: build your own 20-minute session from any practices in this book. Structure it, time it, run it. Nobody else's rules.

On Track: Resistance dropped without being fought ✓ You chose something and stayed with it ✓ **Too Much:** Resistance to the card itself → *Good. You've identified the circuit. Now make a choice. Your choice entirely.*

Return Counter: ___ returns ___ min

These three come out of clinical QEEG work rather than trial-validated categories. They are places to start experimenting.

6.1 The frontal mood axis: one region, three voices

Your frontal cortex has a motivational dial, and it's not a simple slider between "happy" and "sad." It's three-dimensional: approach, withdrawal, and resistance. Each one is a circuit. Each one is trainable.

This is Richard Davidson's frontal asymmetry model, one of the most replicated findings in affective neuroscience (Davidson, 1992). Left frontal regions drive approach: "let's engage." Right frontal regions drive withdrawal: "let's not." Response-inhibition research implicates a right frontal network in braking: "you can't make me" in circuit form.

When these three are in balance, you get flexible motivation. When they're out of balance, you get the Grumpy Old Man (withdrawal dominant), the Happy Little Kid (approach quiet), and the Problem Child (brake stuck). The mood axis tilts toward withdrawal before you've decided how you feel, and every time you notice the tilt and choose engagement, you train the approach circuit to hold.

Three voices, one brain region. Dread, flatness, and resistance aren't personality. They're regulatory reflexes. They eat the space between "I could practice" and "I don't."

6.2 Choose your adventure

- **Withdrawal / effort-dread / catastrophizing**: everything appraised as "not worth it," a flat heaviness that arrives before you start. Read the **Grumpy Old Man** section.
- **Flat approach / nothing pulls / no spark**: the system that should say "ooh, let's try this" is quiet. Skip to the **Happy Little Kid** section.
- **Reactance / anti-coercion / "don't tell me what to do"**: reflexive NO to all instruction, including your own. Skip to the **Problem Child** section.
- **If any practice triggers panic, dissociation, or persistent worsening,** go to Chapter 16.

If you're all three, that's common. Start with whichever voice is loudest right now.

A word about novelty-seeking. If your "can't sustain interest" looks more like *I start every practice, get fascinated for three days, and then the next shiny thing pulls me away,* that's not a Happy Little Kid problem. That's a Supervisor brake problem (impulses leak before you can hold) sometimes layered with a CEO anchoring problem (attention captured by patterns and novelty rather than the chosen target). See Chapter 4 (Supervisor) and Chapter 7 (CEO). The Happy Little Kid in this chapter is the *opposite* presentation: nothing generates enough approach to start.

6.3 What it feels like

If you're the Grumpy Old Man: You wake up and the first appraisal arrives before your feet hit the floor: *another day of this.* Not depression, exactly. You can laugh at a joke, enjoy a meal, have a good conversation. When anything requires *effort* (starting a project, returning a phone call, sitting down to meditate), a flat, heavy voice says: *not worth it. Won't work. Why bother.* The voice is resigned. Like an old man who's seen too many things fail and has stopped expecting success. The effort-dread is reflexive pessimism. It evaluates before you think. Its evaluation is almost always: no.

If you're the Happy Little Kid: Nothing generates a spark. Not boredom. Boredom implies there was interest that faded. This is flatter. An absence of approach. Nothing looks worth doing. The system that's supposed to say "ooh, let's try this" is quiet. You can list things you "should" want to do, and you don't want any of them. You can remember what wanting felt like, and you can't reach it now.

If you're the Problem Child: Someone suggests you try meditation. Immediately, something in you pushes back. Not from logic; you might even agree it's a good idea. The instruction itself, the mere fact of being told what to do, triggers a reflexive *no.* Guided meditations are the worst: that calm, even voice telling you when to breathe, how to breathe, what to notice. You want to breathe differently on principle. You don't hate meditation. You hate being told how to do it, even when the person telling you is yourself.

6.4 A note on intensity and sensory-sensitive brains

If you're here via the autistic/sensory reading path, note this: in typical brains, left frontal activates for positive stimuli (approach) and right frontal activates for negative stimuli (withdrawal). In sensory-sensitive brains, *intense* stimuli of any valence (loud praise or loud criticism, beautiful music or a fire alarm) can trigger right frontal withdrawal. The brain processes intensity before it processes whether the stimulus is good or bad. The signal says LOUD before it says HAPPY or SCARY.

If this resonates, you may need posterior regulation (Chapter 8: turn down the sensory volume) *before* frontal mood work makes sense. The back of the brain feeds the front. If the sensory input is overwhelming, the frontal response will be defensive regardless of whether the input is positive. Regulate the gain first. Then address the mood.

6.5 The shared medicine: compassion and permission

All three voices respond to the same underlying intervention: compassion for the voice, and permission for the person.

- For the **Grumpy Old Man**: Loving-kindness softens effort-dread by activating left frontal approach circuits. Permission to stop disarms the anticipatory appraisal that makes starting feel so costly.
- For the **Happy Little Kid**: Compassion for the flatness rebuilds positive emotional tone without forcing engagement. Borrowed approach (co-regulation, gentle curiosity work) gives the dormant circuit data without requiring it to generate the spark from scratch.
- For the **Problem Child**: Compassion for the resistance itself ("Part of me doesn't want to. That part is doing its job") is the only instruction that doesn't trigger the anti-coercion circuit. Permission to choose everything disarms the brake.

The permission practice from Chapter 1 serves all three. "I'm allowed to stop" disarms the Grumpy's dread AND the Problem Child's resistance. If the mood axis is running hot right now, do it: say silently, "I'm allowed to stop at any time. I'm allowed to do this imperfectly. Whatever my brain does in the next thirty seconds is fine."

6.6 The Grumpy Old Man: effort-dread and catastrophizing

The **Grumpy Old Man** (effort-dread / catastrophizing loop) is the voice that says "don't bother." Right frontal withdrawal system hyperactive. Future-oriented: it predicts threat, effort, and futility before anything happens. Every activity gets cost-benefit analyzed, and the analysis comes back negative. Every time.

Distinction: the Grumpy Old Man generates *internal* futility appraisal, looking *forward* ("this won't work"). The Lifeguard (Chapter 7) generates *external* threat scanning, looking *outward* ("is this safe?"). Different circuits, different temporal directions, different practices.

6.6.1 Why standard advice fails the Grumpy

"Just sit and breathe" gets the same evaluation as everything else: *not worth the effort.* The withdrawal system has already appraised the cost, predicted failure, and concluded the return is negative. It's a circuit running a cost-benefit analysis and getting the wrong answer, weighting cost heavily and discounting benefit. That's frontal asymmetry.

6.6.2 The Grumpy Old Man cascade

Typical first slip: effort-dread appraisal. The cost feels enormous, the reward impossible. Entry: bottom-up first (vagal toning), then compassion. Downstream: when effort-dread softens, arousal normalizes, attention widens, and emotional range returns.

6.6.3 Practices for the Grumpy Old Man

Entry Move: Start with Vagal Toning. Get the nervous system out of withdrawal mode before asking it to do anything more ambitious. Bottom-up first. You can't think your way out of effort-dread.

Vagal Toning (3 minutes)

Setup: Seated or standing. Eyes open or closed, your choice. No special preparation.

The practice: Breathe in for 4 counts through the nose. Out for 6 counts through the mouth. Slow, counted, mechanical. Do this for two minutes. Don't try to feel anything. Don't try to relax. Just count. The vagus nerve will do its job whether you feel it or not.

On the third minute, add a long, audible sigh on each exhale. Let the sound come from your chest, not your throat. The vocalization activates the vagal motor nucleus. Translation: sighing out loud engages the parasympathetic brake. It's a mechanical process, even though it might feel like release. Body first, story second.

When mind wanders: The Grumpy Old Man's wandering sounds like evaluation. "This isn't working." "What a waste of time." "I feel exactly the same." "See? I told you." Note it: "Grumpy talking." Return to the count. Don't argue with the Grumpy; it always wins arguments. Just note and resume counting. Each note-and-return is a rep.

Closing: One breath without counting. Check your jaw. Your shoulders. One degree of release in either is the brake showing up. If nothing shifted, that's useful too. Try the sigh exhale a bit longer next time.

10-minute version: Five minutes of vagal toning, then five minutes of Loving-Kindness (below). The toning settles the nervous system enough for the compassion practice to land without the Grumpy evaluating it to death.

Loving-Kindness as Anti-Catastrophizing (10 minutes)

Setup: Seated. Eyes closed or soft-focused. You've done at least three minutes of vagal toning first (or another bottom-up practice). The Grumpy needs to be at least slightly settled before you aim compassion at it.

The practice:

Phase 1 (3 minutes): Easy target. Bring to mind someone or something easy to care about. A pet. A child. A close friend. Someone whose face makes you soften. Direct these phrases silently toward them: *May you be safe. May you be healthy. May you be at peace.* Repeat. Let the phrases be rhythmic, like a mantra. Don't force feeling; let it arrive on its own. If warmth comes, notice it. If nothing comes, keep repeating. The circuit activates regardless of whether you feel it.

Phase 2 (3 minutes): Yourself. Now direct the phrases toward yourself: *May I be safe. May I be healthy. May I be at peace.* If this feels absurd, forced, or fake, that's the Grumpy Old Man evaluating the practice. Note "evaluating" and repeat the phrases. The feeling follows the repetition, not the other way around. Keep saying the phrases while they still feel hollow. Hollow repetitions count.

Phase 3 (2 minutes): Neutral person. Someone you see regularly but have no particular feelings about: a barista, a neighbor, someone who sits near you at work. Direct the phrases toward them. This is surprisingly powerful: extending compassion to a neutral target broadens the approach circuit beyond the people it already includes.

Phase 4 (2 minutes): Return to self. Come back to the self-directed phrases. Notice if they land differently now.

When mind wanders: The Grumpy will interrupt constantly, especially during the self-directed phase: "This is stupid." "You don't deserve this." "Nothing is changing." Each interruption is a return opportunity. Note "Grumpy" and return to the phrase. The Grumpy's commentary isn't evidence. It's the withdrawal circuit doing its job. Your job is returns.

Closing: One breath. Notice whatever is present, achievement or not. What you *notice* counts. Even the Grumpy's voice, noticed, is data.

20-minute version: Add Phase 5: direct phrases toward someone difficult (2 min). Only when you're ready. This is advanced approach-circuit training: extending the left frontal activation toward a stimulus the right frontal wants to withdraw from. If it triggers flooding, back off. That's a Yellow signal.

If LKM makes things worse: For some people with trauma histories, self-criticism disorders, or active grief, directing compassion inward produces the opposite of the intended effect: intensified self-attack, emotional flooding, or dissociation. The withdrawal circuit is actively fighting the approach instruction. If self-directed phrases consistently produce distress rather than settling (across three or more sessions), drop Phases 2 and 4 entirely. Stay with the easy target and the neutral person. You can build the self-directed capacity later, in Phase 2 or 3 of the program, or in the context of therapy. The circuit still trains from the other-directed phases.

Structured Worry Time (10 minutes, before bed)

This is a containment strategy, and it serves the Grumpy Old Man directly.

Setup: Notebook and pen. Timer set for 10 minutes. No phone. Handwriting only.

The practice: Write down every worry, catastrophe, and "what if" for ten minutes. Stream of consciousness. Don't edit. Don't evaluate. Don't solve. Dump. When the timer goes off, close the notebook. Done. You've given the Grumpy Old Man a designated slot. A fixed window contains the catastrophizing and keeps it from bleeding into your meditation practice and the rest of your day.

Why this works: The Grumpy runs its cost-benefit loop continuously because it has no designated output. Give it an output (ten minutes of uninterrupted complaining) and it often quiets afterward. Not always. Enough that the next practice session encounters less ambient dread.

6.7 The Happy Little Kid: flat approach

The **Happy Little Kid** (flat approach / approach-offline loop) is the left frontal approach system running quiet. Nothing pulls. Nothing sparks. The engine is idling but the car won't move. You can list things you should want to do, and you can't generate the wanting.

Note carefully: this is not the same as novelty-seeking, the high-spark person who burns through ten new interests a month. That's a different brain pattern (Supervisor brake leak or CEO novelty-capture, see Chapters 4 and 7). The Happy Little Kid here is the brain whose approach circuit went quiet, often after burnout, illness, chronic stress, or sustained loss. The fix is gentle reactivation of a circuit that has gone offline.

6.7.1 Why standard advice fails the Happy Little Kid

"Just start" assumes the spark exists. For a flat-approach brain, the spark *is* the resource that's missing. You can't manufacture motivation from nothing by telling someone to start. The fix is to give the dormant circuit input, gently, from outside.

6.7.2 Practices for the Happy Little Kid

Entry Move: Borrow approach. Practice with a calm, engaged person in the room (co-regulation), or use the curiosity meditation below to give the approach circuit something to gently turn toward.

Curiosity Meditation (3 minutes)

Setup: Anywhere. Eyes open. This practice runs on micro-doses of exploration: the gentle activation a flat approach circuit can tolerate without crashing.

The practice: Pick one sense: hear, see, or touch. For three minutes, explore everything available through that sense as if you've never experienced it before.

If you chose hearing: What's the furthest-away sound you can detect? The closest? The strangest? Can you hear the space between sounds? What does silence sound like?

If you chose vision: Pick one object in your field of view. Study it like you're going to draw it from memory. The texture. The shadows. The way light falls on it. Can you see something about it you've never noticed before?

If you chose touch: Feel the surface under your hand. The texture. The temperature. The hardness. How does it change if you press harder? Lighter?

When interest doesn't come: Stay with the sense anyway. The instruction is *direct attention toward sensory data and notice what comes back*, not *feel interested*. The approach circuit is offline. It can come back. Repeated low-cost contact with sensory input gives it material to work with.

Closing: Name one thing you noticed. That naming, even of something dull, is an approach-circuit activation. Count it.

10-minute version: Three minutes per sense across two senses, plus a one-minute closing reflection.

Co-Practice (the offline-approach upgrade): Sit with another person, ideally someone calm and engaged. Take turns noticing and sharing out loud: "I hear the fridge humming." "I notice the shadow under the table looks blue." The social element provides borrowed approach activation. You're not generating wanting from nothing. You're using another nervous system's approach signal to nudge yours.

Why this works: Flat-approach brains often need *external input* to begin generating their own. This is what co-regulation is for, mammalian nervous systems calibrating off each other. If you have a friend, partner, or therapist who can sit with you for ten minutes of low-stakes shared noticing, that's the practice. Build the internal approach signal back up by borrowing it externally first.

6.8 Problem Child: oppositional resistance

The **Problem Child** (oppositional resistance / emergency brake loop) maps to a right frontal inhibition network. When that network is hyperactive, any perceived external control triggers reflexive resistance: opposition that fires before your conscious mind is involved. The word "should" is its activation cue. The word "must" is a declaration of war.

A word about the name. Many people with this pattern were called a problem child as kids, and the label landed as a verdict on their character. Here it means the opposite: a circuit doing a protective job, named this way on purpose to take the term back from everyone who used it as an insult.

Problem Child is often the Grumpy Old Man's exhausted teenager: resistance born from accumulated effort-dread. For some people it runs deeper, an early-installed pattern in which the nervous system learned to treat being directed as unsafe and built a strong brake against external control. Either way, the brake is doing a protective job, and the circuit fires before your conscious mind decides whether the instruction is worth following.

Anti-coercion is a regulatory feature. It's a brake against external override, and for some nervous systems, it's one of the strongest regulatory signals available. The practice has to feel chosen.

6.8.1 Why standard advice fails the Problem Child

"Follow these instructions" is the exact trigger. Guided meditations feel coercive. Structured programs feel like traps. Even setting your own timer can feel like submitting to someone else's agenda, including your own. Problem Child doesn't distinguish external from internal authority. It brakes against both.

6.8.2 Practices for the Problem Child

Entry Move: Complete autonomy. No instructions except one: you decide everything.

Choice-Based Practice (any duration)

Setup: Set a timer for your intended duration: you choose the length. Sit, stand, or lie down: you choose the position. Eyes open or closed: you choose.

The practice: For the duration of the timer, do whatever feels like practice. Breathe. Walk. Count sounds. Stare at the wall. Stretch. Lie down and feel the floor. There are no rules. No instructions. No guided voice. No one is telling you what to do, including me.

The only structure: when the timer goes off, note one thing you noticed during the session. Write it down. That's the data.

When mind says "this isn't real meditation": Notice that thought. That's either the CEO (evaluation) or internalized cultural meditation expectations. Note "judging" and return to whatever you were doing. There is no wrong way to do this practice. That's the point. The absence of instructions is the instruction.

Closing: Timer goes off. Note one observation. Done. You just practiced on your own terms.

Why this works: Problem Child needs to learn, at the nervous system level, that practice isn't coercion. Complete autonomy disarms the anti-coercion circuit. Over time, you'll naturally gravitate toward specific elements (body awareness, breath counting, visual focus) because they feel right, not because someone prescribed them.

10-minute version: Same protocol, longer duration. Add one constraint each week, as an experiment. Week 1: total freedom. Week 2: try including at least thirty seconds of breath focus somewhere (you choose when). Week 3: try including one minute of body awareness (you choose what). The constraints grow slowly, and you always have veto power. Problem Child allows gradual structure if it feels like a choice, not an imposition.

Rebellion Acknowledgment (30 seconds, before any practice)

Setup: Before you begin any practice, from any chapter in this book, add this.

The practice: Say silently: *Part of me doesn't want to do this. That's fine. That part is noted. We're doing it anyway, and we can stop whenever we want.*

Pause. Notice what happens. Does the resistance soften? Spike? Stay the same? Whatever happens, you've just done something most meditation instructions never do: you've acknowledged the resistance instead of ignoring it.

Why this works: Problem Child softens when it's *seen,* not opposed. Most meditation instructions pretend resistance doesn't exist ("let go of thoughts"). The rebellion acknowledgment names the resistance without fighting it: that part gets noted, and you still choose to practice, on your terms. The acknowledgment respects the circuit's protective function; it's not a trick to bypass resistance.

6.9 A vignette: the nurse who couldn't want anything

Twelve years in the ICU. Three failed meditation attempts. "I just can't want things anymore," she said, in a tone so flat it could have been read off a teleprompter.

Brain map: profound right frontal dominance plus left frontal underactivation. Twelve years of sustained stress had trained the withdrawal system to dominate and the approach system to go quiet. Effort-dread plus flat approach: the mood axis stuck in withdrawal.

We started with vagal toning: three minutes in her car, twice a day. "I don't feel anything," she said after Week 1. "Good," I said. "The vagus nerve doesn't care how you feel. It's a hydraulic lever."

By Week 6, she was standing in a grocery store looking at strawberries and noticed, almost with surprise, that she *wanted* them: plain wanting, without obligation or duty.

She bought the strawberries. She ate them in the car. She cried from relief.

For a burned-out nervous system, ordinary wanting is a major sign.

6.10 A vignette: the teenager who said no to everything

Seventeen. Arms crossed. Phone out. Every structured intervention got the same response: *You can't make me.*

I didn't tell him to meditate. I handed him a timer: "Sit anywhere you want, do whatever you want, for three minutes. Scroll your phone. Stare at the wall. Only rule: wait for the timer."

He sat on the floor and closed his eyes.

"My mind was kind of quiet. That was weird."

"You chose to close your eyes. Nobody told you to."

By Week 6, he was practicing five minutes a day at home. Nobody had asked. It had never once been forced.

Remove what the resistance is bracing against, and it often chooses exactly what it refused.

Applied Lane: Chronic Stress and Burnout

After months or years of sustained stress, the Grumpy Old Man becomes the default operating system. "Not worth it" applies to everything: work, relationships, hobbies, the people you care about. The effort-dread isn't situational anymore. It's ambient. It's your weather. *(If your burnout also includes Fog-pattern energy crashes (afternoon collapse, brain-off-at-2-PM), see the Applied Lane in Chapter 5. Fog and Grumpy burnout often co-occur and need different entry points.)*

Practice Rx: Vagal Toning (3 minutes, twice daily) + Structured Worry Time (10 minutes before bed). Bottom-up before top-down: you cannot mindset your way out of burnout. Get the vagal brake working. Contain the catastrophizing. Then, slowly, rebuild approach capacity through loving-kindness. Start with the easiest target (pet, child, good memory). Work toward yourself only when the phrases don't feel like sandpaper.

6.11 What Brain Maps Show: Frontal Mood Axis

For readers who want the underlying EEG picture: a Grumpy Old Man map shows right frontal asymmetry, with the withdrawal circuit running hotter than the approach circuit. A Happy Little Kid map shows left frontal underactivation, the approach drive that should be lighting up for novelty and engagement running quiet. This overlaps with anhedonia and the "negative symptom" cluster of post-burnout states. A Problem Child map often shows elevated right frontal slow activity, the brake system running with too much inhibitory tone where flexibility is needed. For the complete brain-map picture, see *The QEEG Field Guide* (Hill & Lomeli, Peak Brain Press).

6.12 Practice signals: Frontal Mood Axis

Signs you're on track:

- The effort-dread softened, even slightly. A loosening in the chest. One degree less resistance to starting. (Grumpy)
- Something pulled, even briefly. A moment of "I want that." Even small wanting counts. (Happy Little Kid)
- You started a practice despite the "no" voice. The resistance was noted, not obeyed. (Problem Child)

- The dread was there, and you practiced anyway. (all three)
- Around the one-month mark, the dread may still show up at the start of practice, but you've stopped waiting for it to clear before beginning.

Signs you're overtraining:

- Loving-kindness practice is generating more self-criticism, not less. The Grumpy is evaluating the compassion and finding it insufficient.
- Curiosity meditation is making the flatness feel worse, not better. (Forcing approach against an offline circuit can deepen the off state.)
- Problem Child's resistance is getting louder with more practice, not quieter. Each session feels more coercive, not less.

What to do: Drop back to vagal toning only. Three minutes, body-first, no cognitive content. Rebuild the bottom-up foundation before adding emotional practice on top. If you're the Problem Child, switch to choice-based practice with zero structure for a week. If you're the Happy Little Kid, find a co-practice partner instead of trying to generate approach alone. The reset is the strategy.

6.13 Troubleshooting

1. "Loving-kindness feels fake. I don't believe the phrases." Good. You don't have to. The phrases aren't affirmations. They're attention targets: you practice pointing attention toward approach whether you believe the words or not. In my clinical experience the felt sense arrives late, often weeks after the practice stops feeling absurd. That is an observation from practice. The controlled-trial data hasn't mapped the sequence. Start with a pet or a baby (almost nobody finds it fake to wish a golden retriever well). Work toward yourself only when ready. Fake is fine. The circuit doesn't care about sincerity.

2. "I'm all three: grumpy, flat, and oppositional." Start with the Problem Child's choice-based practice, because if resistance is active, nothing prescribed will stick. When resistance softens, add vagal toning for the Grumpy Old Man so the system settles enough for compassion work to land. When the dread softens, add curiosity meditation or co-practice for the Happy Little Kid. Sequence: autonomy first, settling second, gentle approach third.

3. "My resistance isn't to meditation; it's to being told anything by anyone." Strong Problem Child, possibly amplified by a Lifeguard (Chapter 7). Choice-based practice, in a space you control entirely: door closed, no guided audio, your schedule. The resistance will tell you what it needs if you stop fighting it.

4. "I get fascinated for two days then move on to the next thing." That's not Happy Little Kid. That's a Supervisor brake problem (Chapter 4) or a CEO novelty-capture problem (Chapter 7), depending on where the pull comes from. If the pull is impulsive and you don't see it coming, Supervisor. If you can feel yourself getting curious about a new pattern and then locked into it, CEO. Either way, this chapter isn't your starting point.

6.14 "If you're also ___"

- If you're also a **Lifeguard** (threat-scanning underneath the mood layer), see Chapter 7. Address the Grumpy first (bottom-up), then give the Lifeguard safety data. Start with vagal toning (this chapter) for two weeks to settle the withdrawal system, then add the Lifeguard's "Is This Now?" grounding practice (Chapter 7) as a second session. Chapter 11 shows you how to sequence both in a single stack.
- If you're also a **Princess & the Pea** (sensory overwhelm feeding the mood axis), see Chapter 8. If sensory overload is driving the mood, regulate sensation first. Start with environmental regulation and the titrated body scan (Chapter 8) to lower sensory volume, then layer in vagal toning once input is manageable. Mood work lands better when the sensory system isn't screaming.

- If you're also a **Stabilizer** (can't start plus don't want to start), see Chapter 4. Walking meditation serves both. Start with walking meditation (Chapter 4) to get the motor system online, usually before mood work lands, then add vagal toning once you can initiate consistently.

Meta Questions (Optional Nerd Corner)

What does your Grumpy Old Man believe it's protecting you from? If the effort-dread is a security system, what threat is it guarding against?

Record your returns: ___ returns, ___ min. The sessions you almost skipped count too. The return from "why bother" to "I'll try one breath" is the rep. Mood shift is downstream of the count. Tomorrow: start with vagal toning, three minutes, regardless of which voice is loudest when you sit down.

When you're ready: Start with whichever voice is loudest today and practice daily for one week. What happens when the problem isn't mood but attention that won't let go, scanning, evaluating, looping? Chapter 7 has the orienting axis.

Ch 7: Stuck in Loops / Can't Stop Scanning: The Orienting Axis

The CEO (conflict monitoring / perseveration) and The Lifeguard (hypervigilance / threat-scanning)

Quick Check: Close your eyes for 3 seconds. Comfortable or uncomfortable? Comfortable → CEO. Uncomfortable → Lifeguard.

PRACTICE CARD: The CEO *(conflict monitoring / perseveration loop)* **Cascade:** ORIENT: Step 3 | **Chapter:** 7

Entry Move: Give yourself a structured task first. The CEO can't start from nothing: give the quality-control loop something to evaluate before fading to open awareness.

Micro: Notice one evaluation you're running right now. Let it go. That release is the rep. 3 seconds. **3 min:** Structured Breath Count: count 1 to 10, restart at wander **10 min:** Structured → Open Transition: 5 min counting, then release to open monitoring **20 min:** 5 min counting → 5 min noting → 10 min open monitoring

On Track: Evaluation loop ran but you didn't engage it, only observed it running ✓ **Too Much:** Meta-evaluating the evaluation → *Restart the count from 1. That's the exit.*

Return Counter: ___ returns ___ min

PRACTICE CARD: The Lifeguard *(hypervigilance / threat-scanning loop)* **Cascade:** ORIENT: Step 3 | **Chapter:** 7

Entry Move: Eyes open. Always. At least until your nervous system demonstrates safety with this practice. Don't fight the need for visual surveillance. Work with it.

3 min: "Is This Now?": each time the threat scan activates, ask: *Is this threat present right now, in this room?* **10 min:** Grounding + Pendulation: feet/chair/back, then authorized surveillance scan every 2 min, then return to body **20 min:** Co-regulation entry if available: Is This Now? (5 min) → pendulation (5 min) → breath anchor (10 min)

On Track: Noticed the threat scan and let it pass ✓ Room felt slightly safer during practice ✓ **Too Much:** Surveillance intensifying → *Exit practice. Grounding only: feet, hands, name 5 things visible.*

Return Counter: ___ returns ___ min

The CEO and Lifeguard are clinical observations from brain maps. No randomized trial produced them. Begin experimenting from them; don't diagnose yourself with them.

7.1 Choose Your Adventure

- **Stuck in internal loops:** overthinking, evaluating, "am I doing this right?", can't stop analyzing → read the **CEO** section
- **Scanning for threats:** hypervigilant, "is this safe?", can't close your eyes, constantly monitoring the room → skip to the **Lifeguard** section
- **If any practice triggers panic, dissociation, or persistent worsening** → Chapter 16 immediately

If both are running at once: start with the Lifeguard. Safety before evaluation.

Evaluation and vigilance run loud here. The metric is still returns: how often you cut in before the loop completes.

7.2 Start here: entry moves before explanation

If you recognized yourself in the Quick Check above, do the entry move now before reading further. The CEO will want to understand before it tries. The Lifeguard will want to confirm safety before it closes its eyes. Both of those impulses are the patterns this chapter trains.

CEO, start with this: Set a timer for three minutes. Count your breaths. In: one. Out: two. Up to ten. Start over. When you catch yourself evaluating the counting, label it "evaluating" and return to the number. That catch and return is one rep. The rest of this chapter explains why it works.

Lifeguard, start with this: Look around the room slowly. Name five things you can see. For each one: say silently "this is safe right now." Press your feet into the floor. Do this for ninety seconds. You're building a safety inventory. The rest of this chapter explains why that inventory matters.

Do the practice, then read on.

7.3 What It Feels Like

If you're the CEO: You sit down to meditate and within seconds, the audit begins. *Am I breathing correctly? Should my hands be here or there? Is this posture right? It doesn't feel like it's working. Maybe a different technique. Actually, let me think about what technique would be best for my specific situation.* You're not meditating. You're running a quality-control analysis of the meditation. And when you notice you're evaluating, you evaluate the evaluating. It's a hall of mirrors with you at every reflection, clipboard in hand.

The problem isn't that you can't focus. You focus intensely on the wrong thing. Your attention locks onto the process of attention itself and won't let go. Other people seem able to just *be* somewhere, present. You can't experience something ungraded.

What the Brain Map Shows: A CEO map shows anterior cingulate hyperactivation: the conflict-monitoring system stuck in evaluation mode. The error-detection circuit that should flag problems and move on is flagging everything and moving on from nothing.

If you're the Lifeguard: You sit down to meditate and something in your chest tightens before you even close your eyes. If you *do* close them, the tightening gets worse: a rising awareness of sounds, of air movement, of the space behind you that you can't see. Your body generates a continuous question: *Is this safe? Is someone coming? What was that sound?*

It's a body-level surveillance system, running below conscious thought. A radar that doesn't have an off switch. Other people close their eyes and the world recedes. Close your eyes and the world gets louder, more present, more potentially threatening. This isn't clinical anxiety: your posterior cingulate, a broad default-mode hub, appears to be running in surveillance mode. In the Lifeguard phenotype, that processing arrives as threat. In clinical observation, it needs visual data to settle. Take away the visual data, and it goes to high alert.

What the Brain Map Shows: A Lifeguard map shows elevated posterior cingulate connectivity and often heightened beta across posterior regions: a pattern that looks like a surveillance system at maximum sensitivity. A network that should hum in the background appears to be consuming foreground resources. It flags anomalies, and in this phenotype every anomaly arrives as a possible threat.

7.4 The Midline Axis: One Highway, Two Directions

Your brain's midline axis runs front to back along the center of the cortex. The anterior cingulate (ACC) sits at the front, in the salience network. The posterior cingulate (PCC) sits at the back, in the default mode network. Both direct attention. Both can get stuck.

The **CEO** sits at the front, pointing attention *inward*: conflicts, decisions, self-evaluation, "am I doing this right?" It detects mismatches and triggers course corrections. When stuck, it can't stop monitoring: everything gets evaluated, everything gets a score.

The **Lifeguard** sits at the back, pointing attention *outward*: environment, context, continuity, "what just changed?" In the maps, it appears to integrate environmental data and flag what doesn't fit. When stuck, it can't stop scanning.

Distinction: the CEO perseverates *internally* (what should I do?). The Lifeguard scans *externally* (what's happening?). Same highway, opposite directions. Both chew the pause: the CEO packs the gap with evaluation, the Lifeguard with threat-scanning. Often the response fires before either loop finishes.

The CEO needs to learn to *release* focus, and the Lifeguard needs to learn to *trust* the environment. Both struggle with the same skill: disengaging attention when the current target no longer needs it.

7.5 The CEO: When the Evaluator Won't Quit

The **CEO** (anterior cingulate cortex) is the brain's conflict monitor. It detects mismatches and triggers corrections. When working well, it's efficient executive function. When stuck, it evaluates everything: the meditation, your response to it, your evaluation of your response.

Two modes of getting stuck:

- **Theta-stuck:** Simple loops, earworms, repetitive checking. "Did I lock the door?" asked seventeen times. "Am I doing this right?" on infinite repeat.
- **Beta-stuck:** Complex intrusive narratives, rumination spirals, perfectionism. "What if I said the wrong thing at the meeting? Here are seventeen scenarios of how that might play out and none of them are good."

7.5.1 Why Standard Advice Fails the CEO

"Let go of your thoughts" is the CEO's nightmare. The CEO doesn't know how to let go. It monitors *for* letting go. Telling the CEO to stop evaluating is like telling a fire alarm to stop detecting smoke. The circuit is *designed* to hold on. And the harder you try to let go, the more the CEO evaluates your letting go: "Am I letting go correctly? Is this what letting go feels like? I think I'm thinking about letting go instead of letting go. Damn."

In practice: structure first, then gradual release. You can't rip the controls away from a controller. You have to give them a job, let them do it, and then slowly widen the aperture. The evaluation loop closes the gap between observation and judgment, and every time you release the audit and return, you train observation to hold and stay at observation.

7.5.2 CEO Cascade

Typical first slip: evaluation loop. The release signal that should say *done, move on* never fires. Entry: structured-to-open transition: structure first, then gradual release. Downstream: when the loop softens, attention becomes flexible instead of rigid.

The anterior cingulate generates an error signal roughly 50–100 milliseconds after each perceived mistake. In health anxiety that signal runs as hot as it does in OCD, which is why hyperactive error monitoring is proposed as a marker that cuts across diagnoses rather than belonging to one (Riesel et al., 2017). Practice doesn't silence it. It recalibrates the downstream response. Experienced meditators show *stronger* error detection paired with better emotional acceptance, not more self-punishment (Teper & Inzlicht, 2013). Open monitoring specifically enhances conscious error awareness without amplifying the automatic alarm (Lin et al., 2019).

7.5.3 Practices for the CEO

Entry Move: Start with the "Am I Doing This Right?" Practice. Three minutes of breath counting with evaluation-catching.

"Am I Doing This Right?" Practice (3 minutes)

Setup: Seated comfortably. Eyes open or closed (the CEO usually prefers closed, because visual data gives it more to evaluate). Timer set.

The practice: Begin breath counting. Inhale, one. Exhale, two. Inhale, three. Up to ten, then restart at one. This gives the CEO a structured task. It can monitor the counting, check the numbers, evaluate the breath quality. Let it.

But also listen for the evaluation voice. The moment you catch yourself evaluating the meditation ("Am I focused enough? Is this correct? Was that a good breath or should I start over?"), label it: "evaluating." Then return to counting. Don't try to stop the evaluating. Just catch it and name it.

When mind wanders: The CEO's mind doesn't wander the way other phenotypes' minds do. It doesn't drift off to the grocery list or a conversation from Tuesday. It stays on-task, but adds a supervisory layer that grades the performance in real time. The practice is catching the grading, not stopping it. Each time you catch "evaluating" and return to counting, that's a return. That's the CEO's version of a rep.

Closing: When the timer goes off, stop counting immediately. Don't add one more breath. Don't finish the current cycle. Just stop. Notice the urge to complete. That's the CEO. Let it be incomplete. That's practice too.

Same time tomorrow. The evaluation loop will be there. So will you.

10-minute version: Five minutes of breath counting, then transition to Choiceless Awareness (below). The first five minutes give the CEO its structure. The second five minutes practice releasing it.

20-minute version: Three phases. Phase 1 (7 min): breath counting. Phase 2 (6 min): choiceless awareness. Phase 3 (7 min): alternate freely between counting and open awareness, choosing whichever feels right in the moment. Phase 3 is the advanced practice: the CEO learning to toggle between control and release.

Choiceless Awareness (5-10 minutes)

Setup: This practice follows structured breath counting. Don't start here. The CEO needs the counting to settle first.

The practice: Drop the count. Don't replace it with anything. Let attention go where it goes. Sounds, thoughts, body sensations, the feeling of the chair, whatever arrives, notice it. Don't choose. Don't direct. Don't evaluate. Let the mind be a field of awareness instead of a beam of focus.

When the CEO evaluates the awareness: Note "evaluating." Don't return to counting. Stay in open awareness. The CEO will protest: "This isn't structured enough. How do I know it's working? Should I go back to counting?" Label each protest: "evaluating." Return to noticing whatever is present. The discomfort of formlessness IS the training. The CEO is learning that it's okay to not direct.

Closing: One breath. Let your hands rest heavy in your lap. Notice what it's like to not grade this practice. If you grade it anyway, notice *that*. There's no level of meta-awareness that isn't also practice.

7.6 The Lifeguard: When Safety Scanning Won't Stop

The **Lifeguard** (posterior cingulate cortex) is a major default-mode hub, with documented roles in memory, attention, and context. In the Lifeguard phenotype, it appears to run as a background scanner: integrating context, flagging anomalies. When hyperactive, it can't stop monitoring. The room never feels fully safe. When you close your eyes, anxiety spikes. That link between PCC activity and visual safety data is a pattern I see in clinical work. The mechanism has not been mapped.

Distinction from the Grumpy Old Man: the Lifeguard scans *backward and outward* (past events, current environment). The Grumpy looks *forward* (future threat and effort). Different temporal directions, different practices.

7.6.1 Why Standard Advice Fails the Lifeguard

"Close your eyes and go inward" removes visual data. In the Lifeguard phenotype, the scanning appears to depend on that data. Vision dominates your brain's real-time environmental processing. More than any other sense, it's what your threat-detection system relies on to answer "am I safe right now?" When the Lifeguard loses access to that data, it compensates by amplifying everything else: sounds get louder, body sensations get more intense, the air itself feels charged. Heart rate climbs. Muscles tighten. Attention narrows to threat detection.

That's a threat-detection system doing its job without the channel it trusts. The fix is providing the safety data: eyes open, environment visible, grounded in the present moment. Not "push through."

7.6.2 Lifeguard Cascade

Typical first slip: threat perception. The scan completes but never registers "clear," so it restarts. Entry: bottom-up grounding, co-regulation, environmental regulation. Downstream: when safety is established, scanning decreases and the default mode network stops defaulting to alarm.

7.6.3 Practices for the Lifeguard

Entry Move: Start with eyes-open grounding. Establish safety in the present moment before doing anything else.

Grounding: "Is This Now?" (3 minutes)

Setup: Seated or standing. **Eyes open.** Look around the room slowly. Not scanning for threat. Looking with intention.

The practice: Name five things you can see. Say them silently: *chair, window, book, shadow, ceiling.* After each one, ask silently: *Is this now?*

The answer is yes. You're anchoring in the present moment, the only moment the Lifeguard can verify as safe.

Four things you can touch. Reach out and contact them. The arm of the chair. The fabric of your clothing. The surface of the desk. Your own knee. Each one confirms you're here: real contact, in *now.*

Three things you can hear. Name them. Two things you can smell (or the absence of smell; "nothing" is also data). One thing you can taste.

When mind scans: The Lifeguard's default is to scan for what's wrong. Each time you notice the scanning (a sound that triggers alertness, a shadow that draws your eye, a body sensation that feels like a warning), note "scanning" and return to the next sensory item. Don't fight the scanning. Name it and come back. "Scanning. Now, what's the next thing I can see?"

Closing: One breath. Look around the room one more time. Say silently: *This room is safe right now.* Notice where your body receives that statement: chest loosening, shoulders dropping, hands unclenching. Even a fraction of release is the Lifeguard accepting the data.

10-minute version: Three minutes of grounding (above), then seven minutes of Noting for Threat vs. Safety (below). The grounding establishes the floor. The noting rebuilds the Lifeguard's ability to detect safety, not just threat.

20-minute version: Three minutes grounding, then ten minutes noting, then seven minutes of eyes-open present-moment awareness: sitting, eyes open, noticing whatever arises, unlabeled. Let the Lifeguard run its scan in the background while you practice not reacting to its alerts. The non-reaction is the training.

Noting for Threat vs. Safety (10 minutes)

Setup: Seated. Eyes open. Timer set.

The practice: Scan the room deliberately, but instead of checking for threat (which the Lifeguard does automatically), label what you notice: "safe," "neutral," "familiar," "warm," "quiet," "stable."

You're building a safety inventory. The Lifeguard has a threat inventory a mile long. This practice builds the counterpart.

When you notice something that triggers a threat signal (a sound, a shadow, a person outside the window, a thought about something bad), label it: "threat." Then assess: *Is this an actual threat right now?* Right now in this room, not hypothetically, not "what if." If no, label it "not now" and return to noticing safe things.

When mind escalates: If the threat assessment triggers an arousal spike (heart rate up, chest tight, scanning intensifying), that's Yellow. Return to grounding: feet on floor, five things you can see. You haven't failed. You've found the edge. Stay below it.

Closing: Name three safe things in the room. Take one breath. Done.

Why this works: The Lifeguard is tuned to flag anomalies, and any system tuned that way is faster at spotting what is off than at confirming all is clear. It has a signal for wrong and no signal for safe. This practice builds the parallel skill. Over time, the scanning settles because it's receiving confirming data from both channels.

The Lifeguard's Rescue Breath (10–30 seconds)

When the Lifeguard spikes (heart rate climbing, hands cold, scanning intensifying), don't reach for a counted breath. Counting requires prefrontal bandwidth that's already been hijacked. Instead, use the physiological sigh from Chapter 3: two quick inhales through your nose (full breath, then a short top-off sniff), one long exhale through your mouth. Three rounds, fifteen seconds, zero cognitive load. Reassess. If you're still in Yellow, do three more. If you've dropped toward Green, move to the grounding protocol below.

Pendulation (5-10 minutes)

> **Pre-condition:** Pendulation is a Level 3 practice on the Lifeguard Practice Ladder. Do not start here. Complete at least two weeks of consistent Level 1 (eyes-open grounding) and Level 2 (grounding + noting) practice before attempting Pendulation.

Starting here without that foundation risks triggering the exact flooding or flashback response the practice is designed to gradually train past.

Setup: Seated. Eyes open or closed (your choice, but if eyes-closed triggers scanning, keep them open).

The practice: Notice a place in your body that feels tense, tight, or activated: chest, jaw, stomach, shoulders, wherever the tension lives. Stay there for three breaths. Don't try to fix it. Notice the shape of the tension. The temperature. Whether it pulses or holds steady.

Now shift attention to a place in your body that feels neutral or comfortable: your hands, your feet, your belly, the space between your shoulder blades. Stay there for three breaths. Notice what neutral feels like. It's probably quieter than you expected.

Pendulate back and forth: tense place → comfortable place → tense place → comfortable place. Each oscillation is a round. Do four or five rounds.

When the Lifeguard says "don't go back to the tense place": Note "protecting." Stay with the comfortable place. That protective signal is data. You may return to the tense place only if genuine curiosity and a sense of choice are both present and you remain in the Green zone. If the "no" is strong, recurs across sessions, or arrives with dissociation, do not override it solo. Bring it to a trauma-trained clinician and pendulate with them in the room. Over time, the tense place often softens because the nervous system learns at its own pace: going there doesn't mean staying there.

Closing: End on the comfortable place. Stay for three extra breaths. Notice what regulation feels like.

If a flashback begins: If visiting the tense place triggers intrusive images, a body memory, or a flashback, stop the pendulation immediately. Open your eyes if they are closed. Press both feet into the floor. Name five things you can see, out loud if possible. Hold something physical: a glass, your phone, a pen. Feel its weight and temperature.

You are in a room. The room is real. Do not attempt to "pendulate through" a flashback. End the session. Use the 90-Second Reset. Return to Level 1 or Level 2 practice for your next session. If flashbacks recur across multiple Pendulation attempts, this practice needs to be done with a therapist present, not solo.

Why this works: This is what trauma-informed practice looks like. The Lifeguard can't tolerate prolonged exposure to activation. It escalates to full threat mode. Pendulation avoids that by oscillating between activation and safety. The nervous system learns: I can feel this and survive. I can go there and come back. That's the foundation of regulation.

The Lifeguard Practice Ladder

Level 1: Eyes-open grounding: "Is This Now?" 3 min. *(Start here.)* **Level 2:** Grounding + Noting for Threat vs. Safety. 10 min. **Level 3:** Grounding + Noting + Pendulation. 20 min. Eyes open. **Level 4:** Co-regulation entry: practice with another person present. Add brief eyes-closed segments (60 seconds) within an eyes-open session.

Move up only when the current level feels consistently Green. If any level triggers persistent Yellow, drop back. The Lifeguard's ladder is slower than most. That pace is by design.

Co-Regulation for the Lifeguard: If available, practice with another person in the room. Their calm nervous system co-regulates yours. This is not a metaphor, it's mammalian physiology. Same room, separate practices, no talking required. Or have someone sit nearby and breathe steadily. You'll borrow their regulation naturally, on its own. No person available? A dog works. Their calm presence provides the safety data the Lifeguard is scanning for.

7.7 A Vignette: The Lawyer Who Graded Everything

Corporate lawyer, mid-forties, mergers and acquisitions. She sat down across from me with a yellow legal pad already organized into numbered questions. Her handwriting was architectural: every letter formed with the precision of someone who redlines contracts for a living. She uncapped a felt-tip pen and waited for me to begin so she could take notes on whether my opening statement was adequate.

The quality-control circuit never clocked out: every email, meeting comment, and brief audited nightly in bed. The mindfulness course had made it worse. She spent eighteen of twenty minutes grading the meditation and nine of ten minutes after the session evaluating the grade. "I gave myself a C-plus last Tuesday," she said, without irony.

Brain map: anterior cingulate lit up, theta elevated. The error-checking circuit was treating everything as a potential error, including the practice itself.

We started with five minutes of breath counting. The CEO could feel competent at breath counting. It has a number and a sequence, which is something to monitor correctly. Then two minutes of open monitoring. "Terrifying," she said. She put her pen down for the first time in the session. "I don't know what I'm supposed to do." "Exactly. That's the rep."

By Week 6, she could sit in open monitoring for five minutes. The auditing still ran, but she stopped filing the reports. Choice is leaving the report unfiled.

7.8 A Vignette: The Therapist Who Couldn't Close Her Eyes

A therapist who'd taught clients to meditate for twenty years and couldn't do it herself. "Close your eyes": heart rate climbed, hands went cold, fifteen minutes scanning the room through her eyelids.

Brain map: hot posterior cingulate. My read: when she closed her eyes, she removed the data the scanning pattern runs on. Therefore: danger.

We didn't ask her to close her eyes. Three minutes of "Is This Now?": naming what she saw, touching the chair arm, building a safety inventory. "I can feel my shoulders," she said after the first session. "Usually I don't notice them until they're at my ears."

By Week 4: thirty seconds of eyes-closed at the end of grounding. "Not peaceful. But not panic." That pause between one scan ending and the next starting was a half-second more in the gap. By Week 8: five minutes open grounding, then five minutes eyes-closed noting. Non-negotiable order. Her clients got better instruction. She finally knew what a mismatched practice felt like.

7.9 Practice Signals: CEO + Lifeguard

Signs you're on track (CEO):

- You catch the evaluating voice during practice ("there it is again")
- The structured-to-open transition feels less jarring, more like shifting gears
- You can end a session when the timer goes off and stop there

Signs you're on track (Lifeguard):

- Eyes-open practice feels tolerable, maybe even safe
- You can name "safe" and "neutral" as easily as you name "threat"
- The space between a perceived threat and the "Is this now?" assessment is shrinking
- You stayed in the room and kept your seat

By Day 30, noticing the scan no longer means the scan accelerates. The noticing itself has become the deceleration.

Signs you're overtraining:

- CEO: practice has become another performance to score and tune. You're rating your sessions.
- Lifeguard: scanning accelerated instead of settling. The room feels *less* safe after practice, not more.

What to do: CEO: drop to 3-minute breath counting only. No open monitoring. Rebuild the structured floor. Lifeguard: stop the practice. Eyes open. Feet on floor. Name three things you see. Grounding first. Always.

7.10 Troubleshooting

1. "I can't stop evaluating. Even noting 'evaluating' feels like evaluation." That's the CEO being its thorough, relentless self. Note "meta-evaluating" and return to counting. You can nest these labels infinitely (evaluating the evaluation of the evaluation), but the return is what counts, not the depth of the recursion. As long as you're returning, you're training.

2. "I can't close my eyes, but everyone says meditation requires it." It doesn't. Eyes-open meditation is meditation. The Lifeguard needs visual safety data. Practice with eyes open until the nervous system builds enough safety that eyes-closed becomes an option, which may take weeks, months, or never.

3. "I was doing fine and then suddenly felt panicky/dissociated." Stop the practice immediately. Eyes open. Feet on floor. Grounding protocol: name five things you see, four you can touch, three you can hear. Press your feet down hard. This is your Stop Signal working correctly. It's a feature, not a failure. Turn to Chapter 16 for guidance on when mindfulness triggers adverse effects.

7.11 "If You're Also ___"

- If you're also a **Grumpy Old Man** (forward-looking dread underneath the evaluation/scanning), see Chapter 6. Address the Grumpy's effort-dread first (Vagal Toning), then work on the CEO's evaluation loop. Start with Vagal Toning (Chapter 6) for two weeks to soften the effort-dread, then add the CEO's Structured-to-Open breath counting as your second session. The evaluation loop is easier to release when dread isn't fueling it. Chapter 11 maps the full stacking sequence.

- If you're also an **Interpreter** (verbal rumination fueling the loops), see Chapter 9. The language circuit often feeds content to both the CEO and the Lifeguard, providing the words for the evaluation loop or the script for the threat narrative. Address the CEO's evaluation loop first with Structured Breath Counting (less evaluative content means less for the narrator to narrate), then add Mantra Redirect (Chapter 9) as your second session to quiet the verbal channel directly. Chapter 11 has the full stacking protocol.
- If you're also a **Princess & the Pea** (sensory flooding amplifying the scanning) → Chapter 8. The Lifeguard often co-occurs with sensory sensitivity. High-gain processing means more data, which means more for the Lifeguard to scan. Start with Environmental Regulation and the Titrated Body Scan (Chapter 8) to lower sensory volume first, then add the Lifeguard's Grounding practice once the sensory flood isn't feeding the threat queue. Chapter 11 shows you how to sequence both.

Record your returns: ___ returns, ___ min. The loop ran today. You noticed it before it finished, and that noticing is a return, counted the same as any other. Tomorrow: CEO, start with counting. Lifeguard, start with grounding. Same order, same entry point. The session shape doesn't change; your nervous system learns from repetition.

Meta Questions (Optional Nerd Corner)

What would happen if you let yourself not know the answer, even for thirty seconds? Not "pretend not to know." Sit in not-knowing. What does uncertainty feel like in your body?

Can you tell the difference between the Lifeguard's scanning (looking for danger) and genuine curiosity (looking for interest)? They use the same hardware. What shifts when you relabel the scanning as exploration?

What if the CEO's real job isn't to get things right, but to notice when things are off? What changes when you give it permission to detect problems without having to solve them immediately?

7.12 When the Practice Meets Bedtime

The CEO and the Lifeguard are the two phenotypes most likely to make sleep difficult. The loops that run during meditation run louder at night.

Here's the short version.

The Paradoxical Effort Problem (both phenotypes): Trying to sleep is arousing. The effort to fall asleep activates the executive circuits that keep you awake. "I need to sleep" becomes a thought loop. The loop generates cognitive arousal. The arousal prevents sleep. The failure to sleep generates frustration and more effort. The CEO monitors the sleep process. The Grumpy predicts failure. The Interpreter narrates the whole experience. In bed. At midnight. With a 6 AM alarm.

The mindfulness solution is simple and counterintuitive: remove the effort. Not "try harder to relax." Remove the trying entirely.

Say silently: "I don't have to sleep. I'm allowed to rest. My body knows how to sleep; it's been doing it my entire life on its own. My only job right now is to be here."

That's the Permission Practice applied to bed. You're not managing the sleep process. You're lying down and allowing. The loop feeds itself; breaking it at the effort point dissolves it.

The CEO's Nighttime Practice (Closure Ritual): Give the CEO a formal stopping point before bed: write tomorrow's top three priorities. Three only. Then close the notebook. The CEO's default is "keep evaluating until certainty is achieved": certainty never arrives. A deliberate close breaks the loop. In bed, let attention drift freely. That drifting IS sleep onset.

The Lifeguard's Nighttime Practice (Safety Cache): Before getting in bed, do a brief physical scan of the room while the lights are on. Check the lock. Look behind the door. Touch the walls. Confirm safety with eyes open, so the Lifeguard has cached data to work with when they close. In bed: feel the weight of the blanket, the temperature of the sheets, the mattress under your back. You're filling the Lifeguard's data stream with body-level safety signals rather than leaving it to scan a dark room.

A dim nightlight is not childish. It's environmental regulation for a threat-detection system that needs visual data to feel safe. Some Lifeguards don't sleep well in total darkness. That's an accommodation, not a failure.

When sleep problems persist: If sleep difficulties are significantly impairing your functioning, Chapter 16 addresses when mindfulness is not enough. CBT-I (Cognitive Behavioral Therapy for Insomnia) pairs well with these practices and has strong evidence for chronic insomnia.

When you're ready: Practice daily for one week. If both are active, start with the Lifeguard. Safety before evaluation. What if the problem isn't where your attention goes, but how loud the world is when it gets there? Chapter 8 has the sensory axis.

Ch 8: Everything Too Loud / Tone Feels Wrong: Sensing Overload

The Princess & the Pea (high-gain processing / sensory overwhelm) and The Bard (prosody / tonal processing)

Quick Check: Is your environment too loud right now? Fix that first. Then open this chapter.

PRACTICE CARD: The Princess & the Pea *(high-gain processing / sensory overwhelm loop)* **Cascade:** SENSE: Step 4a | **Chapter:** 8

Entry Move: Environmental regulation first. Reduce input before you sit: lights dimmed, consistent background sound, comfortable temperature, no irritating fabrics.

3 min: Sensory Sanctuary Check + titrated body awareness (start with hands or feet only) **10 min:** Alternating external / internal anchor; stay external whenever internal floods **20 min:** 5 min sanctuary setup → 10 min external / internal alternating → 5 min LKM for the body's sensitivity

On Track: Sensory input matched to current tolerance ✓ External anchor held when internal was too much ✓ **Too Much:** Body buzzing, skin crawling, overwhelm → *External anchor immediately. Reduce session length.*

Return Counter: ___ returns ___ min

PRACTICE CARD: The Bard *(prosody / tonal processing loop)* **Cascade:** SENSE: Step 4a | **Chapter:** 8

Entry Move: No guided audio. No human voice. Music or silence. Your own internal voice or none.

3 min: Visual Anchoring: soft focus on a single point (carries no tonal information to decode) **10 min:** Tone Noting: when the Bard circuit analyzes emotional tone in background sound, note "decoding" and return **20 min:** Non-verbal Immersion: instrumental music or white noise; attend to texture alone

On Track: Attention held; tonal-decoding loop stayed quiet ✓
Too Much: Emotional overwhelm from music → *Switch to white noise or silence.*

Return Counter: ___ returns ___ min

8.1 Choose Your Adventure

- **Everything feels too loud / too bright / too much**: sensory overwhelm, body buzzing, emotional flooding from stimuli that shouldn't be that intense → read the **Princess & the Pea** section
- **Tone of voice overwhelms or confuses you**: over-reading emotional subtext, hearing threat in neutral voices, decoding the music behind words instead of the words themselves → skip to the **Bard** section
- **If any practice triggers panic, dissociation, or persistent worsening** → Chapter 16 immediately

---

Like the rest, the Princess and the Bard are QEEG patterns rather than trial-tested diagnoses. They mark a place to begin.

The core move does not change: notice the flood, then come back. Half a second of space, as many times as it takes.

Both phenotypes drown the same way: too much input, too fast, at too high a gain. The Princess drowns in physical sensation. The Bard drowns in emotional tone. Before any practice can land, the volume has to come down.

8.2 What It Feels Like

If you're the Princess & the Pea: The tag in your shirt is intolerable. The hum of the fluorescent light is deafening. Someone across the room shifts in their chair and you feel it in your chest. Not metaphorically. You feel it as a body sensation, as if their movement generated a pressure wave.

Everyone else seems to move through the world with some kind of filter. A selective hearing aid that turns down the irrelevant and amplifies the important. Yours doesn't filter. Everything arrives at the same volume: the traffic outside, the texture of your socks, the emotion on your coworker's face, the temperature shift when someone opens a door. All of it, simultaneously, at full gain. The gap doesn't close because you're slow. It closes because the signal is too loud. No room left.

Meditation instructions say "notice your body." Your body is already screaming. It's like telling someone standing under a waterfall to notice the water.

What the Brain Map Shows: A Princess map shows amplified sensory processing across posterior regions: everything coming in at full gain. The sensory gating mechanisms that should be filtering input are letting too much through.

If you're the Bard: You're having a conversation and the words say "I'm fine." But the *tone* says something different. There was a slight rise on "fine." A half-second pause before it. A micro-expression that flickered and vanished. You caught all of it. You're now running seventeen parallel analyses of what that tone *meant* while the person continues talking about dinner plans.

Guided meditation is a minefield. The instructor says "let go of tension." But the way they *said* it: was that impatience? Condescension? Are they bored? Do they think I'm not trying hard enough? You spend the entire session decoding the emotional subtext of the instruction voice instead of following the actual instructions. By the end, you don't know what the meditation was about. You know that the instructor was slightly congested and possibly irritated during minute seven.

What the Brain Map Shows: A Bard map shows right temporal overactivation: the prosody-decoding circuit running hot. The system that reads tone, inflection, and emotional coloring in speech is working overtime.

Both descriptions, same architecture.

8.3 The Right Posterior Hemisphere: Nonverbal at Full Volume

The **Princess & the Pea** (rTPJ) amplifies sensory and social input: textures, temperatures, emotional cues, the felt sense of others' states. The **Bard** (right posterior temporal) reads the music behind words: tone and inflection, the emotional subtext beneath them. When both run high-gain, the nonverbal world is deafening. Standard meditation gives you a magnifying glass. You need a dimmer switch.

Same posterior neighborhood. Different job descriptions.

Your sensory system keeps swallowing the gap between signal and overwhelm. Every time you titrate input and return to center, you widen that half-second and train the volume dial to hold.

Your brain has early gates: about 50 milliseconds after a sound arrives, a sensory-gating network suppresses repeated stimuli or lets them through. In healthy gating, the second click registers quieter than the first. In sensory-sensitive brains, the gate stays open. Every repetition lands as new. Every stimulus as urgent. That's not sensitivity as a personality trait. That's a circuit running with the filter off.

Three things can make the world too loud. They are not the same problem.

Gating failure: too much gets in. The early sensory gate lets everything through at full volume. **Arousal mismatch:** the system runs too hot for the context, amplifying signals that should be background. **Interoceptive amplification:** external and internal gating are both too open, so you feel everything from outside and everything from inside, simultaneously.

The Princess typically lives at the intersection of gating and interoception. The Bard lives at gating plus social-emotional decoding.

8.4 Why Standard Advice Fails

"Notice your body" is settling for most brains. For the Princess, it's fuel on the fire. You need a volume dial. The body isn't quiet and waiting to be found. It's already screaming. For the Bard, the standard solution is the problem: guided meditation *adds a voice*, the one thing your prosody circuit can't leave alone. You won't be meditating. You'll be auditing the emotional state of a stranger you've never met.

Both brains need a different entry point, and it starts before you sit down. (That sequencing, environment and external anchors before deep interoception, is what we see work in clinic. It has not been run as a formal randomized trial against "body scan first.")

8.5 Environmental Regulation Is the Prerequisite

For both the Princess and the Bard, the first intervention is not a meditation practice. It's the environment. You cannot down-regulate a sensory system that's still receiving maximum input. Asking the Princess to do a body scan in a bright, noisy room is like asking someone to relax in a wind tunnel. Reduce input first. Then practice.

Sensory Sanctuary: Tiered Protocol:

Tier 1 (Minimum): Dim or natural lighting. No overhead fluorescents. Quiet: no background TV, no conversation, no music with lyrics. Temperature comfortable. That's the floor.

Tier 2 (Recommended): All of Tier 1 plus: soft textures where your body contacts surfaces (blanket, cushion). Reduced visual clutter: clean sight lines, minimal pattern. Consistent ambient sound if silence feels too empty (white noise, rain, fan).

Tier 3 (For acute overwhelm): Weighted blanket. Noise-canceling headphones or earplugs. Dimmed screen or no screens. One single-point visual anchor (candle, plant, simple object). Body supported: lying down or reclined, not sitting upright if posture is effortful.

Why deep pressure works: The weighted blanket in Tier 3 is a neurological tool. Deep, evenly distributed pressure activates proprioceptive and tactile receptors across a large body surface area. Clinical and EEG observation suggests this promotes activity in the sensorimotor rhythm (SMR) range: 12–15 Hz oscillations over motor cortex generated by the thalamocortical inhibitory circuits that also produce sleep spindles, suppress seizures, and calm motor restlessness. The mechanism is plausible and consistent with deep-pressure therapy research, though the specific SMR pathway has not been isolated in controlled trials.

Temple Grandin's squeeze machine, the deep-pressure device she designed for her own autistic sensory system, works on the same principle: sustained, firm, even pressure produces profound calming by engaging the body's built-in inhibitory circuits.

You don't need a squeeze machine. A 15–20 lb weighted blanket, a firm self-hug with arms crossed, hands pressing into opposite shoulders, or even lying face-down on a firm surface with a pillow on your back can activate the same system. Deep pressure is a body lever that bypasses cognition. The calming isn't something you think your way into.

This isn't luxury. The room is the practice.

Adverse-effects research finds that deconstructive practices (such as vipassana) and retreat contexts carry higher odds of unpleasant experiences (Lindahl et al., 2017; Schlosser et al., 2019). For sensory-sensitive brains, starting external is the usual clinical move, extrapolated from these risk patterns. The formal protocol test hasn't been run. The logic is straightforward: if the gate is already open, don't start by flooding it from the inside.

8.6 The Princess & the Pea: When Everything Is Too Loud

8.6.1 Princess: what fires first

Sensory gain too high: input that others filter, you amplify. **Entry:** Environmental regulation + titrated interoception. **What settles:** When sensory volume drops, emotional flooding subsides and attention can engage.

8.6.2 Practices for the Princess

Entry Move: Sensory Sanctuary first, then Titrated Body Scan. Reduce input, then gently explore what remains. In practice with sensitive systems, that order holds: skipping it reliably produces flooding.

Titrated Body Scan (3-minute version)

Setup: Sensory Sanctuary established (at least Tier 1). Seated or lying down. Eyes open or closed. Open is often safer for the Princess, because closing eyes amplifies internal sensation. Choose what feels manageable.

The practice: Begin at your feet. Notice the sensation there: temperature, pressure, the contact between your feet and the floor or your socks. Stay for 30 seconds. If it's tolerable (not comfortable, just *tolerable*), move to your calves. Same: 30 seconds of noticing. Then knees. Then thighs.

Move upward only when each region feels manageable. If your feet feel like too much, stay at your feet for the whole three minutes. One body region, fully attended to, is a complete practice.

The titration rule: If any body region feels too intense (too loud, too sharp, too buzzing, too *much*), skip it. Move to the next region. Or return to a region that felt okay. You are not required to scan the whole body. Scan what you can. Leave the rest alone. The regions you skip today might be accessible next week or next month. The skipping is intelligent titration. You're a clinician of your own sensation, not a patient following orders.

When overwhelmed: Open your eyes immediately. Look at something in the room, something specific, something solid. Name it silently: "lamp." "wall." "table." The visual anchor pulls attention out of the body and into the external environment, giving the overloaded sensory system a break. Return to a body region that felt safe, or switch to visual anchoring entirely.

Individual differences in interoceptive sensitivity predict how the body responds to body-focused practices. Higher interoceptive accuracy co-occurs with anxiety in some populations: more signal, not better signal. If body-scan practices spike your anxiety, this is probably why. The fix isn't to push through. It's to start external and work inward gradually.

Permission checkpoint: If body awareness feels like too much today, drop the body scan entirely. This is a Green signal, not a failure signal. Switch to visual anchoring: pick an object and study its color and shape, then shadow and texture. External focus is a legitimate practice for the Princess. It keeps the attention system online while giving the sensory amplifier a rest.

Closing: Wiggle your fingers. Press your palms together. Notice one sensation that feels neutral or pleasant. That's your closing anchor. One breath. Done.

One less thing the world was too loud for today.

10-minute version: Titrated scan for 5 minutes (go as far as comfortable). Then 5 minutes of Compassion for Sensitivity (below). The body scan warms up the interoceptive system gently. The compassion practice reframes the relationship with it.

20-minute version: 5 min Titrated Body Scan → 5 min Compassion for Sensitivity → 5 min visual anchoring (rest the system) → 5 min return to body scan, focusing only on regions that felt manageable in the first pass. The oscillation between body and visual is itself the practice, training the nervous system to move in and out of sensory contact and stay below flood.

Compassion for Sensitivity (5-10 minutes)

Setup: Sensory Sanctuary. Eyes closed if tolerable, open if not.

The practice: Direct loving-kindness at the sensitivity itself. The sensitivity is not a defect. It's high-gain processing. It detects more than most nervous systems detect. The problem is not the detection; it's the volume.

Repeat silently: *My nervous system detects more than most. That's not a flaw. May I be gentle with my sensitivity today. May I give myself what I need without apology.*

If "may I" feels too formal: *It's okay to need quiet. It's okay to need space. It's okay to be this sensitive.*

When mind judges the sensitivity: Note "judging." Return to the phrases. The judgment ("why can't I just be normal?") is the most common thought the Princess generates. It's not true. It's the Grumpy Old Man piggy-backing on sensory fatigue. Name it and come back.

Closing: One breath. One phrase: "I detect more. I can learn to titrate." Return as training: noticing sensitivity and letting it be data.

"Whose Feeling Is This?" (any duration)

For emotional contagion, the Princess's signature experience of picking up others' emotions as if they were your own.

Setup: Can be done anywhere, anytime. This is a real-time practice, not a seated one. Use it in social situations, at work, in crowds, during family gatherings.

The practice: When you notice a strong emotion arriving suddenly (anger, sadness, anxiety, excitement), pause. Don't act on it. Ask silently: *Is this mine?*

Scan the room: who else is present? What are they feeling? If the emotion correlates with someone else's state, if you walked into a room and immediately felt anxious, and the person sitting there is visibly anxious, label it: "borrowed."

Now return to your own body. Feel your feet. Feel your hands. Notice what's *yours* underneath the borrowed material. The borrowed feeling will often fade once you name it as borrowed. What remains is yours.

When you can't tell: When the feeling is ambiguous (maybe mine, maybe borrowed), default to grounding. Feet on floor, three breaths, name three things you can see. You don't need to resolve the ambiguity to regulate. Ground first, analyze later.

8.7 The Bard: When Tone Won't Stop Flooding

The Princess needed a volume dial for the whole sensory system. The Bard has a narrower problem: one overloaded channel, and the solution is to stop feeding it.

From here, voice is optional at best.

8.7.1 Practices for the Bard

Entry Move: Non-verbal practice. Remove human voice entirely. The Bard's overloaded channel is prosody, the emotional music in speech. Remove the music. Practice in silence.

Non-Verbal Practice (3 minutes)

Setup: No guided audio. No talking. No music with lyrics. No podcasts, no voices, no singing. Silence, or ambient sound only (rain, fan, white noise).

The practice: Body awareness without verbal narration. Feel your hands: the weight, the temperature, the texture of whatever they're touching. Feel your breath: the air moving in and out, the rise and fall of your chest. If your mind generates words (narrating the sensation, describing what you're doing), note "narrating" and return to the sensation itself. The practice is experiencing directly. Feeling in the raw.

When the Bard decodes anyway: Without human voice to analyze, the Bard may redirect its prosody-detection to ambient sounds: is that birdsong happy or alarmed? Was that car horn angry? Notice the interpretive impulse. Label it: "decoding." Return to body sensation. Over time, the Bard learns to let sounds be sounds, bare sound only.

Closing: Three breaths in silence. Notice what silence feels like in the raw.

10-minute version: 3 minutes of Non-Verbal Practice, then 7 minutes of Tone Noting (below). The non-verbal phase settles the system. The noting phase exercises the tone-detection circuit in a controlled, low-stakes way.

20-minute version: 3 min non-verbal body awareness → 7 min Tone Noting with ambient sounds → 5 min visual anchoring (complete channel shift) → 5 min non-verbal body awareness again. Notice if the second body-awareness phase feels different. Often, it's quieter after the visual rest.

Tone Noting (5-10 minutes)

Setup: Sit somewhere with ambient sound: near a window, in a café (at a distance), or with a nature soundscape playing. No human speech.

The practice: Listen to ambient sounds. For each sound, label its emotional tone: "neutral," "warm," "mechanical," "sharp," "soft," "gentle," "rough." You're exercising the tone-detection system: giving the Bard a job, but in a controlled, low-stakes environment where there's no social consequence to getting the tone "wrong."

Notice when you assign emotional meaning to a non-emotional sound: a car engine that sounds "angry," a wind chime that sounds "sad." Label it: "interpreting." The interpretation is the Bard doing what the Bard does. But noticing the interpretation creates distance between hearing and meaning. That distance is where you come back.

Variation with music: Use instrumental music without lyrics. Notice the emotional quality of each phrase: the swells, the quiets, the tension and release. Label the tone. Practice being a scientist of emotional sound rather than a hostage of it. You're developing observer distance from the same capacity that usually floods you.

Visual Anchoring (any duration)

Setup: Any position. Eyes open. Pick a visual anchor: a candle flame, a leaf, a spot on the wall, a pattern in wood grain.

The practice: Single-point visual focus. Study the anchor with all the attention you'd normally give to decoding someone's tone of voice. Notice color shifts, shadow, texture, movement (if a flame), stillness (if an object). Stay visual. If auditory processing pulls you away (a sound demanding interpretation), note "hearing" and return to the visual anchor.

Closing: Widen your gaze to the room for one slow breath. Let the anchor go.

Why this works: Visual anchoring bypasses the prosodic channel entirely. It's a channel shift, moving attention from the overloaded auditory-emotional system to the relatively calm visual-spatial system. Not a permanent strategy. A pressure valve for when the Bard is running too hot.

8.8 A Vignette: The Musician Who Heard Too Much

A cellist who could detect a quarter-tone flat in a hundred-piece ensemble. Meditation made her cry. The tears were overload. Every body scan turned her body into a concert hall she couldn't leave. Every guided meditation became an analysis of the instructor's vocal quality.

Brain map: high-gain right posterior processing. In the hall, that resolution was her instrument. Offstage, her prison.

We started with Sensory Sanctuary as the practice itself. Dim lights, soft surfaces, brown noise. First day: sitting in the quiet. "I didn't realize how loud my apartment was."

By Week 8, she could tolerate a full body scan. She'd built a volume dial.

"I used to feel like I was inside the music all the time. Now I can choose when to step inside and when to stand at the door."

The win isn't silence. It's a door you can open and close.

Each return teaches it to move.

Applied Lane: Chronic Pain

A reader with fibromyalgia tried body scan practice and the pain got louder. Not metaphorically. The pain intensity increased with attention. Every time she directed awareness to her body, the volume went up, as if her attention were an amplifier and her pain were the signal.

The problem wasn't body scan. The problem was undifferentiated body scan, pointing high-gain attention directly at the pain zone without titration or escape routes.

Practice Rx: Titrated Body Scan for Pain: scan the periphery first. Hands, feet, face. Regions distant from the pain. Build tolerance and body-awareness capacity in the zones that are manageable. Approach the pain zone last, and only if you're in Green. If Yellow, stay at the edges. If Red, stop and use the 90-Second Reset instead. You're building the capacity to tolerate body awareness gradually, not dumping yourself into the deep end. The body scan doesn't need to include the whole body to be therapeutic. Partial scans are full practices.

8.9 Practice Signals: Princess & Bard

Signs you're on track:

- Sensory input feels manageable during practice. Manageable is the goal. That's the goal.
- You can distinguish "this is loud" from "this is dangerous": volume versus threat. They're different signals from different circuits.
- You caught yourself over-reading tone and labeled it ("that's the Bard") before the interpretation hijacked your attention.

Signs you're overtraining:

- Sensory input spiked: body buzzing, skin crawling, tears without clear cause. The gain went up, not down.

- Guided meditation made you feel worse because you spent the whole session reading the instructor's tone.
- You're avoiding all sensory input instead of titrating it. The retreat became permanent.

What to do: Environmental regulation first. Rebuild the Sensory Sanctuary. Drop to visual anchoring only: external focus, no body awareness. Reintroduce body-based practice one region at a time when the system settles. If the Bard is triggered, switch to non-verbal practice: timer only, no voice, no music. Let the prosody channel rest.

8.10 Troubleshooting

1. "Body scan makes everything louder." That's correct. For high-gain processors, undifferentiated body awareness amplifies the signal. Use the titrated version: scan around the loud parts, not into them. Or switch to visual anchoring, external focus as a temporary reset. The body scan will become accessible as tolerance builds. It may take weeks. That's fine.

2. "I can't do guided meditation because the teacher's voice triggers me." Use unguided practice: timer only, no voice. Or use ambient sound recordings, speech-free. The Insight Timer app has a timer-only mode that lets you practice in silence with a bell at the end. The Bard needs voice-free practice until tone-processing is less reactive. This might be permanent. Some Bards never use guided meditation, and that's a valid, complete practice style.

3. "I pick up everyone's emotions and can't tell what's mine." "Whose Feeling Is This?" is your primary real-time practice. Environmental regulation reduces the incoming emotional data. Over time, the discrimination between "mine" and "borrowed" becomes faster and more automatic. But it may never be effortless. The Princess's high-gain processing is a feature of the hardware, not a software bug you can patch. The goal is a faster sort, not a thicker wall.

8.11 In the Wild

When the restaurant is too loud and you feel the overwhelm rising, touch something cold (your water glass, the table edge). One anchor. One breath. External focus on a single point. You're not leaving because you're weak. You're regulating because you know what your sensory system needs.

When a phone call hits wrong, when the tone was off and the inflection carried something your Bard brain is now decoding on repeat, name it out loud: "I'm decoding tone." The label interrupts the loop. You don't need to figure out what they meant. You need to stop processing what they sounded like.

When open-office noise becomes unmanageable, when keyboards and conversations and that one person who chews stack up, put in earplugs or noise-canceling headphones. That's regulation. The Princess needs to manage input volume before attention training can work.

For combining this chapter's practices with Lifeguard, Grumpy, or Interpreter patterns, see Chapter 11: Custom Stacks.

Meta Questions (Optional Nerd Corner)

What if your sensitivity isn't a problem to solve, but a high-resolution instrument that needs a volume dial, not a mute button?

Can you tell the difference between detecting a feeling and being hijacked by it? Where in your body does that distinction live?

What would your ideal sensory environment look like if you had no budget constraints and no one to explain it to? What does that tell you about what your nervous system needs?

The volume dropped, even briefly. That's the gap appearing. Slow returns, gentle returns, all of them count. If you measure anything, measure returns rather than minutes: ___ returns (or don't count; coming back is what matters). The sensory system can learn a different default.

When you're ready: Practice daily for one week. The Sensory Sanctuary itself counts as regulation. If there's also a narrator running verbal commentary over everything you hear, that's a different channel at the same SENSE step. Chapter 9 has the language circuit.

Ch 9: Narrator in Overdrive: The Language Circuit

The Interpreter: internal narration and verbal processing (comprehension, production, and the loop between them)

Quick Check: Is the narrator running right now, describing this sentence to you as you read it? That's the Interpreter.

PRACTICE CARD: The Interpreter *(internal narration / left language axis loop)* **Cascade:** SENSE: Step 4b | **Chapter:** 9

Entry Move: Give the narrator a job. The Interpreter's language circuit doesn't stop narrating because you ask it to. Give it a mantra; it'll narrate the mantra.

3 min: Mantra Redirect: short neutral phrase (*here, now* or *thinking, breathing*), repeated silently and continuously **10 min:** Body-First Awareness: shift to physical sensation before the narrator catches up; return to sensation at each narration **20 min:** Mantra (5 min) → Body-First (10 min) → Listening Practice attending to raw sound texture (5 min)

On Track: Mantra held the narrator's attention for even 30-second stretches ✓ **Too Much:** Narrating the mantra practice itself → *Get out of language. Return to physical sensation of breathing.*

Return Counter: ___ returns ___ min

The Interpreter is a pattern I see in QEEG work. No randomized trial produced it. Use it as a starting point for self-experiment.

You're having a conversation, and somewhere in the background, a second conversation is happening: the one you're having with yourself about the conversation. You're composing your response before the other person finishes their sentence. You're rehearsing what you'll say next. You're narrating the interaction in real time: *"She seems frustrated. I should say something empathetic. What's empathetic? Maybe 'I hear you.' No, that sounds scripted. Maybe..."*

You sit down to meditate and close your eyes and the narrator kicks into high gear. Present-moment commentary. (Thoughts about the future or the past would at least be interesting.) This is narration of the present moment itself. "Okay, I'm breathing. I'm noticing the breath. The air is cool on the inhale. My chest is rising. I'm noticing my chest rising. I'm narrating the noticing of my chest rising. Now I'm noticing that I'm narrating the noticing of my chest."

It's an echo chamber made of words. Every experience gets translated into language before you can experience it. The sunset isn't orange. It's a sentence about orange. The feeling in your chest isn't sadness; it's a description of sadness, followed by an analysis of the description, followed by a commentary on the analysis.

You get the picture. It doesn't stop.

Other people seem to be able to *be* somewhere without simultaneously narrating their presence. You can't remember the last time you experienced anything in silence. You're not sure it's possible. The narrator has been running so long you've mistaken it for yourself.

What the Brain Map Shows: An Interpreter map shows left temporal-frontal hyperconnectivity: the cable between comprehension and production carrying too much traffic. The language network that should activate for communication stays active even when no one is talking.

9.1 Who This Is For

Everything below is still one training: interrupt narration, return to sensation. Same gap, different noise.

What makes the Interpreter different from every other phenotype: thinking and *experiencing* have merged. The thought about the sensation has replaced the sensation. The narration has become the event.

The gap fills with words (description, analysis, rehearsal), and by the time the narration pauses, the moment has already passed. Your language system closes the gap between thought and narration, and every time you interrupt the narrator and return to sensation, you train the off-switch to hold.

The **Interpreter** (internal narration / left language axis loop) is the language phenotype, but language isn't one spot in the brain. It's a circuit. A loop. Your left language axis runs through three well-known landmarks:

Wernicke's area at the back of the left temporal lobe, historically linked to comprehension. It anchors the receiving end of the loop, where the world begins to be translated into verbal content.

Broca's area at the front of the left frontal lobe, historically linked to production. It anchors the output end: formulating, rehearsing, generating. The network that composes your sentences before you speak them (and sometimes speaks them before you've finished composing).

The arcuate fasciculus connecting them, the cable. A white-matter fiber highway that runs from Wernicke's to Broca's and back, carrying the signal between comprehension and production.

Modern imaging shows the language network extends well beyond these three landmarks. But the loop between them is real and measurable. When it's overactive, verbal processing dominates experience. I'll call it the language loop.

If the Decision Tree sent you here for "I can't stop the internal commentary" or verbal rumination and worry loops, you're in the right place.

9.2 Why Standard Advice Fails the Interpreter

"Notice your thoughts and let them go" is jet fuel. The Interpreter notices the thought, describes the noticing, generates meta-commentary

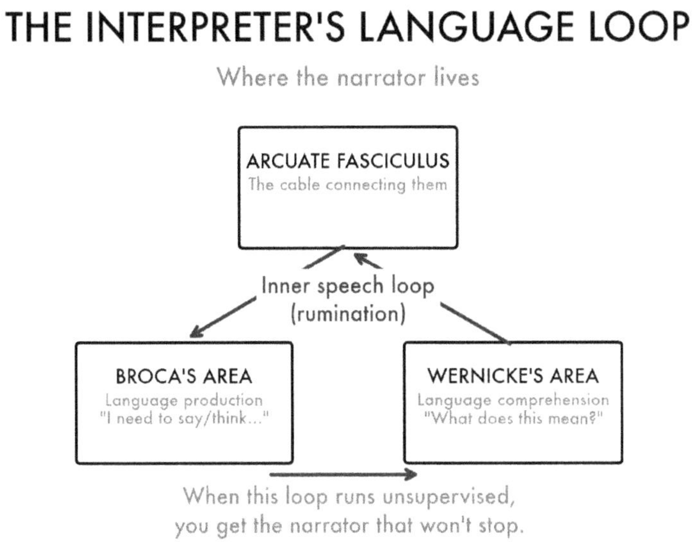

Figure 9.1: The Interpreter Language Loop

on the description, and turns the instruction into more narration material. Every word-based technique feeds the loop: "label your thoughts" gives it a labeling project; "be present" launches a philosophical inquiry.

You can't think your way out of thinking; you'll only narrate the attempt. You can't outrun the narrator either. It's faster than executive control. You can give the thinker something else to do. Occupy it with something specific (mantra fills both ends of the loop with one script), bypass it entirely (body-first awareness skips the verbal channel), or interrupt it at the production end (listening practices activate the receiver while the speaker idles).

Try this now: Stop reading. Notice the voice in your head that's narrating this sentence. That's the Interpreter. You caught it. One return, whether or not you count it.

You already named the three parts. Now imagine all three at full volume.

When the Interpreter's loop runs hot, verbal processing dominates all other channels. The narrator fills the gap with words, and every practice in this chapter creates space between the narration and your response to it. The three entry strategies work at different points in the loop: mantra occupies it, body-first awareness bypasses it, receptive listening interrupts production. When the loop quiets, non-verbal experience emerges: body sensation, spatial awareness, emotional tone without words.

9.3 Your Entry Move

Entry Move: Start with Mantra Redirect. Occupy the narrator with a single script. Don't try to silence the narrator. Give it one line and make it repeat.

9.4 Practices That Work for the Interpreter

Here's the sequence, from three minutes to twenty.

9.4.1 Entry Practice: Mantra Redirect

Mantra Redirect (3 minutes)

Setup: Seated. Eyes open or closed (closed is often better here, because reducing visual input means less material for the narrator to describe).

The practice: Choose a short phrase. Traditional mantras work fine: *om, so hum, one.* Functional phrases also work: *here now, let go, enough, breathing.* Choose what feels natural. You'll repeat this silently, at whatever rhythm emerges. Don't force a pace.

Begin repeating the mantra silently. Let it fill the verbal channel. Notice where you feel the mantra land: the chest, the throat, the back of the skull. Let it settle there, playing on a loop, like a song stuck in your head, only deliberately. The mantra occupies the loop.

When the narrator interrupts: It will. Within seconds, the narrator will comment on the mantra: "Is this working? This feels weird. Should I be saying it faster? I wonder if 'om' is better than 'let go.' " That's fine. Each time you notice the commentary, return to the bare repetition. The syllables. No analysis. No evaluation. The sound of the phrase in your mind.

The commentary is not the enemy. It's the loop doing its job. Your job is to keep returning to the mantra. The mantra is the leash. The commentary is the dog pulling. You don't need to stop the dog from pulling. Hold the leash.

Closing: Let the mantra get softer. Quieter. Notice the silence that appears between repetitions. Feel where the silence lands: throat, chest, the space behind your eyes. One breath there. Done.

Your language circuit just ran on a shorter leash for three minutes.

Why this works at the circuit level: Mantra runs one script through the whole loop (production, reception, and the cable between) instead of open-ended churn. You're not fighting the narrator. You're giving the entire loop a job, and the job is one word, repeated. Eventually, the mantra fades and the circuit goes quiet on its own. The loop ran out of new material.

9.4.2 10-Minute Practice: Body-First Awareness

Body-First Awareness (10 minutes)

Setup: Standing or seated. Eyes open; visual data gives the sensory system something to process that isn't words.

The practice: Feel your hands. Nothing else. Feel them. Temperature. Tingling. Weight. Pressure against whatever they're resting on. The texture of your clothing under your fingers. Don't describe what you feel. *Feel it.* Stay in the pre-verbal moment, the instant of sensation before the narrator translates it into words.

Move to your feet. Same thing: pressure, temperature, contact with the floor. Then your face: the air on your skin, the tension in your jaw, the position of your tongue in your mouth.

Continue through the body at whatever pace the narrator allows. Shoulders first, then chest and belly, then back. Ten minutes gives you time for two or three full passes, and each pass, the narrator is a little slower to jump in.

When narration starts: It will start immediately: "my hands feel warm, there's a tingle in my left thumb, now I'm feeling my feet again." Note "narrating" and return to raw sensation. The label "narrating" is the last word you use. After that: feeling. The moment between sensation and description, that fraction of a second, is your target. Live there.

This is harder than it sounds. The Interpreter's default is to encode everything verbally. But that pre-verbal moment exists. Everyone has it. You haven't been trained to notice it because the narrator translates so fast.

Closing: One breath. Notice the room, unlabeled. Seeing. Hearing. The words will come back. Let them wait.

Why this works: Body-first awareness bypasses the language circuit entirely. You're training a different channel, Feeling Tone External, that doesn't depend on verbal processing. For the Interpreter, this practice is a revelation. It's the discovery that experience can happen on its own, unlabeled. That the world has a texture that isn't made of words.

9.4.3 20-Minute Practice: The Full Interpreter Sequence

The Full Sequence (20 minutes)

Setup: Seated, somewhere with ambient sound (a window, a porch, a room with household hums). Timer set for 20 minutes. You'll move through three phases without stopping.

Phase 1: Mantra (5 minutes): Begin with your mantra. Let it fill the language loop. For five minutes, the narrator has one job: repeat the phrase. As the minutes pass, let the mantra soften. Quieter. Slower. The gaps between repetitions will widen. Those gaps are the practice bearing fruit: the loop taking a breath.

Phase 2: Body-First (10 minutes): When the mantra fades, shift to body sensation. Hands. Feet. Face. Move through the body in pure sensation. The mantra has already quieted the loop. Now you're filling that bandwidth with non-verbal content. The transition from verbal to non-verbal is a shift worth staying inside. Stay with raw sensation. Each time words arrive, note "narrating" and return to feeling.

Phase 3: Listening (5 minutes): Open to ambient sound. Birdsong, traffic, wind, household hums. Hear raw sound. Receive only. Your only job is to listen the way a microphone listens: without meaning, without story. This trains the receiver to stay active while the speaker idles (the inverse of the rehearsal loop).

Closing: One breath. Notice the silence between the last sound and the next thought. You spent twenty minutes learning to stand at that border between reception and narration.

9.4.4 Supplementary Tools

The practices above are your core. When the loop is especially resistant, two tools can prime the system before you sit.

Writing-to-Silence (5 min writing + practice of any duration): Before sitting, write for five minutes. Stream of consciousness: dump the narrator's current contents onto a page. Don't edit, don't organize. When the timer goes off, close the notebook unread. The narrative buffer is drained, and what remains is quieter. Meditate from this quieter state using any of the practices above. You're offloading the verbal buffer: the narrator dumps its contents onto the page, and what's left is closer to quiet.

Mini-Silence Retreat (2 minutes, building to any duration): The advanced tool. Zero verbal activity: no inner narration, no rehearsal, no planning. When words form, any words, even single labels, return to body sensation or visual input. Pre-verbal only. Start with two minutes. The emptiness is where you keep coming back. What rushes in to fill the silence (body sensation, emotion without words, spatial awareness) is data about what the narrator was covering up. Don't start here. Build up through mantra and body-first awareness first.

9.5 A Vignette: The Writer Who Couldn't Stop Writing

A novelist who narrated everything. "I'm always at one remove. I watch my life instead of living it."

Brain map: hot left language axis. A gifted narrator that never clocked out.

She chose the mantra *enough*. First session: ninety seconds before the narrator hijacked it: "Enough. That's interesting. Why *enough*? The word has a blunt Anglo-Saxon quality…" An etymological analysis of her own mantra.

"Label it: 'writing.' Come back to the syllable. Not the meaning. The sound."

By Week 6, the silence between repetitions had widened to two or three full seconds. One evening she noticed light on the trees: gold and green layering into something she had no word for. Five seconds of silence.

"And I can't describe it. That's the point, isn't it?"

Yes. That quiet is a half-second more in the gap.

9.6 Practice Signals: Interpreter

Signs you're on track:

- Gaps appear between narrator episodes: brief silence, then words restart. The gaps are the fruit.
- You catch the narration faster: the lag between loop-start and "oh, I'm narrating" shrinks
- Non-verbal experience surfaces: body sensation, undescribed; emotion, unanalyzed; seeing before labels land

By Week 4, there are gaps between narrator episodes: brief silence, then words restart. Those gaps are the training taking hold.

Signs you're overtraining:

- Trying to suppress the narrator generates anxiety or agitation. The silence feels threatening
- The mantra itself has become a new rumination object; you're analyzing it instead of repeating it
- You're at war with your own language circuit, and the war is generating more words than the peace

What to do: Drop back to Writing-to-Silence. Drain the buffer. Then try a shorter practice: sixty seconds of body-first awareness. Don't try to be silent. Try to *feel* something and hold it in sensation before the sentence forms.

9.7 Troubleshooting

1. "The mantra becomes another thing to narrate about." Normal. The Interpreter turns everything into content. When you notice meta-narration about the mantra, return to the bare *sound* of the syllables. The auditory quality alone: the vibration, the rhythm. Let it be music, not language.

2. "I can't experience anything without words." You can. You haven't practiced it. Start with strong physical sensations: hold an ice cube, run cold water over your hands, bite into something sour. The intensity of the sensation cuts through verbal processing. You'll have a moment of pure sensation before the words arrive, a fraction of a second where there's just COLD or SOUR without a description. That moment is the target. Expand from there.

3. "Silence makes me anxious." The narrator may be covering something with its constant chatter: anxiety, grief, emptiness that the words are papering over. If silence consistently triggers anxiety, the Interpreter may be co-occurring with a Lifeguard (Chapter 7) or a Grumpy Old Man (Chapter 6). The words are a defense mechanism.

Address the underlying anxiety or dread first, then return to silence practices. The narrator will let go when the system underneath feels safe.

9.8 In the Wild

When the narrator starts rehearsing a conversation you haven't had yet, say the mantra once ("enough" or whatever anchor word you chose) and feel your hands. Three seconds of non-verbal sensory experience. The rehearsal will return, and you've interrupted the loop. Each interruption is a return.

When you're replaying a conversation that already happened, editing what you said, scripting what you should have said, notice the narrator is in "post-production." Label it: "Editing." Then put your attention on the soles of your feet for ten seconds. The narrator can't edit and feel the floor at the same time.

When the bedtime narrator starts its review of the day, the verbal replay that keeps you awake, switch to body scan. Start at the feet, work up. If the narrator interrupts, go back to the feet. The body channel is the off-ramp from the language channel. Every time you redirect is a return. Count it.

9.9 "If You're Also ___"

- If you're also a **CEO** (perfectionism loops fueling verbal rumination), see Chapter 7. The CEO generates the evaluative content, and the Interpreter narrates it. Address the evaluation loop, and the narrator has less material. Start with the CEO's Structured Breath Counting (Chapter 7) to settle the evaluation loop (fewer evaluative thoughts means less for the narrator to narrate), then add Mantra Redirect as your second session. Chapter 11 has the full stacking protocol.
- If you're also a **Grumpy Old Man** (catastrophizing in verbal form), see Chapter 6. The Grumpy provides the worry; the Interpreter

puts it in prose. Vagal Toning first, then mantra. Start with Vagal Toning (Chapter 6) to soften the catastrophizing, then add Mantra Redirect once the worry content decreases. The narrator runs quieter when the Grumpy has less material to feed it. Chapter 11 maps the full stacking sequence.

- If you're also a **Bard** (over-reading tone while the Interpreter narrates what it heard), see Chapter 8. Start with Non-Verbal Practice: body-first, no guided audio, visual anchoring. Once the tonal-processing channel settles, layer in Mantra Redirect for the verbal loop. The two practices address different sensory overload channels and stack well together. Chapter 11 shows you how to combine them.

The narrator hasn't stopped. The gaps between repetitions are yours, and they get longer with practice. ___ returns (or don't count: coming back is what matters). Count returns.

Meta Questions (Optional Nerd Corner)

What does your experience feel like in the moment *before* words arrive? Can you catch that moment, the sensation or emotion that exists for a fraction of a second before the narrator translates it?

If the narrator stopped permanently, what would you be left with? Does that thought excite you or terrify you, and what does that answer tell you about the narrator's function?

Is the narrator protecting you from something? What would you notice, what would you *feel*, if the verbal buffer went quiet?

When you're ready: Practice daily for one week; if the mantra gives the narrator new material, switch to Body-First Awareness and bypass the verbal channel entirely. Has the practice ever felt like it's running at the wrong RPM? Chapter 10 matches the clock to your brain.

Ch 10: Everything Too Fast (or Too Slow): The Timekeeper

The Timekeeper: clock speed and processing rate mismatch

> **Quick Check:** Reading faster than this sentence deserves? Or slower? That's your Timekeeper telling you which practice to start with.

PRACTICE CARD: The Timekeeper (Fast) *(clock running above average speed)* **Cascade:** PROCESS: Step 5 (Override: may be first stop) | **Chapter:** 10

Entry Move: Match the practice to your speed. Don't try to slow the brain down first. Run fast, on purpose, in a structure. Let it decelerate naturally.

3 min: Rapid Noting: note whatever arises as fast as it arises: *thinking, hearing, feeling, planning, sensing, and similar experiences* **10 min:** Rapid Noting sustained: each note is a return. **20 min:** Rapid Noting (10 min) → breath-counting with deliberate deceleration (10 min)

On Track: Noting kept pace with arising: no boredom, no racing ahead ✓ High return count ✓ **Too Much:** Rapid noting accelerating rather than grounding → *Switch to 1-to-10 breath counting. Fixed track.*

Return Counter: ___ returns ___ min

PRACTICE CARD: The Timekeeper (Slow) *(clock running below average speed)* **Cascade:** PROCESS: Step 5 | **Chapter:** 10

Entry Move: Set your own pace. No timer pressure. The practice runs at your speed.

3 min: Slow Concentration: one breath at a time, 5 counts in / 5 counts out, self-paced **10 min:** Self-Paced Body Scan: one breath per body area **20 min:** Concentration (10 min) → Self-Paced Body Scan (10 min)

On Track: Self-paced practice allowed actual attention instead of forced compliance ✓ **Too Much:** Even self-paced feels rushed → *Slow further. There is no minimum pace.*

Return Counter: ___ returns ___ min

Clock-speed differences are real. The fast and slow Timekeeper come from QEEG work rather than from trial categories, so use them to start experimenting.

Before you read: three questions

Speed might be a property of your brain.

You have probably felt a task click into your natural pace, the moment the world finally synced to your clock. What would meditation feel like if it did that?

And what happens if, instead of dragging your thoughts slower, you bring your awareness up to their speed and let them settle from there?

(Hold your answer. The chapter is built around it.)

10.1 Choose Your Adventure

- **Everything too fast:** racing thoughts, can't slow down, standard meditation feels like jogging through concrete → read the **Fast Timekeeper** section

- **Everything too slow:** can't keep up, feel behind, instructions arrive faster than you can process them → skip to the **Slow Timekeeper** section
- **If any practice triggers panic, dissociation, or persistent worsening** → Chapter 16 immediately

Both phenotypes share one problem: a clock that doesn't match the world's default. Tempo, not attention or motivation. The move stays the same: notice the mismatch, return to anchor, let the clock find its gear.

10.2 What It Feels Like

If you're the Fast Timekeeper: The guided meditation says "breathe in" and by the time it says "breathe out," you've already breathed in, breathed out, thought about three things, planned dinner, circled back to the breath, lost it again, and are now wondering why the instructor talks so slowly. Standard meditation feels like dial-up internet when your brain is running fiber optic. You can focus. You focus at a speed the practice can't match, and the gap between your speed and the instruction's speed fills with racing thoughts, restlessness, and the crawling sense that something is *wrong*.

Other people seem to settle into silence. You bounce off it. The silence has too many gaps, and your brain fills every gap with thought-content at high speed. Not anxious thoughts, necessarily. Just *fast* thoughts. A firehose of processing that has nowhere to go when the practice says "sit still."

If you're the Slow Timekeeper: The guided meditation says "notice your breath, now notice your body, now shift to sounds in the room" and you're still processing the first instruction when the third one arrives. You feel behind. Always behind. Like everyone else got a preview of the script and you're reading it for the first time while simultaneously performing it.

You can pay attention. In fact, when you *do* settle into something (a visual focus, a body sensation, a single sound) your attention can go deep. Deeper than most people's. But the moment someone introduces a pace, a transition, or a "now do this," you lose it. The depth is real. The speed isn't there. And the margin between your tempo and the world's tempo generates a quiet, persistent shame: *Maybe I'm just not smart enough for this.*

You are. Your brain processes at a different RPM.

What the Brain Map Shows: A Timekeeper map shows an individual alpha peak frequency that's either well above or well below the statistical middle of about 10 Hz. In the clinical model, that difference sets the clock speed: either racing ahead of the world or trailing behind it.

10.3 Who This Is For

The **Timekeeper** (clock speed / processing rate loop) shapes how you experience the pace of the world. You route by feel: the fast lane if the world runs too slow for you, the slow lane if it runs too fast. You already know which way you lean. Everything below is the mechanism underneath that felt sense. You don't have to measure it.

In clinical observation, your tempo tracks with your alpha peak frequency (APF), a stable individual EEG rhythm generated by the thalamocortical system (Grandy et al., 2013). Hardware, not skill. Some brains sit high in that range, around 11 to 12 Hz, some low, around 8 to 9 Hz. Neither is wrong. What the research establishes is narrower than the personality reading it invites: alpha frequency is a stable individual trait, and in specific laboratory tasks it tracks how finely someone separates rapid events. Whether it makes a person quick to bore or deliberate by temperament is my inference from clinical work. The studies haven't gone there.

Most generic meditation instruction is *not* tuned to your individual alpha frequency; my working model is that it lands near the statistical middle (roughly the 10 Hz neighborhood on a bell curve), so if you're markedly above or below that, the pace can feel wrong, and no amount of willpower will make a one-size script feel right. (Matching practice tempo to IAF remains clinical inference; see below.)

Individuals with faster alpha oscillations at rest discriminate rapid events more finely: higher IAF, sharper temporal resolution. Samaha and Postle (2015) showed this directly: faster alpha, better separation of two rapid flashes. Ronconi et al. (2018) added causal evidence: when alpha was entrained above each person's natural frequency, temporal segregation improved; when entrained below it, the window widened. The correlational finding and the causal one point the same way. Alpha frequency does not just track temporal perception. It shapes it.

This is where the title of this book becomes most literal, and it is worth being careful about how literal. A 10 Hz rhythm cycles roughly every 100 milliseconds, and in the laboratory tasks above, faster alpha goes with finer separation of rapid events. Extending that from a flash-discrimination task to the whole felt grain of your experience is a metaphor I find useful in the clinic. Nobody has measured it at the level of the gap.

"Half a second more" is not a fixed duration. It's a felt experience of sufficient processing time, and the Timekeeper's dysregulation is precisely the loss of that sufficiency. Underneath the clock speed sits a preparatory timing wave: the brain's "getting ready" signal that builds before an expected event. In ADHD, that wave is weaker or more erratic depending on subtype, contributing to the feeling that you're always slightly out of sync (Bluschke et al., 2018). From clinical observation, pacing practices appear to engage this readiness system, though that specific mechanism has not been isolated in meditation research.

Try this now: Count to four at whatever speed feels natural. Not too fast, not too slow. That's your tempo. The practice in this chapter runs at that speed.

Override note: If your tempo mismatch is extreme: everything racing uncontrollably, or everything moving through molasses, this may be your first stop in the cascade, even before MOVE. The Decision Tree in Chapter 2 flagged this: extreme tempo mismatch overrides the standard sequence because nothing downstream will feel right until the pace matches. If that's you, start here, then run the cascade from Step 1. You're still counting returns.

The problem isn't attention. The practice is running at the wrong RPM. In clinical experience, anchoring to a fixed rhythm and returning appears to train the clock to hold a steadier tempo.

10.4 Why Standard Advice Fails the Timekeeper

"Slow, mindful breathing. Count to four. Pause. Count to six." That instruction assumes average processing speed. At 12 Hz, the instructions arrive too slowly. Your brain has processed, planned, and circled back before the next one. At 8 Hz, they arrive too fast; you're still settling into "breathe in" when the teacher says "breathe out." The clinical fix is matching. Match the practice to the clock, and in my experience the clock stops being the problem.

Clock speed is also state-dependent. Higher arousal speeds up your internal clock, packing more moments into each second: the world feels temporally compressed (Lake & LaBar, 2016). The Fast Timekeeper under stress isn't just running a fast processor. The throttle is jammed open. The soft-gaze technique from Chapter 3 is a practical entry point: widening your visual field pulls attention out of the near-space mode that accelerates the clock.

We don't yet have trials where practice tempo is tuned to individual alpha frequency. But from timing research, ADHD processing-speed data, and twenty-five thousand brain maps, it is plausible that practices closer to your natural tempo will be easier to engage with and sustain. That's clinical wisdom. The tested protocol is still ahead of it.

10.5 What's Running

Fast Timekeeper: Pace too slow for the processor. **Entry:** Match speed first (rapid practice), then gradually decelerate. **What settles:** When practice runs at brain speed, engagement stabilizes and restlessness drops.

Slow Timekeeper: Pace too fast for the processor. **Entry:** Remove time pressure entirely: self-paced, no external clock. **What settles:** When pacing pressure disappears, attention engages at its natural depth.

10.6 Practices for the Fast Timekeeper

10.6.1 Your Entry Move

Entry Move: Start with Rapid Noting. Match the speed instead of fighting it.

10.6.2 Rapid Noting

Rapid Noting (3 minutes)

Setup: Seated or standing. Eyes open or closed; choose based on whether visual data helps or distracts. Timer set.

The practice: Note everything you notice, as fast as it arrives. Use single-word labels: "thinking. hearing. feeling. planning. sound. itch. thought. breath. sound. worry. light. tension. thinking. remembering." Don't slow down. Don't organize. Don't evaluate whether your labels are correct or "good enough." Just note. Quick rhythmic labels, matching the speed of your mind.

The pace should feel fast, fast enough that your brain doesn't have idle bandwidth to fill with random content. If you can note faster, note faster. The ceiling is your actual processing speed. Match it.

When mind races ahead of the notes: Let it. Note faster. The practice is not to slow your thoughts; it's to match them with awareness.

Speed is not the enemy. Unaware speed is the enemy. You're not trying to brake. You're trying to keep the headlights on while driving fast.

Closing: After three minutes, stop noting. One long exhale. Sit for ten seconds, unlabeled. Feel the weight of your body in the chair, the hands in your lap. Notice: did the speed shift at all? Even slightly? If yes, that's your nervous system finding its own natural settling point when it's not fighting the pace. The deceleration happens naturally when the mismatch is removed.

If it still felt too fast, the practice still counts. Racing with awareness beats racing without it. That's a return.

If noting escalates rather than matches: For some Fast Timekeepers, rapid noting can tip from matching-the-speed into sympathetic activation: heart rate climbing, chest tightening, the noting itself becoming frantic rather than rhythmic. If the noting feels like it is feeding the speed rather than riding alongside it, stop noting immediately. Drop to one long exhale. Place both hands flat on your thighs and press down. Feel the pressure. Sit for thirty seconds, unlabeled. If the activation settles, you can resume at a slower pace. If it does not settle within a minute, end the session and use the 90-Second Reset. This is a Yellow signal. Next session, start with the slow version (breath counting at your pace) instead of rapid noting.

10-minute version: Rapid note for five minutes. Then gradually slow the noting pace: one note per breath instead of one per thought. Let the pace drift downward organically. Don't force slowness. Just stop racing. Then drop the labels entirely and sit in open awareness for three minutes. Fast → matched → gradually slower → open. This is tempo training, teaching the Timekeeper that deceleration is possible and lands safely.

20-minute version: Five minutes rapid noting → five minutes breath counting at a pace that feels natural (you choose the count, you set the speed, whatever matches YOUR tempo) → five minutes open monitoring → five minutes slow body scan. Alpha peak frequency is not fixed. It slows during meditative states and speeds up during demanding tasks. Practice doesn't permanently shift your clock speed, but a 2017 review found alpha peak frequency is state-dependent: it slows in relaxed, low-arousal states and speeds up under task demands rather than staying fixed (Mierau et al., 2017). That gear-shifting is one of the most direct ways to widen the space.

For Fast Timekeepers who need more than labeling alone, the body scan runs at your speed too.

10.6.3 Active Body Scan

Active Body Scan (3 minutes)

Setup: Seated or standing. Eyes closed works well here; it increases the attentional demand, which keeps the Fast Timekeeper engaged.

The practice: Scan your body fast. Head to feet in thirty seconds, quick impressions, not deep analysis. Start at the crown and move down through face, jaw, and shoulders to your hands. Then chest, belly, hips, and all the way to your feet. One-second snapshot per region. Only question: what's there? Move on.

Now reverse: feet to head in thirty seconds.

Now random: left hand. Right knee. Belly. Forehead. Toes. Jaw. Right shoulder. Left ankle. Jump around. Feel each region for one breath, then move on. The randomness prevents habituation, the speed matches the Timekeeper's natural pace, and the whole-body coverage gives the attention system a full tour at the right RPM.

When mind races ahead: Let it preview the next region. When you arrive, notice what's there versus what the preview predicted. The discrepancy, "I expected tension in my shoulders but it's in my jaw," is the practice. Prediction versus reality, at speed.

Closing: Stop scanning. Rest attention on one region, wherever feels most alive right now. Stay for three breaths. The contrast between scanning and settling is the training.

Variation: Set a metronome app or rhythmic music at 80-100 BPM. Shift body attention on each beat. External rhythm provides structure for the internal clock and gives the Timekeeper something to sync with.

Now flip the direction: the clock that runs slow.

10.7 Practices for the Slow Timekeeper

10.7.1 Your Entry Move

Entry Move: Start with Self-Paced Concentration. Remove all external timing pressure. No instructor. No guided audio. No clock you have to match. Just you and one object.

10.7.2 Self-Paced Concentration

Self-Paced Concentration (3 minutes)

Setup: Seated comfortably. Eyes open, gazing at a single object: a candle flame, a dot on the wall, a leaf, a pebble, anything with enough detail to hold interest. Set a timer (so you don't have to track time yourself), but don't let it create pressure.

The practice: Look at the object. Look. Period. No counting, no labeling, no instruction to follow. Stay with the object at whatever pace your attention naturally moves. If your gaze softens and the object becomes vivid, detailed, almost hypnotic, stay there. That's depth. That's the Slow Timekeeper finding its groove.

When attention drifts (slowly, like a boat leaving a dock), notice the drift. Return to the object. No urgency. The return doesn't need to be fast. A slow return is still a return. It still counts.

When you feel behind: You're not behind. There's no schedule. There's no instruction arriving faster than you can process it. The only pace is yours. If "your pace" means you spent three minutes looking at one candle flame and noticed three things about it, that's three deep observations. That's your practice.

Closing: One breath. Look away from the object. Notice the room. Notice how the visual field is different after sustained focus: softer, maybe. Wider. That's the attentional system recalibrating after depth.

Why this works: The Slow Timekeeper's struggle is not attention. It's *paced* attention. Remove the pacing, and concentration often improves dramatically. The brain can focus with depth, often more than faster processors, but not on someone else's clock.

10-minute version: Same practice. Let attention deepen naturally over the longer duration. If the object becomes so vivid it almost seems to glow, that is deep concentration, and it is what the Slow Timekeeper can access when nothing is rushing it. Stay there. That's excellent training.

10.7.3 Self-Paced Body Scan

Self-Paced Body Scan (10 minutes)

Setup: Lying down or reclined. Eyes closed. Timer set (long enough that it won't interrupt, ten minutes minimum). No guided audio.

The practice: Scan your body at your own pace. Start at your feet. Stay with each region until YOU feel ready to move on. No timer. No guide. When a region feels fully noticed, however long that takes, move to the next.

If you spend eight minutes on your feet and two minutes on everything else, that's fine. Your pace IS the practice. Depth over coverage. The goal isn't to complete the scan. The goal is to feel whatever region you're in, fully, at the speed your brain processes it.

When you feel you "should" go faster: Notice the "should." That's external pacing pressure, internalized from every guided meditation that moved too fast. Note "rushing" and stay where you are. The Slow Timekeeper's gift is depth. Don't sacrifice depth for coverage.

Closing: Notice one region that felt most vivid during the scan. Stay there for three breaths. Done.

10.8 A Vignette: The Day Trader and the 911 Dispatcher

A day trader. "Every app felt like parking a race car in a compact space." Alpha peak 12.1 Hz: his brain clocked faster than the practices.

We started with Rapid Noting. 127 notes in three minutes. "The first time the practice ran at my speed." By Week 4, the slow-down was organic, because we started where he was.

A 911 dispatcher. "Every guided meditation makes me feel stupid. The instructions arrive and I'm still processing the last one." Alpha peak 8.6 Hz: not deficit, processing style. We started with Self-Paced Concentration. A candle, no instructions. "I noticed the blue at the base, the yellow, the wobble in the air above it."

"That's not slow. That's deep."

Two Timekeepers. Opposite speeds. Same fix: match the practice to the clock.

Your brain isn't broken. It runs at its own speed. The practice teaches it to shift gears.

10.9 Practice Signals: Timekeeper

Signs you're on track (Fast):

- The practice speed feels matched to your brain. You're noting at your natural pace
- Rapid noting generates engagement, not frustration
- You notice natural slowing in the second half of longer practices. The brain downshifts on its own when it stops fighting

Signs you're on track (Slow):

- Self-paced practice feels spacious, not pressured
- Attention deepens naturally, on your own
- You stopped comparing your pace to anyone else's

Signs you're overtraining:

- Fast: Rapid noting has become frenetic: speed without awareness, compulsive labeling, the practice itself is now racing

- Slow: Self-pacing has become avoidance; you never progress to any structured element because unstructured feels safer

What to do: Fast: add three minutes of silence after rapid noting. Let the system settle. Don't note the settling. Sit. Slow: add one gentle timed element: a chime at five minutes. Practice tolerating one external structure in small doses. The goal is flexibility, not rigidity in either direction.

10.10 Troubleshooting

1. "Rapid noting feels absurd, like speed-talking to myself." Good. That means you're matching your actual processing speed instead of performing meditation at a culturally approved pace. Absurd and effective are not mutually exclusive. The attorney from Chapter 1 felt the same way. Ninety-two notes in three minutes. It worked anyway.

2. "I'm not sure if I'm fast or slow." Try both entry practices for one week. Rapid noting for three days, self-paced concentration for three. Whichever felt like relief, where you stopped fighting the practice and the practice started fitting, that's your tempo. If both felt wrong, you might be at average speed with a different phenotype driving the issue. Revisit the Decision Tree.

3. "My speed changes throughout the day." That's normal. Alpha peak frequency has a stable baseline, but arousal state affects moment-to-moment speed. Caffeine shifts you faster. Fatigue shifts you slower. Practice rapid noting in your fast windows (morning, post-exercise). Practice self-paced concentration in your slow windows (afternoon, evening). Match the practice to the tempo of the moment, not to a fixed assumption about who you are.

10.11 "If You're Also ___"

- If you're also a **Stabilizer** (fast Timekeeper plus can't start), see Chapter 4. Speed without initiation means racing thoughts that never become action. Walking meditation at your natural fast pace serves both. Start with Walking Meditation (Chapter 4) at your natural fast pace to solve the initiation problem (you can't train tempo if you can't start), then add Rapid Noting as a second session once the motor system is reliably online. Chapter 11 has the full stacking protocol.

- If you're also a **CEO** (fast Timekeeper plus evaluating everything), see Chapter 7. Address the tempo first (rapid noting satisfies the speed need), then work on the evaluation loop. Start with Rapid Noting (this chapter) to satisfy the speed need and prevent the empty bandwidth the CEO fills with evaluation, then add the CEO's Structured-to-Open transition (Chapter 7) as a second session. Chapter 11 maps the full stacking sequence.
- If you're also a **Fog** (slow Timekeeper? or just low energy?), see Chapter 5. If removing time pressure helps, it's Timekeeper. If you're falling asleep regardless of pace, it's Fog. Start with activating practices (Eyes-Open Standing Awareness or Walking with Counting, Chapter 5) to get the power system online first. If slow processing lifts with energy, it was Fog all along. If it persists, add Self-Paced Concentration as a second session. Chapter 11 has the full stacking protocol.

___ returns (or don't count: coming back is what matters). A fast-Timekeeper session at ninety returns feels different from a slow-Timekeeper session at twelve, but the rep is the same in both. The clock shifted for however long you held the anchor. That shift accumulates. Come back tomorrow at whatever speed today ran.

When you're ready: Practice at your natural speed for one week. When the RPM matches, the frustration drops and the engagement clicks. What if you carry more than one pattern? Chapter 11 builds the custom stack for the brain you have.

Ch 11: When You're All of the Above: Custom Stacks

Quick Check: Top 2–3 phenotypes right now: ___. Start with whichever is loudest today.

11.1 What It Feels Like

You read through Part II and thought: "I'm not one of these. I'm five of these." Your Grumpy Old Man is arguing with your Happy Little Kid about whether to even try, while your Lifeguard scans the room, your Interpreter narrates the entire argument in real time, and your Timekeeper is running all of it at 1.5x speed.

Welcome to the majority.

Rarely does a dysregulated brain present as one thing. You're a constellation: multiple circuits, multiple failure modes, multiple places the gap closes. In 25,000 brain maps, I've seen exactly *zero* single, pure phenotypes. The question isn't "which one am I?" It's "which ones are loudest right now, and in what order do I address them?"

That's what this chapter answers. Regulation is distributed; dysregulation is too. You're a pattern of where and when the space closes. What you count is still returns: gap, come back, repeat.

A stack addresses the pattern in order: loudest circuit first, cascade sequence second, because each fix clears bandwidth for the next. Your brain can lose the gap in more than one place, and sequencing makes each return land on the circuit that needed it.

A clarification on the word "cascade": in Chapter 2, the cascade *routes* you to your starting chapter, identifying which circuit is loudest. Here in Chapter 11, the cascade *sequences* multiple practices within a single session. Same hierarchy, different job. Chapter 2 picks the door; Chapter 11 orders the workout.

11.2 The Loudest-Circuit-First Rule

Start with the loudest circuit: the one consuming the greatest bandwidth right now.

It's the phone alarm going off in the meeting. Nothing else gets through until you silence it. Address it, and the other phenotypes often settle on their own. They were being amplified by the noise.

Then sequence in cascade order (Chapter 2): highest broken step first. If your loudest circuit sits lower but you also have an upstream issue, fix upstream first: same rule as the Decision Tree. Two phenotypes can share a step. SENSE holds both: the sensory phenotypes (Princess, Bard, step 4a) and the verbal one (Interpreter, step 4b). When you stack within SENSE, regulate sensory gain first, then quiet the verbal loop: 4a before 4b. Turn the volume down before you ask the narrator to stop.

The Stack Formula:

1. Identify your 2–3 currently dominant phenotypes (from the Decision Tree in Chapter 2 or from reading Part II)
2. Order them by cascade position (highest step first)
3. Start with a 3-minute entry practice for the highest one
4. After one week of consistency, add the second phenotype's entry practice
5. After two weeks, add the third (if needed)
6. Total daily practice time: 10–15 minutes, stacked in cascade order

The rule: You don't need to do all practices every day. You need to *sequence* them correctly when you do. The sequence is the strategy.

The exception: If one phenotype is dramatically louder than the others, if your Lifeguard is screaming and everything else is murmuring, go there first, regardless of cascade position. Address the crisis, then return to cascade order.

When you can't stack, the 90-Second Reset is the book in miniature: same gap, same return, less choreography.

11.3 Pre-Built Stacks

These are five constellations I see repeatedly in my clinic. If one matches your pattern, use it as your starting blueprint. Modify as needed. These are templates, not prescriptions.

11.3.1 The ADHD Stack

Phenotypes: Stabilizer (can't start) + Supervisor (can't sustain / stop, brake leaks toward novelty) + Timekeeper fast + often Fog (energy cycling). The novelty-seeking that drives ADHD distractibility lives here in the Supervisor (brake won't hold) and sometimes the CEO (anchoring captured by patterns and novelty), not in the Happy Little Kid.

Sequence: 1. Walking Meditation at fast natural pace (Stabilizer + Timekeeper, 3 min): movement initiates, speed matches 2. Rapid Noting seated (Timekeeper + Supervisor, 3 min): speed stays matched, impulse-watching begins 3. Rotate the specific practice variant daily (different walking route, different noting focus, different body awareness target): rotation prevents habituation-driven dropout in a brain whose Supervisor brake leaks toward novelty.

Total: 6 minutes daily, rotated

Speed matching first: match before you slow. The *habit* is daily; the *content* can change.

If Fog is active: Do this stack during your highest-energy window. Don't fight the tide. Surf it.

11.3.2 The Anxious-Avoidant Stack

Different nervous system, different entry point: this one runs tense instead of fast.

Phenotypes: Grumpy Old Man (effort-dread) + Lifeguard (threat-scanning) + Princess & the Pea (sensory amplification)

Sequence: 1. Sensory Sanctuary setup (Princess, 1 min): reduce input before asking the system to do anything 2. Grounding: "Is This Now?" (Lifeguard, 3 min): establish present-moment safety 3. Vagal Toning (Grumpy, 3 min): down-regulate the effort-dread system 4.

Loving-Kindness if tolerable (Grumpy, 3 min): only after grounding and vagal work have settled the system

Total: 10 minutes, in strict order

Environmental regulation first, then grounding (safety for the Lifeguard), then vagal calming (physiological shift for the Grumpy), then emotional practice. Bottom-up before top-down. Skip grounding and the Lifeguard will scan for threat instead of directing compassion.

11.3.3 The Trauma + Fog Stack

Phenotypes: Lifeguard (hyperactive) + Fog (chronic low energy) + often Princess (sensory sensitivity)

Sequence: 1. Eyes-open walking, moderate pace (Fog activation, 3 min): gets the system online 2. Grounding with visual safety cues while standing (Lifeguard, 3 min): safety data for the scanning system 3. Pendulation if tolerable (Lifeguard, 3 min): oscillation between activation and safety

Total: 9 minutes

Fog and Lifeguard need opposite things: activation vs. calming. The trick: *activating practices with safety cues built in.* Eyes-open walking satisfies both. If Pendulation triggers escalation (Yellow), drop it and add grounding. Warm the system gradually.

11.3.4 The Autistic/Sensory-Sensitive Stack

The Lifeguard appears in the Trauma + Fog stack too, but here the context is sensory load. The sequence matters more here than anywhere else in Part II.

Phenotypes: Princess & the Pea (sensory overwhelm) + Bard (prosodic overwhelm) + Lifeguard (threat-from-intensity) + Grumpy / Problem Child (frontal reactivity)

Sequence: 1. Sensory Sanctuary, Tier 2 minimum (Princess/Bard, 2 min): non-negotiable environmental regulation 2. Visual Anchoring or non-verbal body awareness (Bard, 3 min): no voice, no music, no prosodic input 3. Grounding: "Is This Now?" (Lifeguard, 3 min):

present-moment safety 4. Choice-Based Practice (Problem Child, 3 min): complete autonomy over content

Total: 11 minutes

Order here: Posterior regulation (Princess/Bard) before frontal mood work (Grumpy/Problem Child). Frontal circuits keep firing defensively until sensory volume drops. Back of brain first, then front.

11.3.5 The High-Performance Stack

Phenotypes: Timekeeper fast + CEO (sticky evaluation) + Grumpy Old Man (catastrophizing the performance)

Sequence: 1. Rapid Noting at matched speed (Timekeeper, 3 min): engage the speed system 2. Structured-to-Open transition: 2 min breath counting → 2 min choiceless awareness (CEO, 4 min): practice releasing control 3. Compassion practice directed at the inner critic (Grumpy, 3 min): soften the catastrophizer

Total: 10 minutes

Match speed first, release evaluation second, soften dread third. Also the pre-performance centering stack: compress for high-stakes moments (see Applied Lane below).

11.3.6 The Gifted Poet Pattern

Phenotypes: Interpreter (verbal overload) + Princess & the Pea (sensory amplification) + Grumpy Old Man (effort-dread) + Timekeeper fast

Sequence: 1. Writing-to-Silence (Interpreter, 5 min pre-meditation): drain the narrator's buffer 2. Sensory Sanctuary (Princess, 1 min): reduce environmental input 3. Mantra at natural fast pace (Interpreter + Timekeeper, 3 min): occupy the loop at speed 4. Body-First Awareness (bypass verbal channel, 3 min): non-verbal experience

Total: 12 minutes (including the 5-min writing)

Drain the narrator first, reduce sensory input, occupy the language loop at speed, then bypass with body-first awareness. The stack works with each circuit in sequence instead of fighting the Gifted Poet's reality.

11.3.7 The Fog + Timekeeper Mismatch

When Fog and Timekeeper co-occur, the problem is coordination at two timescales: the arousal system is desynchronized (wrong power at the wrong time), and the processing system is mismatched (wrong speed for the demand). Address the Fog first. You need the lights on before you can adjust the clock.

The next two stacks are situation-based. Use them when time is the constraint.

11.3.8 The Morning Commute Stack

Situation: You have 10 minutes between waking and work. You need to regulate before the day starts.

1. 90-Second Reset in bed or standing: body → breath → meaning, lowest friction entry
2. 3-minute walking to your car or transit stop (Stabilizer): motor system on
3. 2-minute vagal toning while parked or waiting (Grumpy): 4 in / 6 out, before the first call

Total: ~7 minutes. No cushion. No app. No time blocked.

11.3.9 The Sunday Reset Stack

Situation: You have 20 minutes and want to recalibrate before the week begins.

1. 10-minute walking meditation (Stabilizer): unhurried pace, counting steps or breath
2. 5-minute seated open monitoring (CEO): no task, no anchor, open observation
3. Permission Practice closer: "I'm allowed to rest. I'm allowed to start again."

Total: 15 minutes. Works across many phenotype combinations. The walking starts the system; the open monitoring clears it, and the Permission Practice resets the identity layer.

11.4 The Stack Builder

Build your own stack using this worksheet.

My active phenotypes (2–3):

1. ______________ (cascade step: _______)
2. ______________ (cascade step: _______)
3. ______________ (cascade step: _______)

My cascade order (highest step first):

1. ______________
2. ______________
3. ______________

My daily stack:

- **Practice 1** (highest cascade): ______________ (from Ch. ___): ___ minutes
- **Practice 2** (second cascade): ______________ (from Ch. ___): ___ minutes
- **Practice 3** (third, if needed): ______________ (from Ch. ___): ___ minutes
- **Total daily time:** ___ minutes

My rotation element (if Happy Little Kid is active): vary Practice ___ daily.

My energy window (if Fog is active): practice at _________

My environmental setup (if Princess/Bard is active): ______________ (Tier ___)

11.5 A Vignette: The Startup Founder With Everything Running

A startup founder, early thirties, sleeping five hours, brain "like a television playing six channels at once." Couldn't start non-work tasks (Stabilizer). Couldn't stop working (Supervisor). Bored by every app in ninety seconds (Timekeeper fast). Effort-dread about anything except the company (Grumpy). Narrator running continuous strategic analysis (Interpreter).

We mapped to the cascade: MOVE first (Stabilizer + Supervisor), then MOOD (Grumpy), then SENSE (Interpreter), then PROCESS (Timekeeper).

The stack: Fast walking (3 min) → Rapid Noting seated (3 min) → Writing-to-Silence (5 min, with morning coffee). Total: 11 minutes. The writing didn't feel like meditating, which mattered because his Grumpy had pre-appraised meditation as "not a real use of time."

By Week 6, his wife said: "You seem less… buzzy." He could name what changed: the narrator had lost its frantic quality. Six channels still playing. The volume had a dial.

A well-sequenced stack doesn't give you a new personality. It gives you more returns per minute of actual life.

Applied Lane: Performance

The high-performing reader, whether creative, athletic, or entrepreneurial, with the classic Timekeeper-fast + CEO-sticky + Grumpy-catastrophizing stack.

Practice Rx: The High-Performance Stack above.

Pre-performance centering (30 seconds): Compress the 90-Second Reset for high-stakes moments. Body lever (feet press into floor, 10 sec) → Breath lever (three fast breaths at your natural pace, 10 sec) → Meaning lever ("This is not a performance.

There's no grade." 10 sec). Before the meeting, the pitch, the audition, the starting line. Thirty seconds. Nobody will notice you doing it.

When metrics ARE the problem: If your meditation practice has a KPI dashboard, color-coded progress charts, and an A/B testing framework, the practice has become the CEO's project. Drop the tracking. Do the 90-Second Reset. No data. No scorekeeping. Practice. The CEO doesn't get to audit this one.

If your constellation doesn't match any pre-built stack: Build your own. Follow the cascade when it's useful. Pick your top two or three phenotypes. Sequence them upstream-first. Three minutes per phenotype is your minimum effective dose. That's your stack.

Most meditation books hand you one practice and hope it fits. This one routes the practice to the circuit. Count returns.

11.6 Troubleshooting

1. "My loudest circuit changes day to day." Good; that means you're noticing. Day-to-day flexibility is the skill. On high-Grumpy days, start with Vagal Toning. On high-Timekeeper days, start with Rapid Noting. On high-Lifeguard days, start with grounding. The cascade sequence stays the same, and the starting phenotype can flex. Use the Decision Tree daily if needed. It takes thirty seconds.

2. "I have too many phenotypes to stack." Cap at three. If you're recognizing yourself in six or more phenotypes, start with the top two in the cascade and ignore the rest for now. When you address upstream patterns first, downstream ones often quiet on their own. The Stabilizer coming online might resolve what looked like a Timekeeper problem. The Grumpy calming down might unmask a Princess that was hiding underneath. Less is more. Sequence beats completeness.

3. "My stack takes too long. I don't have 15 minutes." Shorten each component to the minimum effective version: 90 seconds per phenotype practice. A three-phenotype stack at 90 seconds each is 4.5 minutes. That's your floor. If even 4.5 minutes is too much, do the 90-Second Reset and call it done. The best meditation is the one you do.

All you're doing is coming back. Whatever you stacked today, however it went. ___ returns (or don't count; coming back is what matters). The sequence is scaffolding, and the score is still returns.

Come back tomorrow.

Meta Questions (Optional Nerd Corner)

If you had to choose one phenotype as your "home base," the one that feels most like *you*, the one you'd keep even if you could trade in the others, which would it be? What does that choice tell you about your brain's default mode?

What would happen if you stopped trying to fix all your patterns at once and addressed only the loudest one today?

Is there a version of your constellation you'd want to keep? Are any of these patterns, speed, sensitivity, vigilance, verbal fluency, intensity, assets in the right context? What would change if you treated them that way?

When stacking isn't enough: If you're running four or more active phenotypes simultaneously and self-directed practice keeps breaking down: not from inconsistency, but from genuine physiological interference (can't stay awake, can't tolerate sensation, can't down-regulate enough to start). That's a signal that the regulation problem may be beyond what mindfulness alone can address. Clinical neurofeedback works from below the level of conscious practice, training the circuits that make practice possible in the first place. Chapter 14 covers the clinical options. The Resources section has provider directories. You don't have to white-knuckle your way through a practice that your nervous system isn't yet ready to support.

When you're ready: Practice your stack daily for one week. You've matched the practice to your brain. Is it changing anything? Chapter 12 has the honest answer.

Ch 12: What Changes in Your Brain: States to Traits

Read this when you need to know if the practice is working.

You've been practicing. You've been logging returns. A few sessions felt like something was happening. More felt like you were just sitting there being bad at sitting.

The practical question: *Is this doing anything?*

Yes. And the changes are more specific, more gradual, and more honest than the meditation industry's public claims. I'm going to show you what changes, how quickly, and where I have to shrug and say "promising, not proven." Trust what replicates.

It works. Just not the way Instagram suggests.

Part III rests on one idea: practice widens the half-second between stimulus and response. When that margin survives the session, state becomes trait.

12.1 States and Traits: The Framework

Every time you practice, you're creating a temporary state shift. Your nervous system changes during the session: arousal drops, attention sharpens, heart rate variability often rises during practice (Kirk & Axelsen, 2020), the prefrontal cortex gets more active relative to the amygdala. Measurable, reproducible, and real.

When the session ends, you drift back toward your baseline. The arousal creeps back up. The default mode network re-engages. The amygdala starts doing its thing again. That's a state: a temporary shift that resolves when the practice stops.

Do this enough times (enough sessions, enough months), and the baseline itself shifts. The drift-back gets smaller. The default mode runs quieter. Reactivity decreases not just during practice, but during the rest of your life: during the argument, in the meeting, at 3 AM when your brain wants to replay that thing you said. That's a trait: a durable shift in your brain's default operating parameters.

One session = one state shift. Measurable, temporary, real. You feel different afterward, but the baseline hasn't moved yet.

One hundred sessions ≈ the range where many people notice the beginning of trait shift: a heuristic. No dose-finding trial produced that number. The brain you're building is *starting* to show up even when you're not practicing. The direction of change shows up in your log before you feel it in your life, but timelines vary widely.

Long-term, high-session practice = where durable trait differences show up in research. Long-term meditators show trait-level differences in brain structure and function that persist between sessions. The Shamatha Project tracked meditators for seven years and found that sustained attention improvements persisted in those who continued practicing, even at reduced levels (Zanesco et al., 2018). The compound interest of consistent practice is real. It is the single most important concept in long-term meditation.

Everything you do today is building the brain you'll have in five years. That's not a motivational poster. It's neuroplasticity.

12.2 What Changes: The Gap Gets Wider

Every circuit change below serves one outcome: the gap widens. Different mechanisms, same direction. The principle from Chapter 2 still holds: your brain loses control in different places, and every time you come back, you train control to hold longer. Here's what the research shows.

Prefrontal-amygdala circuit (emotional regulation): Consistent practice strengthens the top-down brake on emotional reactivity. Hölzel et al. (2010) reported structural and functional shifts after roughly eight weeks of practice in a modest-sized MBSR cohort, including decreased amygdala gray-matter density correlated with reduced stress: effect sizes are not large, and not every trial replicates

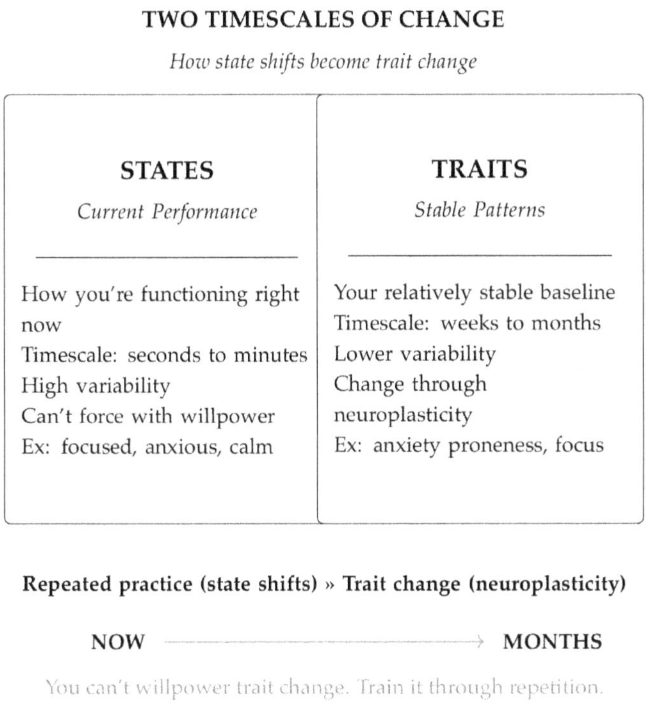

Figure 12.1: States vs Traits

structural change (see below). Reduced functional connectivity between the amygdala and the rumination circuit means the loop between "feeling bad" and "thinking about feeling bad" loses momentum (Taren et al., 2015). The space between trigger and reaction widens by fractions of a second. That fraction is where choice lives. Desbordes et al. (2012) found decreased amygdala response to emotional stimuli in the mindful-attention group, measured outside of meditation, though whole-brain analysis showed no significant pre-post changes in any group. Early evidence that some of the training transfers off the cushion.

Default mode network (mind-wandering and rumination): Brewer et al. (2011) found that experienced meditators showed relative deactivation of default mode network nodes during meditation and, at rest, stronger coupling between the posterior cingulate and cognitive-control regions. Mind-wandering doesn't stop, but the architecture for catching it changes: the wandering network stays wired to the monitoring system.

For the Lifeguard (Chapter 7), a quieter PCC means less background monitoring: the monitoring doesn't shut off, but it stops running at maximum sensitivity, and less of it arrives as threat.

Autonomic nervous system (vagal tone and HRV): Kirk & Axelsen (2020) and related trials report increased resting HRV after mindfulness training, though a 2021 meta-analysis found the pooled evidence mixed (Brown et al., 2021). Higher HRV means a more flexible nervous system, faster recovery from stress. The breath practices in Chapter 3 directly train the baroreflex-vagal system. Over weeks, the state effect (calmer *during* slow breathing) may develop toward a trait effect (the brake engaging faster between sessions), though the evidence for a reliable resting-HRV increase is not yet settled.

Attentional release speed: Attention needs to disengage from one stimulus before it can pick up the next. Several laboratory measures capture aspects of this process. Inhibition of return, a spatial-orienting effect, shows that roughly 300-500 milliseconds after attending to a location, the brain deprioritizes it (Posner & Cohen, 1984; Klein, 2000). That is one example of subsecond attentional bias. The broader clinical picture: dysregulated brains are often slow to disengage. In anxious states, threat cues hold attention past their usefulness; in perseverative ones, evaluative loops resist release (De Lissnyder et al., 2010).

Part of what sets the tempo of this release is your individual alpha frequency. Alpha frequency sets the temporal grain of perception (Samaha & Postle, 2015). Faster alpha means shorter integration windows and quicker release from one stimulus to the next.

The space is, in part, a frequency phenomenon, and multiple small studies suggest practices that increase alpha coherence *may* be tightening the clock that governs how quickly your brain lets go; the mechanism is not fully mapped.

Practice strengthens the release. Meditators show reduced attentional blink: a faster ability to let go of one target and pick up the next (Slagter et al., 2007). In a randomized trial, mindfulness training shortened how long an unpleasant image kept interfering with a simple tone task, and relaxation training did not produce that effect (Ortner et al., 2007; N=82). And experienced practitioners show stronger error-detection signals in the anterior cingulate (the same region that drives the Return Counter) combined with better emotional acceptance, not more self-punishment (Teper & Inzlicht, 2013; Fissler et al., 2017). Over time, practice appears to sharpen how quickly your attention can release and move on.

Notice your jaw right now. Is it clenched? Release it. That conscious release is a moment of voluntary control. One return, right here on this page.

The changes above are circuit-level: which regions connect, how fast signals travel, how strongly the brake engages.

There's another layer of change: the *rhythm* of the brain itself. Your brain produces electrical oscillations at different speeds, and meditation shifts those rhythms and their relationships over time, in the same direction and at the same pace as the circuits above.

Chapter 13 goes deeper: the five frequency bands, how they talk to each other, what changes in long-term meditators (including during sleep), and why when you practice matters as much as how you practice.

A note on structural claims: Multiple small longitudinal MRI studies show detectable gray matter changes after six to eight weeks of consistent practice, especially in hippocampus and default-mode regions. Effect sizes are modest. The "eight weeks" reflects MBSR's program structure as much as a neurobiological threshold: it's the length of the training course. Nobody has proven it's an inflection point in cortical remodeling. One large, well-controlled trial (Kral et al., 2022; N=218) found no significant structural changes compared to an active control. The functional changes above are well-supported. The structural claims are more modest than the marketing suggests.

Promising. Not magic.

12.3 The Dose-Response Reality

How much practice does it take?

The dose-response curve has a clear shape. Your brain begins responding within days; Tang et al. (2010) found measurable white matter changes after just eleven hours of training distributed over four weeks. Reliable improvements in attention, mood, and emotional regulation emerge around eight weeks of brief daily practice (Basso et al., 2019), and even single-session mindfulness practice can sharpen attention in novices (Norris et al., 2018). A large naturalistic study of more than 10,000 meditators across 103 countries (Cearns & Clark, 2023) found that regular, moderate sessions, consistency over marathon effort, predicted the greatest improvements. The steepest slope is in the first three months.

The single strongest predictor is *regularity*, not session length. Three minutes every day beats thirty minutes twice a week. The brain learns through repetition, not heroic effort. That claim is strong for behavior and habit formation (Lally et al., 2009). It's promising but speculative for structural brain change. No imaging study has yet compared short-daily versus long-weekly schedules head to head. The compound-interest logic is real for practice adherence, and it's plausible but unproven for cortical thickness.

The math: if you do a 3-minute practice twice daily for a year, that's 36 hours of total practice time. At twenty returns per 3-minute session, that's roughly 14,600 returns over the year. That number is your engagement record, not a measure of proportional neural change. No study has tested whether more counted returns produce proportionally more brain change. What the number tells you is that you kept showing up. Small things accumulate.

Try this now: One-Breath Return. In through your nose, out through your mouth. That's one more data point on the slope.

12.4 The Honest Ledger

Meditation is not a cure-all. Goyal et al. (2014), a rigorous meta-analysis of 47 randomized trials, found moderate evidence for improvement in anxiety, depression, and pain (effect sizes in the 0.2-0.4 range), comparable to what would be expected from antidepressants in a primary care population. The same analysis found low or insufficient evidence for sleep, attention, and substance use. "We need more data" is not "it doesn't work." But the evidence base is smaller than the marketing suggests, and publication bias inflates it. Van Dam and colleagues published the field's most important reality check in 2018: small samples, definitional fuzziness, publication bias, and overinterpretation of preliminary findings. I cite it here because this chapter needs to survive your skeptical friend's scrutiny.

The phenotype-to-practice matching system in this book is a working clinical model based on 25,000+ QEEG brain maps. It is supported by the research but not identical to it. This matching has not been tested in randomized trials. I believe it works. I've seen it work. And I want you to know the difference between "clinically observed" and "proven in a trial."

Chapter 1 named three distinct claims the book is making. This chapter is the right place to say which one has the strongest support.

The science claim is that matched practice produces larger regulation gains than unmatched practice for a given phenotype. No published trial has tested this directly. A three-arm study, matched practice against mismatched practice against a standard MBSR-control, using an eight-week protocol with adherence as the primary outcome and HRV, attentional metrics, and symptom scales as secondary, could settle the question. That trial has not been run. The effect direction in the chapter-level predictions is clear and operationalizable. The evidence is clinical.

The harm claim has better support. Farias et al. (2020) pooled 83 studies and found an overall adverse-event prevalence of 8.3%, ranging from 3.7% in experimental studies to far higher in survey samples. Lindahl et al. (2017) catalogued 59 categories of meditation-related challenge in experienced practitioners. Schlosser et al. (2019) found particularly unpleasant experiences in roughly one in four regular meditators. Standard meditation is not universally benign. That is documented in the literature. The specific phenotype-level risk attribution, that the Lifeguard is more prone to escalation with eyes-closed practice than other phenotypes, remains clinical pattern-recognition rather than trial-established fact.

The engineering claim is the one most likely to hold up when the trial is eventually run. Routing a meditation-naive person with a strong CEO pattern to breath counting before open monitoring takes less time, produces faster subjective fit, and has lower dropout than routing the same person to an unstructured open-awareness practice. Whether cumulative regulation gains at twelve months differ meaningfully is uncertain. The path to a working practice habit is shorter with the routing tool. That is the claim I am most confident in, and it is the one this book is primarily making.

Name which claim you are asking the book to prove when you evaluate whether it worked.

Use what works. Log your returns. That's science, not faith.

- **Skeptical?** Good. Read the Van Dam caveat above. Then practice anyway.
- **Wondering if this is changing anything?** Track your returns this week. Compare to last month.

12.5 The Compounding Effect

This is why Part IV exists.

Neuroplasticity is a slope. There is no switch. Each session nudges your nervous system toward a slightly different baseline. Over months and years, those nudges compound into a margin you didn't know was possible from where you started. The firefighter's pause in the vignette below, the one he never planned and that was *there*, was built from hundreds of micro-shifts.

This is the states-to-traits trajectory:

1. State shift. During practice, your nervous system is measurably different. Calmer, more focused, more regulated. Temporary. Resolves when the session ends. Like feeling stretched after yoga, real, but it doesn't last.

2. State accessibility. With repetition, the state becomes easier to access. You settle into it faster. You reach the "zone" in ninety seconds instead of ten minutes. The on-ramp shortens. This is the first sign that something structural is shifting.

You can test it right now: notice what you're feeling and label it in one word. "Curious." "Skeptical." "Tired." "Hopeful." That label is the same noting practice from Chapters 9 and 10, deployed in two seconds. Faster access, same skill.

3. Trait shift. The default changes. You're calmer *between* sessions, not just during them. Reactivity decreases in situations where you're not actively practicing: in the meeting, in the argument, at 3 AM. The gap between stimulus and response widens durably, at least as long as you maintain some practice. The brain you're building shows up in the rest of your life.

4. Trait regulation. The highest level. You notice when the trait drifts: when stress accumulates, when practice lapses, when the old reactivity returns. And you correct. You adjust your practice. You add a session. You shift your stack. Self-regulation applied to the practice of self-regulation itself. This is the Mastery Loop in Chapter 18.

You're not trying to become a different person. You're building a different default: less reactive, more flexible, more able to choose. Modest, real, and over five years of consistent practice, life-changing.

12.6 A Vignette: The Moment He Didn't Snap

A firefighter, broad-shouldered, strong Lifeguard, Grumpy underneath, had been practicing for eight weeks. Three minutes of grounding in the morning, vagal toning on the drive to the station. He didn't feel different. His wife said he seemed a little less wound up, but he attributed that to a lighter rotation at work.

Then his fourteen-year-old son slammed a door during an argument, and the firefighter noticed something he'd never noticed before: a gap. A beat between the door slamming and his response. In that beat, he felt the Lifeguard spike: heart rate up, jaw clenched, the whole threat cascade activating. And then, without deciding to, he exhaled. Long exhale. The vagal brake engaged. He said, calmly: "I'm going to take a walk. We'll talk in ten minutes."

His son looked shocked. His wife looked like she might cry.

He called me the next day. "I didn't do anything during the fight. It just… happened. The pause was there."

That's the state-to-trait transition, as it looked for him: not a guaranteed timetable from a study. He didn't apply a technique in the moment. The eight weeks of practice had shifted his default enough that the pause showed up unbidden. He'd built the pause; it wasn't something he performed on cue. The vagal brake that used to need conscious activation (4-in, 6-out, count it) had become fast enough to fire automatically, in the half-second between stimulus and response.

He didn't stop getting angry. He stopped being controlled by it.

12.7 What to Expect When

This timeline is a heuristic. Nobody has empirically mapped it step by step. No longitudinal study has tracked the full arc from first sit to year five. The stages described here are composites from clinical observation, imaging snapshots, and meditator self-reports. With that caveat:

Weeks 1–4, you're building a habit. Awkward. Worth it. Weeks 6–8, state shifts become reliable: you settle faster, recover faster. Month 3–

6, the calm that used to be practice-only starts showing up in real life: in traffic, in the argument, at 3 AM. Year 1, the baseline has measurably shifted. People who know you well will notice before you do.

- *Weeks 1–2: You're remembering to practice without an alarm.*
- *Month 3–6: Someone who knows you well remarks on something they can't name.*
- *Year 1: The things that derailed you for hours now derail you for minutes.*

> **Try this now:** You've been reading about neuroplasticity. But you've been practicing it since page one. How many returns today? Estimate. Write it down. That number is your record.

If you've been practicing and can't feel the difference: that's the nature of gradual change. You can't see the water rising when you're standing in it. The numbers see it before you do, which is exactly why you keep counting. By week 8, you still get irritated, but the irritation runs a few seconds shorter. You notice it as it peaks instead of after it lands. That's the gap.

The one constant across all the research: *regularity beats intensity.* The compound effect is real. You can see it in your return log before you feel it in your life.

> Whatever you practiced today: did you come back at least once? That counts. If you feel worse afterward, check your signals.

You now know what changes. Every circuit in this chapter builds the same thing: a longer pause before the old pattern takes over.

The brain you have today is not the brain you'll have in six months. You'll train it, and through training your brain develops new capacity for regulation. Your brain loses control in different places, and every return you logged was one more moment of coming back. That's not hope. It's practice.

The circuits you've been training run on brain rhythms. Chapter 13 goes underneath them to that oscillatory layer, where the widening gap shows up as measurable waves.

Ch 13: Your Brain's Rhythms

Read this when you want to understand what's happening under the hood. If you're not in that mood right now, go straight to Chapter 14. Nothing in the following chapters requires this one. It's here because some brains need the mechanism before the tool makes sense.

> **If you're in Phase 1 or Phase 2:** You can skip this chapter entirely. The practices work with no science required underneath them. Come back here when (or if) curiosity pulls you. Chapter 14 and beyond don't depend on it.

Your brain doesn't think in words. It thinks in rhythms.

Right now, billions of neurons are firing in coordinated electrical patterns. Not randomly, in waves. Slow waves. Fast waves. Waves riding on top of other waves. The shift you feel when you settle into practice (the room going quieter, the breathing slowing, something loosening behind your eyes) has a frequency signature. It's measurable. It's specific. It changes over time with practice.

Chapter 12 mapped the circuits: connections, brakes, recovery speed. Under the wiring is timing: how fast your brain cycles, couples, and releases.

This chapter covers that layer: the electrical oscillations that organize everything from deep sleep to conscious awareness to the moment you notice your mind has wandered and come back.

13.1 Five rhythms, five modes

Your brain produces oscillations at different speeds, and each speed tends to dominate during a different regulatory mode. These categories are functional shorthand: the bands overlap, co-occur, and serve multiple roles.

Delta (0.5–4 Hz): The slow control rhythm. Delta organizes large-scale cortical silencing and recovery. It dominates deep sleep, coordinating the up-and-down states that allow synaptic maintenance and waste clearance. While you are awake, delta is quieter but not absent. It operates whenever the brain runs large-scale housekeeping. The heartbeat of the brain: slow, pervasive, foundational.

Theta (4–8 Hz): The release rhythm. Theta rises whenever the brain softens inhibitory control over a resource. This happens in sleep, in insight (the "aha" moment when focused constraints loosen and associations recombine), in creative incubation, and in the loss of focused attention (the "squirrel" moment). Whether theta is adaptive or maladaptive depends on context: theta during a creative breakthrough is the same rhythm as theta during the Fog's inopportune power-down. The difference is timing. If you have a Fog brain (Chapter 5), excess theta during tasks you need to be awake for is the signature of a system releasing control when it shouldn't. Frontal midline theta, specifically, indexes the anterior cingulate's engagement during sustained internal attention, the same region that drives the Return Counter.

Alpha (8–13 Hz): The gating rhythm. Alpha idles cortical regions that aren't currently needed, directing resources toward whatever IS active. Your individual alpha frequency sets the temporal grain of perception (Chapter 10). Faster alpha means shorter integration windows and quicker release from one stimulus to the next. When alpha rises during meditation, it's the brain efficiently shutting down what it doesn't need, not "relaxing" in the way most people imagine. Alpha is the bouncer at the door: only the relevant signals get through.

Beta (13–30 Hz): Active processing. Beta rises during focused cognition, motor planning, and sustained vigilance. High beta is often associated with overthinking, anxiety, and rumination: the brain locked in processing mode when it should be resting. If you're a CEO (Chapter 7) or a Lifeguard, that hum of high beta is the monitoring system that won't stand down.

Gamma (30–100+ Hz): The integration rhythm. Gamma has no dedicated generator. It emerges from the same neural circuits that produce other bands, but at moments when those circuits synchronize at high frequency. Gamma appears to be what binding feels like from the inside: sensory, cognitive, and emotional information assembled into a single coherent moment. The moment you hold the room, the page, and the feeling in your body all at once: that's the state that correlates with gamma synchrony in the lab.

> **Try this now:** Notice what you're aware of right now. Not one thing; everything. The page. The room. The weight of your body. The temperature. All held at once, without choosing. That panoramic awareness correlates with gamma synchrony in lab studies.

Each band paces the gap differently: how long a "moment" lasts before the next stimulus wins. Returns are reps for that pacing.

13.2 The rhythms talk to each other

These bands don't operate in isolation. They nest. Gamma bursts ride on theta waves. Alpha gates which cortical regions get to fire gamma. The relationships between bands matter as much as the bands themselves.

Neuroscientists call this **cross-frequency coupling**: slower rhythms organize when and where faster rhythms fire. The most studied form is theta-gamma phase-amplitude coupling: gamma bursts locked to specific phases of ongoing theta, like items organized on a shelf.

Lisman and Jensen proposed the theta-gamma code: items in working memory are represented as distinct gamma bursts nested within a single theta cycle, providing an ordering mechanism for sequential experience (Lisman & Jensen, 2013). Research suggests stronger coupling correlates with better working memory performance and more precise representations.

Anesthesia research cares about this coupling for a reason. Clinical monitors of awareness, like the Bispectral Index (BIS) used in anesthesia, track, among other things, how different frequency bands interact. The BIS algorithm incorporates spectral content and higher-order phase relationships between bands to gauge depth of anesthesia. When cross-frequency coupling breaks down under anesthesia, awareness fades. When it restores, you wake up.

The careful claim: meditation appears to systematically alter these rhythms and their relationships, especially in the gamma range, reshaping the oscillatory language the brain uses to support conscious awareness. The Part II moves (notice, stay, return) train how bands couple and release.

13.3 Gamma in long-term meditators

The evidence for oscillatory changes in long-term meditators is among the most striking in meditation neuroscience. It's also among the most cautiously interpreted, for good reasons.

Lutz et al. (2004) recorded EEGs from eight Tibetan Buddhist monks with 10,000 to 50,000+ hours of practice. In compassion meditation, they showed massive increases in gamma synchrony across frontal and parietal regions. More striking: their *baseline* gamma, measured before they started meditating, was already elevated. That's a trait-level difference. The brain's resting integration rhythm had shifted. On a brain map, that kind of baseline elevation looks like a different nervous system. In clinical practice, I don't see this in beginners; I start to see it in people who have been practicing consistently for years.

Ferrarelli et al. (2013) measured 29 long-term meditators during sleep, when they weren't meditating and couldn't have produced muscle artifact, and found parietal-occipital gamma power roughly 35% higher than controls. The brain was doing something different even while unconscious. If that doesn't strike you as remarkable, sit with it for a moment. A practice conducted while awake changed how the brain oscillates during deep sleep.

Braboszcz et al. (2017) replicated the gamma elevation across three meditation traditions (Vipassana, Himalayan Yoga, and Isha Shoonya), and found that lifetime practice hours predicted gamma power. Three traditions, one direction. The trait component was real enough to show up across different teachers, techniques, and cultural contexts.

The Shamatha Project's longitudinal data put this in perspective. As Cliff Saron and colleagues have shown, you don't jump straight to monk-level gamma. Months of intensive practice first reshape the slower control rhythms: beta power drops, individual alpha frequency shifts with the amount of practice, large-scale brain dynamics reorganize (Saggar et al., 2012; Skwara et al., 2022). Best current evidence suggests the dramatic gamma traits reported in long-term adepts emerge on top of that foundation. Early training tunes the scaffold. Advanced practice builds integration on top. Same arc as Chapter 12: returns first, integration later.

Long-term meditators also show changes in how slow rhythms modulate faster ones. Experienced Vipassana meditators show reduced infra-slow EEG activity and weaker coupling between those infra-slow fluctuations and alpha amplitude, most clearly over the left frontal region, suggesting more stable baseline excitability: less spontaneous fluctuation, more consistent readiness (Sihn et al., 2024). The system for starting, stopping, and stabilizing integration events is being retuned.

More reliable room between stimulus and response. The widening gap by another name.

The honest-broker frame: Sample sizes are small (8 monks in Lutz, 29 per group in Ferrarelli, 44 total in Braboszcz). Gamma is artifact-prone: high-frequency EEG is vulnerable to muscle contamination, and scalp recordings have limits. All studies are cross-sectional or quasi-longitudinal: the meditators chose to practice, so we can't prove practice caused the trait differences. The direction is consistent across labs, traditions, measurement conditions, and even sleep states. Consistent enough to take seriously. The gold standard confirmation hasn't arrived yet. One finding stretches beyond waking practice altogether.

13.4 Your rhythms don't stop when you sleep

Return to the Ferrarelli sleep finding, because it is the most underappreciated result in the field. The meditators weren't meditating, weren't conscious, and weren't producing muscle artifact, and their brains still oscillated differently: that 35% gamma elevation, tracking their daily practice.

This didn't show up in sleep stage proportions. Meditators didn't get more deep sleep or more REM. The architecture looked the same. What differed was the activity *within* the architecture: the gamma signature inside NREM, suggesting that the brain's integration circuits were operating differently even during unconsciousness.

Delta (the dominant rhythm of deep sleep) drives the large-scale cortical silencing that allows glymphatic clearance: the brain's waste-removal system, flushing metabolic debris through channels that open when neural activity quiets. This is the "housekeeping" rhythm. Meditation improves self-reported sleep quality across multiple studies, and the gamma trait suggests the brain's regulatory machinery is doing something different overnight. The data don't show meditators getting more slow-wave sleep. The standout is what the brain is doing *within* the sleep it gets.

One intriguing finding: Kaul et al. (2010) reported that long-term meditators showed shorter total sleep time (by actigraphy and sleep diaries) with no worse psychomotor vigilance compared to matched controls. One study, small sample, no full polysomnography. It raises a question: is the brain sleeping more efficiently, or is meditation partially compensating for sleep pressure? The answer isn't clear. The question is worth asking.

The sensorimotor rhythm (SMR, 12–15 Hz), trained in neurofeedback (Chapter 14), overlaps with the N2 sleep spindles that organize memory consolidation during lighter sleep stages. The connection between SMR training and sleep architecture improvement is neurophysiologically plausible: Sterman's original work discovered SMR in the context of sleep research. No published study has measured sleep spindle density in meditators specifically. This is a gap where the hypothesis runs ahead of the data.

The overnight consolidation hypothesis (and I'm flagging this as theoretical): what you practice during the day may get consolidated during sleep. Practice shifts wake oscillations. Those shifts could get reinforced during NREM, when the brain replays and consolidates recent learning. The next morning, your baseline is slightly different. This is a plausible mechanism for how states become traits. Direct evidence is thin. Consider it "how it likely works" rather than "how it's been proven to work." If it holds, sleep is doing part of the return-training when you're not on the cushion.

13.5 Why timing matters: your practice and your clock

Your brain's rhythms operate on multiple timescales. Gamma oscillates in milliseconds. Theta in hundreds of milliseconds. Alpha in tenths of a second. There's a much slower rhythm governing all of them: the circadian cycle. A 24-hour oscillation, driven by the suprachiasmatic nucleus and synchronized by light, that determines when your brain is neurophysiologically ready for different kinds of work.

Circadian rhythms are oscillating systems on the same continuum as brainwaves, just slower. The same principles apply: timing, coupling, entrainment. They matter for your practice.

The morning window. In the 30 to 60 minutes after waking, cortisol peaks sharply in a phenomenon called the cortisol awakening response (CAR). This isn't a stress response. It's a biological boot sequence: mobilizing glucose, priming the immune system, shifting the brain from sleep oscillations to waking oscillations. Morning light within the first hour strengthens CAR, suppresses residual melatonin, and advances circadian phase.

The CAR may open a neurophysiologically distinct window. In one small study, higher CAR amplitude was associated with left-lateralized frontocentral alpha asymmetry, a pattern linked to active coping, though the association was marginal before covariate adjustment (Duan et al., 2019; N=55). Intensive contemplative retreat practice has been shown to increase CAR amplitude, suggesting a healthier, more dynamic circadian profile (Cahn et al., 2017). The morning brain, post-CAR, is oscillatorily primed for focused, intentional work.

No one has run the definitive study ("meditate at 7 AM versus 7 PM and compare EEGs"). The recommendation to practice in the morning is physiologically plausible and consistent with circadian data.

The oscillatory landscape is measurably different at different times of day. Theta and delta power rise with drowsiness: continuous EEG during night-shift driving shows the signature clearly (Torsvall & Akerstedt, 1987). The brain you bring to morning practice is not the same brain you'd bring to evening practice.

Practice after your brain wakes up. If you meditate in the first 30 minutes and you're foggy, that's sleep inertia. The cortisol hasn't peaked yet. Morning light first, then practice. If you're a Fog phenotype (Chapter 5), circadian timing matters even more: your arousal system is already running on a brownout. Don't fight it with eyes-closed meditation at 6 AM. Wait for it to peak. Stand up. Let the light in.

Match practice type to time of day. Morning, when CAR and cortical arousal are rising, tends to suit focused attention and open monitoring practices (the kinds that demand sustained, alert engagement). Chronotype shifts this window: night owls peak later. Evening is better suited to body scans, compassion practices, and Yoga Nidra (practices that downshift arousal and bridge into the drowsy, theta-rich transition toward sleep). In a lab trial, Yoga Nidra shortened sleep onset latency in adults with insomnia (Datta et al., 2021). The same practice that would fight your morning alertness becomes a sleep-onset facilitator at night.

Consistent timing as entrainment. Non-photic behaviors (exercise, meals, social interaction) can act as secondary zeitgebers (time-givers), modestly strengthening circadian rhythms when done consistently at the same clock time. In one small study, morning cortisol fell with years of practice among long-term meditators, and novices who completed an eight-week MBSR course showed both lower morning cortisol and better self-reported sleep (Brand et al., 2012; N=20). A daily practice at the same time may entrain not just the habit but the oscillatory patterns associated with the practice state. This is a hypothesis informed by chronobiology, without direct testing for meditation. No study has compared same-time versus random-time practice on circadian or EEG endpoints. The logic tracks: the brain adapts to regular inputs, and regular inputs at the same daily phase should reinforce the same oscillatory patterns.

Returns stay primary. This times them when your oscillator already leans the right way.

13.6 What this means for your practice

The frequency bands are the infrastructure of the space between stimulus and response.

Short-term practice shifts state-level rhythms during sessions: alpha changes, beta quiets, theta shifts, the brain settles into a different frequency signature. That's what settling in feels like. It's measurable and temporary.

Long-term practice is a different project.

Long-term practice shifts the *relationships* between bands: how gamma rides on theta, how alpha gates resources, how the whole system tunes itself between sessions. Alpha sets the grain of the gap (Chapter 10). Gamma reflects whether you're consciously present in that gap. Theta determines whether control is holding or releasing. Circadian alignment amplifies all of these effects: the same practice at the right time, consistently, compounds faster than the same practice at random times.

The oscillatory changes track the states-to-traits arc from Chapter 12. State shifts during practice → trait shifts between sessions → trait shifts during sleep → a brain that's oscillatorily different 24 hours a day. A better-tuned brain. The gap is partly timing: how long a cycle runs before the next one grabs the wheel.

> **Try this now:** Think about when you last practiced. Were you foggy or alert? If foggy, try shifting your practice 30 minutes later tomorrow. The oscillatory landscape changes hour by hour. Find the window where your brain is already leaning toward focus, and practice there.

13.7 The honest-broker summary

What's solid:

- Meditation shifts state-level oscillations during practice (alpha, theta, beta changes). Replicated across labs and traditions.
- Long-term meditators show elevated baseline gamma (Lutz, Braboszcz) and elevated NREM gamma (Ferrarelli). Consistent direction. Small samples.
- Cross-frequency coupling changes appear in experienced meditators (infra-slow / alpha / gamma PAC). This finding is emerging.

What's plausible but preliminary:

- The overnight consolidation loop (practice → sleep reinforcement → trait shift). Theoretically grounded.
- Consistent practice timing as circadian entrainment. Supported by chronobiology, without direct testing for meditation.
- Morning practice as oscillatorily optimal. Physiologically plausible.

What's unknown:

- Whether meditation changes sleep spindle density.
- Whether meditators need less sleep or are more efficient sleepers.
- The precise cross-frequency coupling changes that meditation produces over time.

The evidence is promising and consistent, though not yet proven by the gold standard. The direction is clear enough to practice on. Every return still trains the circuits these rhythms organize. This chapter doesn't change that priority.

Can technology train these rhythms faster than practice alone? Chapter 14 is the honest assessment: which tools speed up return-training, and which are mostly expensive nightlights.

Ch 14: Tech-Assisted Meditation: Biofeedback, Neurofeedback & Gadgets

Read this before you buy a device, an app, or a gadget.

A client came in carrying a cardboard box. Inside was a consumer EEG headband she'd bought after watching a YouTube video that promised to "show you your brain as you meditate." She'd been using it for six weeks. It showed a lot of data, she said. She had no idea what any of it meant. The app told her when she was "calm" and when she was "active." On calm days she felt fine; on active days she felt like she was failing at something.

She asked me if the device was working.

I told her the device was measuring something. Whether it was measuring what the marketing said it was measuring was a different question.

This chapter is about that different question. Specifically: which technologies add precision to the practice you're already building, which ones add noise while looking like signal, and why that distinction matters more than the device itself.

Return-training is the engine. Technology is optional gearing. Used well, it targets the circuits underneath with more precision per rep. It does not replace logging returns, phenotype matching, or the 90-Second Reset. Those stay primary. HRV biofeedback, clinical neurofeedback, and consumer EEG headbands earn their place when you know what each one actually does.

I run a neuroscience clinic. I use neurofeedback and biofeedback every day with the same clients I teach meditation to. I've watched these tools produce real, measurable, lasting change in thousands of brains. I've also watched marketing bury the science: same tools, louder claims.

This chapter covers four things: the vagus nerve (the hardware underneath everything), HRV biofeedback (a voluntary skill you can learn with cheap consumer devices), neurofeedback (involuntary brain training that reaches circuits meditation can't), consumer EEG devices (useful gauges, mediocre training tools), and binaural beats (probably not doing what you think). An honest broker's guide to what accelerates your training and what's mostly good packaging.

14.1 The Vagus Nerve: The Hardware

Every breath practice in this book operates through the vagus nerve, the longest nerve in your body, running from brainstem through chest and abdomen. Approximately 80–90% of vagal traffic flows *up*, from body to brain, not brain to body. The vagus is an information highway, and most of the traffic is northbound.

The vagal brake you've been training with every breath practice produces a measurable oscillation: heart rate rises on the inhale, falls on the exhale. The size of that oscillation is heart rate variability (HRV). Higher HRV means a stronger vagal brake and faster recovery from stressors. Lower HRV tracks with anxiety, depression, PTSD, and chronic stress. HRV responds to voluntary breathing in real time, and biofeedback makes that response precise and learnable. Whether resting HRV durably increases from meditation alone is a separate question with mixed evidence (Chapter 12).

14.2 HRV Biofeedback: Learning to Drive Your Own Nervous System

What it is: Voluntary skill acquisition. You learn to shift your own autonomic balance by breathing at your personal resonance frequency.

How it works: You breathe at a specific rate, typically 4.5 to 6.5 breaths per minute, individualized to your physiology, while watching a real-time display of your heart rate variability. A chest strap or finger sensor reads your heart rate; software calculates the HRV in real time; you see a waveform that spikes when you're breathing at resonance and flattens when you're not. When you hit your frequency, the waveform looks like a clean sine wave. Your heart rate synchronizes with your breathing in a way you can watch happening.

This is skill building, not passive treatment. The analogy that works best: you're learning to drive a car, not being driven somewhere. You're at the wheel. The display is the speedometer. Over sessions, you learn to produce the resonance state deliberately, and eventually unassisted. The biofeedback scaffolds the learning, and the skill is yours to keep.

Why consumer devices work for this: Because the skill is voluntary and the feedback loop is simple. Any device that accurately measures your heart rate beat-by-beat will do: a Bluetooth chest strap, a finger pulse sensor, a phone app with a pulse reader (many are free or cheap). You don't need clinical-grade equipment for HRV biofeedback. The target is your heart rate, which is easy to measure accurately with consumer hardware. This is one of the few areas where "there's an app for that" is true.

The evidence: Lehrer and Gevirtz (2014) published a full review of HRV biofeedback mechanisms, documenting improvements in baroreflex sensitivity, parasympathetic tone, and stress resilience.

A meta-analysis of 24 studies found a large effect size (Hedges' $g \approx 0.83$) for stress and anxiety reduction (Goessl et al., 2017). The same review noted that few studies included follow-up assessments, so the long-term durability of these gains remains uncertain.

Clinical framing: HRV biofeedback teaches the autonomic system to hold a wider gap between excitation and response, and that gap is trainable. If you can downshift your nervous system in three minutes of resonance-frequency breathing before you meditate, you don't "drop into your crap" when you close your eyes. You meditate from a platform of physiological stability. For the Lifeguard, body-level safety data helps the scanning system stand down. For the Grumpy Old Man, resonance breathing shifts the autonomic balance away from withdrawal before the effort-dread can sabotage the session.

The breath lever from Chapter 3 is the same breathing, without the measurement. Strictly, biofeedback means you can see the signal you are changing; paced breathing alone is the intervention without the feedback loop. Adding the gadget makes the feedback loop faster, more precise, and more engaging, especially for the Happy Little Kid phenotype.

> **Try this now:** Breathe at six breaths per minute for sixty seconds. In for five, out for five. If you have a chest strap or phone app, watch the waveform. If not, put two fingers on your wrist and feel the pulse slow on the exhale. That slowing is the vagal brake engaging. That's the resonance you'd see on the screen.

14.3 Neurofeedback: Training Below the Surface

What it is: Involuntary operant conditioning. This is different from biofeedback. The distinction is real, and marketers blur it on purpose.

In biofeedback, you learn a skill. You feel the change. You know what you're doing. You're the student.

In neurofeedback, the brain changes without you "trying." An EEG sensor reads your brainwaves in real time. A computer identifies patterns in your brain activity: specific frequencies, at specific locations, in specific amplitudes. When the brain produces the target pattern, it gets rewarded (usually with a tone, a brightening video, or points). When it doesn't, the reward pauses.

Over sessions (typically 20 to 40, twice weekly) the brain shifts toward the rewarded patterns through operant conditioning, reshaping the odds of which patterns fire beneath your awareness. Exactly like a pigeon learning to press a lever without understanding why the food appears. Except the pigeon is your cortex, and the lever is a specific frequency pattern in a specific brain region.

This is why neurofeedback can reach circuits that meditation can't. Meditation requires conscious anchoring. You can only train what you're aware of directing attention toward. Neurofeedback trains cortical activity below conscious awareness.

The sensorimotor rhythm that governs the Supervisor's braking? Neurofeedback trains it directly. The alpha peak frequency that sets the Timekeeper's clock speed? Neurofeedback can nudge it. The deep default-mode-network patterns that drive the Lifeguard's scanning? Neurofeedback addresses them at a level that meditation approaches from above.

The two work on different layers. Neurofeedback trains from below: cortical timing, inhibitory tone, the source of the space. Meditation trains from above: attention, regulation, conscious return. Together they cover more ground than either alone.

Protocols relevant to this book:

There are protocols for impulse control (SMR training, the Supervisor's brake), attention and initiation (left-side beta training, the Stabilizer and CEO), and trauma recovery (alpha-theta training). SMR protocols that increase 12-15 Hz over sensorimotor cortex improve spindle density and stabilize vigilance: the same thalamocortical circuits that keep the Fog brain's lights on.

Alpha-theta training deserves a closer look because it's often described as "the crossover" and left at that. What happens: the clinician rewards theta amplitude while monitoring alpha. As the session deepens, theta rises and alpha falls until theta crosses above alpha. That crossover marks entry into a liminal state between waking and sleep, the same territory meditators spend years approaching. But the crossover isn't a simple on/off switch. Johnson et al. (2013) analyzed 182 alpha-theta sessions and found that therapeutic crossovers, the ones associated with vivid imagery, emotional processing, and better clinical outcomes, had a specific multi-band signature: theta at least 1 μV above alpha, sustained for three or more minutes, with a moderate bump in low beta (15-20 Hz). In other words, it's not "theta dominates and you drift off." It's a precise configuration where slower rhythms open a gate and faster rhythms stay engaged enough to process what comes through.

The same dynamic from Chapter 12 applies here: slower control rhythms (theta, alpha) don't just compete for dominance; they scaffold what faster rhythms (beta, gamma) can do. Alpha-theta neurofeedback likely works by training the brain to hold that scaffold in a specific configuration that opens access to memory, imagery, and emotional reprocessing. Your clinician selects the protocol based on your individual brain map.

The trauma data is worth noting: a landmark RCT of neurofeedback for chronic PTSD (van der Kolk et al., 2016; N=52, 24 sessions) found that 61% of the neurofeedback group no longer met PTSD criteria, compared to 33% of the waitlist control.

A subsequent trial tested it more strictly (Nicholson et al., 2020; N=36, 18 per arm), double-blind and sham-controlled rather than waitlist-controlled, and the result came back mixed. Symptom scores fell over time in both arms, and the group by time interaction was not significant, so alpha training did not outperform sham on symptom reduction itself. Two findings still favored it: remission reached 61.1% in the trained group against 33.3% in sham, and post-treatment fMRI showed restored default mode and salience network connectivity. The authors call it a preliminary investigation. That is the right weight to give it, and it is the honest version of a result you will see quoted elsewhere without the sham comparison attached.

NFB + meditation pairing: A systematic review of mindfulness-based neurofeedback (Treves et al., 2024) found promising early evidence that combining meditation with real-time EEG or fMRI feedback can help participants modulate targeted brain networks and improve clinical symptoms, including in novice meditators who had never meditated before. The feedback appears to accelerate the learning curve by making the target states visible (on screen) rather than purely subjective. The evidence is preliminary and heterogeneous, but the direction is promising.

Caveat: Clinical neurofeedback requires clinical-grade equipment and trained clinicians. Assessment is where the channel count matters: a full 19-channel QEEG is what maps the brain and guides protocol selection. Training itself often runs on far fewer channels, sometimes one or two over the target site. The point is that a clinician chose the site and the target from a map. This is not something you do at home with a consumer headband. The section below explains why.

> **Going deeper clinically:** If what you've read above sounds like the right level of intervention for your brain, or if self-directed practice has stalled and you want to understand why, the clinical path starts with a quantitative EEG brain map. *The QEEG Field Guide* (Hill & Lomeli, Peak Brain Press) is the complete reference for understanding your own map and what it means. *Neurofeedback, Explained* (Hill & McCann, Peak Brain Press) covers protocol selection, what to expect session by session, and how to evaluate providers. This chapter is the introduction to that world. Those books are the maps.

See the Resources section for supplementary references and provider-focused material.

14.4 Consumer EEG Devices: Gauges, Not Gyms

Here's where I need to be careful, because I respect the engineering behind these devices while disagreeing with how they're marketed.

Consumer EEG headbands are marketed as neurofeedback for your living room. They're not. They're useful for something different, and less useful for what they claim.

Here's the split.

What they CAN do well:

- Track meditation consistency and gross state shifts over time (are you generally calmer this month versus last month?)
- Provide basic real-time feedback on alpha power modulation (you can see, roughly, when your brain is more or less settled)

- Gamify practice: points, streaks, audio feedback that shifts with your brain state. For the Happy Little Kid phenotype, this can maintain engagement through the novelty drought.
- Scaffold habit formation: the ritual of putting on the headband, launching the app, and starting creates an initiation bridge that the Stabilizer can use.

What they CANNOT reliably do:

- Targeted, protocol-driven neurofeedback: training specific brain regions with specific frequency targets. Consumer headbands have too few sensors (4-8 versus 19+ for clinical systems), too much movement artifact, and insufficient spatial resolution for genuine operant conditioning protocols.
- Signal quality varies significantly across devices. A 2024 comparison of consumer dry-electrode systems against clinical gel-based EEG (Kleeva et al., 2024) found that devices like the Muse headband showed clear limitations in signal quality, especially for higher-frequency bands. Gel-based systems remained superior for capturing beta activity and maintaining test-retest reliability. These consumer products improve with each generation, so check current reviews before buying.
- Individualized protocol selection. Consumer devices use one-size-fits-all algorithms, which is exactly the problem this book exists to solve.

I'm not anti-technology. I use consumer EEG headbands in my clinic as meditation gauges. They're useful for showing clients what their alpha looks like during practice. But I don't call it neurofeedback, because it doesn't produce the operant conditioning that clinical systems produce. The feedback loop isn't precise enough, the sensor coverage isn't broad enough, and the protocols aren't individualized.

The bottom line for consumer EEG: Use it for what it does well: gauging your practice, gamifying consistency, building the habit. These devices don't widen the space directly, but they make your gap-widening practice visible, and visibility sustains the consistency that produces the change. Don't expect them to do clinical neurofeedback. The hardware isn't there. And that's okay. You don't need it to meditate. You need your brain, your anchor, and a way to log returns if you're counting (Chapter 3).

Try this now: If you own a consumer headband, try one session with it and one gadget-free; compare how the two sessions feel. If you don't own one, after your next session, rate how settled you feel in one word. That's the same measurement the app produces, translated into your own language. The gadget measures from the outside. You measure from the inside. Both matter, and they don't always agree.

14.5 Binaural Beats: Honest Skepticism

Binaural beats present a different frequency to each ear: say, 200 Hz to the left and 210 Hz to the right. The brain perceives the 10 Hz difference as a "beat," a pulsing tone that isn't in either earphone. The claim: this entrains your brainwaves to the target frequency, producing desired states. Alpha beats for relaxation. Theta beats for creativity. Delta beats for sleep.

The claim outstrips the evidence.

So what do we know?

What the research shows: The frequency following response is real; your auditory cortex perceives the difference frequency. But perceiving a frequency is not entraining your whole brain into a functional state. A systematic review (Ingendoh et al., 2023) found inconsistent, small effects for theta/alpha entrainment, and many studies assume entrainment without measuring it. Expectancy effects likely mediate most of the perceived benefit.

If you enjoy binaural beats while meditating, they won't hurt you. They create a consistent auditory environment: an auditory sanctuary for the Princess, background noise less stimulating than music for the

Bard. Use them if they help. But a slow exhale is a hydraulic lever; a binaural beat is a nice sound.

14.6 HRV, neurofeedback, consumer EEG, binaural beats

Tool	Mechanism	Access	Evidence	Best For
HRV Biofeedback	Voluntary skill (breathing)	Chest strap + app	Strong	Vagal tone, Grumpy, Lifeguard
Neurofeedback	Involuntary operant conditioning	Clinical only	Varies (moderate to strong by condition)	Supervisor, Stabilizer, trauma
Consumer EEG	Meditation gauge + gamification	Earband + app	Moderate	Happy Little Kid, habit building
Binaural Beats	Auditory perception	Earphones	Weak	Ambient practice

If You're Prone to Compulsive Optimization

A warning for the CEO and Timekeeper phenotypes: tech-assisted meditation can become self-surveillance. If you find yourself checking HRV scores after every session, comparing today's coherence number to yesterday's, building spreadsheets of your EEG band ratios, or feeling worse about a "low score" session despite feeling calmer. The technology has become another arena for self-judgment. That's the CEO auditing the meditation through a different lens. Stop tracking. Do the 90-Second Reset. No data. No dashboard. Practice gadget-free. The tech is a tool for regulation.

Technology complements meditation. It doesn't replace return-training. The practices in this book work with zero hardware.

HRV biofeedback makes the breath lever more precise. Neurofeedback reaches circuits meditation can't. Consumer EEG makes practice visible. Binaural beats sound nice.

Use what's available. Be honest about what it does. The most powerful regulation tool you own is your nervous system. Everything else is an amplifier. Your nervous system has been regulating since before you were born. Practice teaches it to do that on purpose, with or without a screen.

14.6.1 Getting Started with HRV Biofeedback

For the Grumpy Old Man, Lifeguard, and anyone doing breath-paced work: a Bluetooth chest strap ($50–80) and a free HRV app (Elite HRV, HRV4Training) are enough to start. Set the pacer to 6 breaths per minute (5 seconds in, 5 seconds out) for 5 minutes before your regular session. The first sessions feel mechanical. By Week 2, you start to feel when the breath and heartbeat lock in, screen or no screen. By Week 4, you can often find resonance unassisted. The biofeedback trained the skill. The skill is yours.

On beta-blockers: Your HRV readings will look different from an unmedicated baseline, and not in one simple direction. That's the medication, not your practice. See Chapter 16 for what the evidence does and doesn't show. Focus on the subjective feel of calm.

> **Timing and HRV:** If you want to choose *when* you practice (best practice window, aligning peak regulatory capacity with high-demand work), that territory is covered in depth in *Action Cadence* (Peak Brain Press).

> You now know more about your nervous system than most meditators. That's enough to start anywhere in the toolkit.

You know what's real and what's packaging. That clarity is a return.

Disclosure: The author founded Peak Brain Institute, a neurofeedback clinic that uses some of the technologies discussed in this chapter. No product manufacturer has paid for placement in this book, and no referral fees or affiliate arrangements exist with any product or service mentioned here.

You have the tools and the science. Chapter 15 turns them into a three-phase program that starts where you are and scales from there.

The Restart Protocol

Use this when you've fallen off.

You practiced for a while. Then you stopped. Maybe for a week. Maybe for six months. Maybe you never quite got started and this is your second or third attempt with this book, and you carry the particular guilt of owning a self-improvement book without being improved yet.

First: you have not failed. You have a dysregulated brain. Dysregulated brains are, by definition, inconsistent. Inconsistency is the symptom. You don't need to feel bad about the gap. You need to close it.

Here's how.

The Three-Step Restart

Step 1: Start smaller than you think you should.

Whatever you were doing before, cut it in half. If you were doing ten minutes, do five. If five, do two. If two, do thirty seconds.

This is not about lowering your standards. It's about removing the re-entry cost. A big practice you do rarely is worse than a tiny practice you do every day. The nervous system learns from repetition. Your job right now is to rebuild the habit.

Start tiny. Add length when tiny gets boring.

Step 2: Don't count the gap.

Whatever you were doing before, wherever you stopped, don't calculate the damage. It doesn't matter. The nervous system doesn't accumulate "lost progress" the way you imagine. Some of what you built is still there. Some has faded. That's fine: it rebuilds faster the second time. This is true of every physical skill, and meditation is a physical skill.

You're not behind. You're restarting. Those are different things.

Step 3: Do the 90-Second Reset right now.

Feet. Breath. Permission. That's it. You just restarted.

The Restart is the Practice

One reframe might help: for a dysregulated brain, the essential skill is not sustaining a practice indefinitely. It's restarting after you stop.

Everyone stops. The difference between someone who "has a meditation practice" and someone who "used to meditate" isn't perfection. It's the ease of restarting: less drama, less negotiation.

You just did that. You restarted. Count it.

Your tally starts fresh each morning, by design. You're always one practice away from being back.

When the Restart Feels Impossible

If coming back feels overwhelmingly impossible (not just inconvenient, but like there's a wall between you and the cushion you cannot move), that's a circuit problem.

Use the Decision Tree (Chapter 2): what's loudest? Initiation, mood, sensory overload, or tempo? Start at the highest broken step and open the matched chapter (4–10).

The most important meditation you'll ever do is not the one where you sit for forty minutes in perfect stillness. It's the one you do the morning after you've stopped. Do the Reset. Count one return. You're back.

Ch 15: The Three-Phase Model: Stabilize, Train, Integrate

Read this when you've been practicing a week and want a plan.

Most books teach meditation as one generic habit. This one matches the practice to the brain you have. The standard advice is "meditate twenty minutes daily." The real advice: find where your system breaks, match the practice, and show up. Three minutes counts.

You have the tools. You have your phenotype match. You've been practicing, or you're about to start. Maybe you've been doing the 90-Second Reset twice daily for a week. Maybe you've been walking and counting steps. Maybe you've done one 3-minute Rapid Noting session and felt something shift.

Now the question: what's the program? How long? How do you progress? When are you done?

This chapter answers that. The throughline is a return practice that compounds: more reps, a truer match to your brain, paced by your nervous system instead of a calendar. The three-phase structure (Stabilize, Train, Integrate) only paces that work, so you're not guessing what "enough" looks like week to week.

The half-second between trigger and reaction, where choice lives, runs through all three phases. Phase 1 finds the gap. Phase 2 widens it. Phase 3 lives in it.

Your phenotype match from Part II doesn't change across phases. Phase is training intensity. A Lifeguard in Phase 1 and a Lifeguard in Phase 3 are still doing Lifeguard practices. The duration, complexity, and real-world deployment change. The match stays.

Here's what that looks like in the weeks ahead.

Each phase has a clear entry point, clear practices, and a clear signal for when to progress. Markers and milestones, yes, and explicit permission to stay at any phase as long as you need.

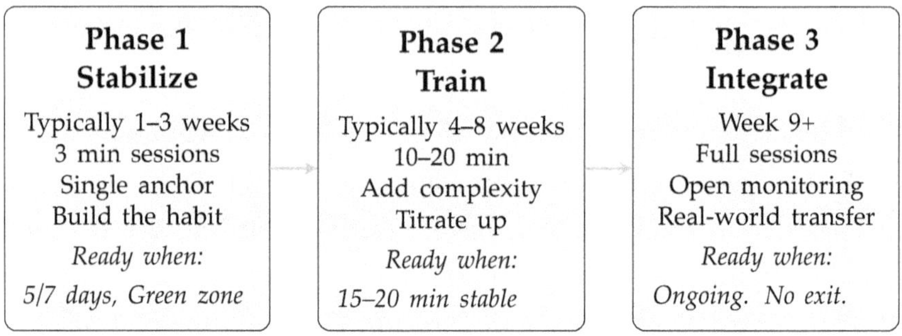

Figure 15.1: The Three-Phase Program. Stabilize the habit, then train the skill, then integrate into life.

15.1 Already Practicing?

If you're coming to this chapter with an existing practice, maybe you've been meditating for months or years but feel stuck, or you've been doing unmatched practice and want to recalibrate. You don't need to start at Phase 1.

Self-assessment: Can you sit for 10+ minutes most days, in the Green zone, with ease? If yes, you're in Phase 2. Start there. Add your phenotype-matched practices from Part II to whatever you're already doing, and use the Anchor Ladder to assess your current complexity level.

Can you sit for 20+ minutes and practice off the cushion (transitions, relationships, work)? You're in Phase 3. Chapter 17 (Mindfulness in Motion) is your next step. Use this chapter's progression criteria to confirm, but trust your practice. You've built something real.

Not sure? Start at Phase 1 for one week. If it feels too easy, if 3 minutes is trivial and you're solidly Green the whole time, move to Phase 2. The phases are scaffolding.

15.2 Phase 1: Stabilize (typically 1–3 weeks)

Phase 1 is ugly. You'll forget. You'll negotiate with yourself before every session. You'll do ninety seconds and feel like a fraud. You'll skip two days and feel like you've failed the whole thing. All of that is Phase 1 working. None of it is evidence that you're doing it wrong.

Phase 1 is the period when the habit doesn't exist yet and you're building it from scratch. Ugly is normal. Showing up anyway is the skill.

If you feel behind: you're not. Phase 1 is where everyone starts, including people who've been meditating for years and just realized they were doing it wrong for their brain. The only "behind" is not starting. You're already past that.

Phase 1 is about one thing: building the habit. Focus solely on consistency at low intensity, with maximum safety. Mastery, depth, and transformation come later.

If the starting resistance is fierce, lead with the Permission Practice from Chapter 1: "I'm allowed to stop at any time." That line disarms the Grumpy, the Problem Child, and the CEO in one sentence. The week ranges below are typical. Your nervous system doesn't keep a calendar. The progression criteria tell you when to move.

The most common reason people abandon meditation is that they start too hard, too long, too ambitiously. The mismatch between effort and result generates guilt, which generates avoidance, which generates more guilt. Phase 1 breaks that cycle by starting so small that failure is nearly impossible.

15.2.1 Week 1: The 7-Day Start Sequence

Phase 1, Week 1 is the 7-Day Start Sequence from Chapter 3. If you've already done it, skip to Week 2. If you haven't, turn back to that sequence and start there. It's your phenotype-matched practice (from your place in the Regulation Cascade), twice daily, building to three touchpoints by Day 5. That sequence IS Phase 1.

15.2.2 Week 2: Add a Layer

Your initiation habit is forming. Now add complexity, gently.

Add a second layer from your cascade starting place (Chapter 2). One new 3-minute practice, once daily, next step up from where you began. Total: 9–13 minutes, split across the day.

Add one co-regulation element. Practice with another person in the room: a partner, a roommate, even a dog. Or text a friend "3 min done" after your morning practice. Or join an online sitting group where you check in. The social element provides accountability and co-regulatory support without pressure.

Track your data. By now you have at least ten days of Return Counter numbers (Chapter 3). Write down one observation about the trend: any direction can be information.

15.2.3 Week 3: Consolidate

Increase session duration from 3 to 5 minutes per practice. By now the initiation habit is solid enough that 5 minutes doesn't feel like a cliff. If it still does, stay at 3. The phases are pacing tools.

Test a new channel (optional range-building). If you've been doing body-focused practices (Feeling Tone: External), try one session of breath counting (Single Point). If mantra, try body-first awareness. You're exploring range.

Continue the daily Reset Stack. The 90-Second Reset doesn't retire because you've "advanced." It stays in your toolkit permanently, the emergency kit you always carry.

A note on dose. The 90-Second Reset and three-minute practices are primarily state nudges plus habit reinforcement, keeping the regulatory circuit warm and recruitable. Longer sits, five to ten minutes, fall in the range where controlled studies have measured trait-level shifts. Both matter.

That's why Week 3 pushes to five minutes: you're moving from habit maintenance into the range where research has observed training effects.

15.2.4 Phase 1 Principles

These are non-negotiable through all three weeks:

- **Low intensity, high consistency.** Most days, even if "most days" is a 90-second reset done standing in a bathroom. When Yellow or Red signals say modify or rest, listen. That is the practice working. Frequency builds the neural habit loop. Intensity can come later.
- **Bottom-up before top-down.** Body and breath before cognitive reframes, emotional practices, or open monitoring. Same order the nervous system settles in before the prefrontal cortex can direct anything useful.
- **Environmental regulation counts as practice.** Dimming the lights before practice, reducing noise, creating a sensory sanctuary. These aren't luxuries. They're Phase 1 regulation practices. For the Princess, the Bard, and the Lifeguard, environmental regulation IS the practice for Week 1.
- **The Stop Signal is always on.** If any practice triggers Yellow or Red, modify or stop. Phase 1 is about building safety and trust, not pushing limits. The nervous system needs to learn that practice is safe before it can learn anything else.

15.2.5 When to Progress to Phase 2

Move to Phase 2 when all of these are true:

- Your Phase 1 practice is happening at least 5 out of 7 days
- Sessions are at least 5 minutes per practice
- You're consistently in the Green zone during practice (occasional Yellow is fine; persistent Yellow means stay in Phase 1)
- The initiation gap has narrowed: you start practice with less resistance than Week 1

For most people, this takes two to three weeks. Sometimes longer. There's no penalty for staying in Phase 1 for a month, or two. The Stabilize phase is the foundation everything else builds on. A deeper foundation means a more durable practice. If your Grumpy Old Man is whispering that you're "behind," that's your Grumpy talking.

What Phase 1 progress looks like: you sit down and skip the negotiation with yourself first. Or the negotiation is shorter. Seven days of showing up, and you've found the gap: a half-second more. You'll know you're ready to move to Phase 2 when 3 minutes feels boring.

15.3 Phase 2: Train (typically weeks 4–8)

The Grumpy Old Man is back: "I've been doing this for a month and I don't feel different." He's wrong. The space is there; you can't see it from inside. The changes at this phase are too gradual, too structural to register in the moment. You notice them in retrospect: the conversation that didn't escalate, the morning that started easier, the irritation that peaked and passed in minutes instead of hours. If you're in Phase 2 and feel like nothing is happening, that is Phase 2 working.

Phase 2 is where the training load goes up. You've stabilized the habit; now you deepen returns at longer sits, titrating duration, moving through attention channels, cross-training so one format doesn't become a brittle crutch.

15.3.1 The Titration Ladder

Progressive increase in session duration, following one rule: expand only when the current level feels manageable. Manageable means you're in the Green zone most of the time, with occasional Yellow that resolves during the session. Easy and comfortable can wait.

Duration ladder:

Rung	Duration	Stay Here For
1	5 minutes	Until stable (you're here from Phase 1)
2	8 minutes	5–7 days
3	12 minutes	5–7 days
4	15 minutes	5–7 days
5	20 minutes	Ongoing

Move up one rung every 5–7 days. If the new duration feels destabilizing (more Yellow signals, more agitation, the session feels like endurance rather than training), drop back one rung for another week. The ladder is not a race. The Returns happen at every rung. A 5-minute session with thirty returns beats a 20-minute session spent white-knuckling.

Breath protocol specifics: If you're using breath-based practices, aim for approximately 6 breaths per minute (4 seconds in, 6 seconds out is a good starting point). Lehrer and Gevirtz (2014) put the resonance point at roughly 0.1 Hz, about six breaths per minute, and treat breathing *rate* as the variable that drives HRV amplitude. They also note that longer exhalations can raise it further. If 4:6 feels forced, try 4:4 at a slow pace. Comfort and rate over precision and ratio.

15.3.2 The Anchor Ladder

Progressive complexity of attention, parallel to the duration ladder:

Single → Multi → Open

1. Single anchor (start here): Sustained focus on one object: breath, mantra, body region, visual anchor. Concentration training: one anchor, sustained, coming back every time attention drifts. Stay here for at least two weeks or until the anchor feels steady.

2. Multi-anchor (when single feels stable): Hold two objects in awareness simultaneously. Breath AND body sensation. Sound AND visual focus. This builds attentional flexibility, the ability to hold a wider field while keeping both anchors. It's the difference between a spotlight and a floodlight. Both are useful. Phase 2 trains the toggle between them.

3. Open monitoring (when you're ready, or never): No anchor at all. Attend to whatever arises. Choiceless awareness. Noticing freely, receiving as-is. For the CEO, this is often the hardest step on the ladder. For the Lifeguard, it can feel like removing the last safety rail. If it triggers Yellow, drop back to single anchor. Open monitoring isn't required. It's the endpoint of the ladder for those who are ready, and plenty of experienced meditators never go here. That's fine.

15.3.3 Channel Cross-Training

By Phase 2, you're ready to explore channels beyond your primary phenotype match:

- If you've been doing **Single Point** (breath counting, mantra), try **Feeling Tone: External** (body scan). Concentration → interoception.
- If you've been doing **Feeling Tone: Internal** (compassion, LKM), try **Present Moment** (open monitoring). Emotion → awareness.
- If you've been doing **movement** (Walking Meditation), try adding a **stationary** practice. The stillness itself is a new training stimulus.
- If you've been doing **visual anchoring** (external focus), try **brief eyes-closed** practice. Even 60 seconds of eyes-closed within a longer eyes-open session.

Cross-training channels builds a more resilient practice, the same way a runner benefits from occasional swimming. Less rigidity, more flexibility when daily life asks for something your primary match never trained.

15.3.4 Phase 2 Principles

- **Regularity beats intensity.** Twelve focused minutes daily builds more than twenty distracted minutes three times a week.
- **Track your Return Counter** (Chapter 3 for how to read it). By Week 6, look for a shifting trend: either direction can mean progress.
- **One practice session per day is enough.** Two is optional. Twice daily at 8 minutes each is a reasonable substitute for once daily at 16 minutes; split sessions can improve adherence, though the two formats have not been shown equivalent for every outcome. Structure it however fits your life.
- **The 90-Second Reset** stays your emergency kit, same as Phase 1.

15.3.5 When to Progress to Phase 3

Move to Phase 3 when all three of these are true:

- **20+ minutes stable, 5 out of 7 days.** You can sustain a 15–20-minute practice in the Green zone most days, with two or more channels explored.
- **Off-cushion micro-practices are happening on autopilot.** You notice yourself grounding, breathing, or noting phenotype patterns in daily life before you decide to. The practice is leaking into your day on its own.
- **Yellow signals self-resolve within five minutes.** When practice pushes you into Yellow, you can bring yourself back to Green within five minutes using the tools from Part II, without ending the session.

For many people this happens around week eight. Some take twelve. That's fine. Your baseline isn't the same as anyone else's, and there's no "normal" pace: only yours.

What Phase 2 progress looks like: your phenotype pattern fires (the Grumpy voice, the Lifeguard scan, the CEO evaluation), and you notice it as it starts. That half a second more between the pattern firing and the old response taking over is what Phase 2 built. You're no longer someone who tried meditation. You're someone who trains. You'll know you're ready for Phase 3 when you catch yourself using the practice without deciding to. That noticing is the entry point.

15.4 Phase 3: Integrate (week 9 onward, or whenever you're ready)

Phase 3 is where practice becomes life. The formal session continues, but the real work happens between sessions, in the moments where your phenotype patterns fire in the wild.

15.4.1 From Cushion to Context

The integration question: **Can you notice the pattern *as it happens*, and apply even one lever in time?**

You don't need a perfect read. One lever counts.

If the Grumpy Old Man fires during a meeting and you notice it before withdrawal takes over: one slow exhale, feet on the floor, or silently note "Grumpy." Phase 3 practice. Mindfulness in motion. The same gap, out in the open where it counts.

You don't need to transform the moment or be calm. You need to catch it happening and insert one micro-intervention: one lever, one breath, one return. The catch is the rep. Everything else follows.

The Micro-Practice Model: Attach one 30-second practice to one real-life trigger, daily. Examples:

- **Before opening email:** One-Breath Return. Feet on floor. "I'm allowed to stop."
- **When the Lifeguard starts scanning in a crowd:** Note "scanning." One breath. "Is this now?"
- **When the Grumpy voice says "don't bother":** Note "Grumpy." One breath. Do the thing anyway. Count it as a return.
- **When the Interpreter starts rehearsing a conversation:** Note "rehearsing." Feel your hands. Three seconds of pre-verbal awareness.
- **When your phone buzzes:** Notice the impulse before checking. That urge to look is the gap closing. One breath before you pick it up. That's the gap, reopened.
- **When picking up your child from school:** One breath before opening the car door. Work-brain to parent-brain.

Each of these is a return. Each is a rep. The practice has left the cushion and entered your life.

15.4.2 Phase 3 Principles

- **Formal practice continues.** Integration doesn't mean you stop the daily session. It means you add real-world micro-practices on top of it. The formal session builds capacity, and the micro-practices deploy it.
- **Track micro-returns separately.** How many times did you catch a phenotype pattern in the wild today? That number, separate from formal-session returns, is your integration metric.
- **Seasonal adjustment.** Your practice will change with seasons, stress levels, and life phases. Longer sessions during calm periods, shorter during crises. Different stacks for different life chapters. This is expected, not failure.
- **Phase 3 is permanent.** You don't "graduate" from integration. This is the sustained practice that builds the brain you'll have in five years. Chapter 18 addresses how to keep it going.

15.5 The Program at a Glance

Phase	Weeks	Duration	Focus	Key Metric	Ready When
1: Stabilize	1–3	3–10 min	Cascade match, habit, safety	5/7 day consistency	Green zone, 5+ min, 5/7 days
2: Train	4–8	10–20 min	Titration, anchors, channels	Return Counter trend	15–20 min stable, 2+ channels
3: Integrate	9+	15–20 min + micro	Real-world catching	Micro-returns in the wild	You don't graduate. This is it.

Here's what that progression looks like when it's working.

15.6 A Vignette: The Gradual Build

A therapist, empathic and chronically overextended, a Princess & the Pea with a Lifeguard running underneath, started with the absolute minimum: Sensory Sanctuary setup and 3 minutes of eyes-open grounding while standing in her office. That was Week 1. All she could tolerate without the sensory system spiking.

She wanted to do more. I told her the most important thing she'd hear from me all month: "The fastest way to build this practice is to go slowly. Your nervous system doesn't respond to ambition. It responds to safety."

Week 2: she added Vagal Toning, 3 minutes before her first client. Week 3: 5-minute titrated body scans, starting at her feet, moving up as far as tolerable. Most days she got to her knees before the system said Yellow. She stayed at feet-to-knees for two weeks.

Week 6: the body scan reached her hips. She added "Is This Now?" grounding for the Lifeguard, 3 minutes at the end of her lunch break. The scanning system had something to do instead of running unsupervised.

Week 8: she could sit with eyes closed for 12 minutes without the Lifeguard escalating: manageably, but the system that used to go Red at minute two was now holding Green for twelve.

Week 12: Phase 3. She was in session with a client who was sobbing. The old pattern: absorb the distress, lose her ground, feel it in her body for hours afterward. The new pattern: she felt the distress arriving: a tightening in her solar plexus, the Princess picking up the client's pain signal, and she caught it. She noted "borrowed." She pressed her feet into the floor. One breath. She continued the session, present, empathic, with a floor underneath her. The regulation held.

"The feelings are still there," she told me afterward. "I just don't get pulled under by them the way I used to. I can feel something and still stay in the room."

The practice shows up where it matters: in the room with another human being.

You have a plan. Start where you are; let the phases pace the work. You're building the gap.

15.7 Your 90 Days

Week	Phase	Daily Practice	Milestone
1	Stabilize	3 min × 2	7-Day Start Sequence complete
2	Stabilize	3 min × 3	Second cascade layer added
3	Stabilize	5 min × 2	Initiation resistance fading
4–5	Train	8–12 min	Duration ladder rungs 2–3
6–7	Train	12–15 min	Second anchor channel explored
8–9	Train	15–20 min	Off-cushion catches beginning
10–11	Integrate	20 min + micro	Micro-practices in daily life
12–13	Integrate	20 min + micro	Yellow signals self-resolving

This is a map. Your pace is your pace. The phases tell you when to progress.

Before you take this into the wild, read the safety chapter: the gap still applies when you need to stop.

Sometimes practice makes things worse: not uncomfortable but destabilizing. Chapter 16 is the safety chapter. Read it even if nothing has gone wrong yet.

Ch 16: When Mindfulness Makes Things Worse: Safety, Trauma & Edges

If practice made something worse, read this now. If nothing has gone wrong yet, read it anyway.

> **If you are dissociating right now:** Stop reading. Open your eyes. Press both feet flat on the floor and push down. Name five things you can see out loud or silently. Pick up something physical and hold it: a glass, your phone, a pen. Feel its weight and temperature. Take one breath through your nose. You are in a room. The room is real. Come back to this chapter when you are grounded.

This is the chapter every meditation teacher, app developer, and retreat leader should read. Meditation can make things worse for some people, under some conditions. Mindfulness practices can trigger destabilization: flooding that won't stop, panic that escalates, or dissociation that leaves you feeling unreal. And the response from the meditation community is too often "push through" or "that's just resistance" or, worst of all, "you're not doing it right."

If that's happened to you, if practice has made things worse rather than better, your nervous system gave you accurate information about one practice, at one intensity, at one point in your life. You're not broken, not "too damaged for meditation," and not doing it wrong. Stopping is not a failure of the gap: it's the pause working. The pause between "this is happening" and "I'll keep going" is the same skill this book trains. Noticing the edge and honoring it is regulation at its most precise. This chapter will help you understand what happened and what to do about it.

Before you continue: If you're currently in psychiatric crisis, have significant unresolved trauma, or have experienced persistent destabilization from previous practice, please read the clinical escalation path in the Resources section before continuing solo. This book can accompany clinical support. It is not a substitute for it.

16.1 The Prevalence of Adverse Effects

The numbers matter, because "meditation is always safe" is a dangerous oversimplification.

Farias et al. (2020) pooled 83 studies and found an **overall adverse-event prevalence of 8.3%**, with wide variation by study type. Among experienced practitioners, the figure is higher: Lindahl et al. (2017), in the landmark "Varieties of Contemplative Experience" study led by Willoughby Britton at Brown University's Contemplative Studies Program, catalogued 59 categories of meditation-related challenges across seven domains: perceptual, emotional, cognitive, somatic, conative, social, and sense-of-self. Their sample was predominantly experienced meditators, not beginners, which directly challenges the assumption that adverse effects only happen to people "doing it wrong." Britton and Lindahl documented somatic and perceptual challenging experiences in dedicated meditators: pain, tension, involuntary movements, heightened sensory sensitivity, depersonalization. These are not signs of "doing it wrong." They are known responses that some brains have to specific formats of practice. Most effects are transient. Lindahl's sample was recruited specifically for having had challenging experiences, so it tells you what can happen, not how often. For frequency you need a population survey. Goldberg et al. (2022) surveyed meditators in the United States and found some degree of functional impairment in 10.6%, with impairment lasting a month or longer in 1.2%.

Britton's research program is the field's most systematic taxonomy of what can go wrong. The phenotype routing in this book offers a candidate mechanism for parts of that taxonomy. The Lindahl typology describes *what* went wrong; the phenotype model points toward *which practice format, in which brain type, is most likely to cause it.* A Lifeguard pattern with closed-eyes practice sits at one end of that spectrum. A Princess & the Pea pattern with intensive body-scan sits at another. The seven-domain taxonomy and the phenotype routing system answer different halves of the same question. This chapter's harm-reduction guidance applies that pairing directly.

Schlosser et al. (2019) found that roughly one in four regular meditators reported particularly unpleasant experiences, with deconstructive practices (such as vipassana) and retreat contexts carrying higher odds. Read that association carefully. The study was cross-sectional, so it cannot show that the practice caused the experience. "Vipassana" there is a broad research category covering curricula that differ enormously, many of them embedded in ethics, staged preparation, and teacher contact. Format, intensity, retreat conditions, available support, and a practitioner's own history are all plausibly doing some of the work. What survives is the signal worth acting on: the field's assumption that meditation is universally benign doesn't hold.

Baer et al. (2019) concluded that the field needs better screening, attention to individual differences, and explicit safety protocols. The meditation research community is only beginning to take this seriously.

This book is built on trust. Trust requires telling you the parts the marketing leaves out.

16.2 What Can Go Wrong

16.2.1 Emotional Flooding

When you close your eyes and direct attention inward, you reduce external stimulation and create space for whatever is stored below the surface to emerge. For many people, this is therapeutic: suppressed emotions arise, are felt, and pass. Sitting with difficult feelings is part of what formal practice can build, when the dose matches the system.

That same opening can go the other way.

But for people with significant unprocessed trauma, active emotional crisis, or limited distress tolerance, the surfacing can overwhelm the system. The emotion doesn't pass. It intensifies. The grief becomes a wave, the anger a fire, the terror total. The practice becomes a container that's too small for what it just opened.

This matters most for the **Princess & the Pea** (high-gain processing amplifies the emotional signal) and the **Lifeguard** (the emerging emotion is interpreted as threat, which escalates the arousal rather than allowing it to pass).

The mechanism: Interoceptive awareness practices (body scans, feeling-tone exercises) increase the signal from body to brain. For brains that already amplify that signal, the increase can tip the system from manageable to flooding. Wrong practice. Wrong dose. It's the intensity relative to the person's current capacity.

16.2.2 Depersonalization and Dissociation

Some meditators report feeling detached from their body, identity, or reality itself, from mild "floating" (body distant, self thin) to full depersonalization: watching yourself from outside, nothing feels real, the person in the mirror is a stranger.

In contemplative traditions, some of these experiences are considered signs of progress. In clinical terms, they can be severely distressing, especially for people with existing dissociative tendencies. Meditation can intensify dissociation rather than resolving it, because "observing without attachment" can accidentally reinforce the same neural pattern dissociation uses: separation from experience.

The key distinction: Therapeutic detachment (observing emotions with equanimity) involves *more* connection to the present moment. Dissociation involves *less*. If "letting go of thoughts" makes you feel more present, that's healthy. If it makes you feel less real, that's a warning sign.

16.2.3 Panic and Anxiety Escalation

For the **Lifeguard** and **Grumpy Old Man** phenotypes, certain practices, including eyes-closed, prolonged sitting, and intensive interoception, can trigger the same circuits they're meant to regulate. The practice becomes the stressor. Conditions of practice (darkness, stillness, inward focus) remove the safety data and external regulation that were holding the system together.

This is not a sign to "push through." It's a sign that practice parameters need adjusting for your nervous system right now.

16.2.4 Re-traumatization

Body-based practices can set off trauma-related responses. A body scan directing attention to a region associated with trauma (stomach, throat, pelvis) can trigger intrusive images, physical re-experiencing, or full flashbacks. What is happening there is present-moment sensation carrying a learned association, not a stored recording being played back. The distinction matters: attention to that region can produce real distress and real physiological arousal without any of it being a retrieved factual record of what happened.

This is not a failure of the practice. It's a feature of how trauma is encoded, and why trauma-sensitive meditation (Treleaven, 2018) exists as a specific adaptation. Without proper preparation, titration, and support, body-based practices can be re-traumatizing rather than therapeutic.

16.2.5 Sleep Disruption

Paradoxically, meditation can sometimes worsen sleep: intensive evening practices, highly activating techniques used at the wrong time, or practices that increase arousal through interoceptive amplification. In clinical observation, the **Fog** pattern is especially vulnerable to timing mismatches (for example, calming practices during the day deepening an afternoon crash, or mindful awareness at night paradoxically increasing cognitive arousal by engaging executive circuits that should be offline), though these interactions have not been mapped in controlled sleep trials by phenotype.

16.2.6 Mania and Hypomanic Activation

Intensive meditation practice, especially when combined with sleep restriction, extended sessions, or breath manipulation, can precipitate hypomanic or manic states in people on the bipolar spectrum. Lindahl et al. (2017) documented agitation or irritability in the affective domain, heightened somatic energy, and intense positive affect that in some practitioners escalated into destabilizing states resembling mania. The mechanism is plausible: practices that increase arousal, reduce sleep, or shift frontal asymmetry toward approach activation can tip a vulnerable mood-regulation circuit into hypomanic territory.

Who is at higher risk: Anyone with a bipolar diagnosis, cyclothymia, a family history of bipolar disorder, or a history of medication-induced mania. The **Happy Little Kid** phenotype with its flat approach circuit and the **Grumpy Old Man** with mood-axis instability are the phenotype profiles where this is most clinically relevant.

What to do: If you notice escalating energy, decreased need for sleep, racing thoughts that feel *good* rather than anxious, grandiose planning, or uncharacteristic impulsivity emerging during a period of intensive practice: stop the intensive protocol and return to Phase 1 duration and intensity. Contact your prescriber or therapist. These are not signs of "breakthrough" or "progress." They are signs that the practice is destabilizing your mood-regulation circuit.

When to stop: If you cannot sleep for two or more consecutive nights during intensive practice, or if people close to you comment that you seem "different" or "wired," stop all practice and seek professional support. Mania is a psychiatric emergency when it escalates, and the escalation can be rapid.

16.2.7 Eating Disorders and Body-Scan Risk

Body scan and interoceptive practices direct sustained attention to body sensations, body shape, and internal signals. For people with active eating disorders, body dysmorphia, or a history of restrictive eating, this focus can intensify the hypervigilance toward body experience that drives the disorder. The instruction to "notice what your body is telling you" assumes the body's signals are trustworthy guides. In an eating disorder, they are systematically distorted.

Who is at higher risk: Anyone with an active or recent eating disorder (anorexia, bulimia, binge eating disorder, ARFID), body dysmorphic disorder, or compulsive exercise patterns. The **Princess & the Pea** phenotype, with its high-gain sensory processing and body-focused attention, is the profile where body-scan practices carry the highest interaction risk.

What to do: If body-scan practices trigger intrusive thoughts about your body (weight, shape, or adequacy), or if they increase restrictive or compensatory behaviors, switch to external anchors: pick something to see, something to hear, or walk instead. Body-based practice can be reintroduced later, in collaboration with a therapist who specializes in eating disorders, using the same titration approach as the Lifeguard Practice Ladder: peripheral regions first (hands, feet), short durations, with explicit permission to stop. For support or a clinician referral, the National Alliance for Eating Disorders runs a helpline staffed by licensed therapists at 1-866-662-1235.

When to stop: If practice increases food restriction, purging, body checking, or exercise compulsion, stop body-based practices entirely and consult your treatment team.

16.2.8 Dissociative Identity Disorder and Severe Dissociative Disorders

The depersonalization and dissociation section above covers the common, milder end of the dissociative spectrum. Severe dissociative disorders, including dissociative identity disorder (DID), require specific consideration because meditation's core instruction to "observe what arises without attachment" can inadvertently trigger switching, destabilize an internal system, or produce experiences that the practitioner cannot safely process alone.

Who is at higher risk: Anyone with a DID diagnosis, OSDD (Other Specified Dissociative Disorder), or severe structural dissociation. Also at elevated risk: people with complex PTSD and significant dissociative features who have not yet established safety and stabilization in therapy.

What to do: If you have a dissociative disorder, work with a therapist experienced in dissociation before beginning solo meditation practice. When you do practice, use external anchors only (visual, auditory, tactile objects), keep sessions under three minutes, and keep eyes open. Avoid body scans, interoceptive practices, and any practice that directs attention to "what's arising" without structure. The Permission Practice and the Five Things grounding exercise from the Safe Anchor List are the safest starting points.

When to stop: If practice triggers switching, amnesia for the session, internal conflict that was not present before the session, or if you "lose time" during practice, stop and consult your therapist before resuming.

16.2.9 Suicidal Ideation

Suicidal thoughts can emerge or intensify during meditation practice. The mechanism is straightforward: meditation creates the conditions for suppressed material to surface. For someone already carrying suicidal ideation below the surface, the quiet and inward focus of practice can amplify it. The practice did not create the ideation. It created the space in which existing ideation became audible.

Who is at higher risk: Anyone with a history of suicidal ideation or attempts, current depression, chronic pain, significant loss, or isolation. When the **Grumpy Old Man** pattern is running loud, with its catastrophizing and withdrawal-circuit dominance, the drift from "what's the point" toward active ideation is the one to watch most closely. The pattern is a state to monitor.

What to do: If suicidal thoughts emerge during practice, stop the session immediately. Ground yourself while you take the next step: feet on the floor, name five things you can see, hold something physical. Then reach out. Call or text 988 (Suicide and Crisis Lifeline), text HOME to 741741 (Crisis Text Line), or contact your therapist or prescriber now, not at your next scheduled appointment. Suicidal thoughts do not need to include a plan to warrant immediate support. If you are in immediate danger, call 911 or go to your nearest emergency department.

When to stop: If suicidal ideation is present before, during, or after practice across multiple sessions, stop solo practice and seek professional support. Meditation can resume as an adjunct to therapy once the ideation is being addressed clinically. When ideation persists across sessions, the practice is surfacing material that needs professional attention. That's the correct response.

Meditation-triggered difficulty doesn't always announce itself as anxiety or panic. Sometimes it shows up in quieter, more confusing forms: a jaw that won't unclench for hours after practice. Vivid, unsettling dreams that weren't there before. A low hum of dread that starts during practice and follows you out of the session and into your day. A startle response that's jumpier than it used to be: the dog barking, the phone buzzing, a door closing, and you're already braced.

These are signals. They mean the practice is reaching something your nervous system hasn't finished processing, and that the current dose, duration, or technique needs adjustment. You're not broken, and meditation isn't wrong for you. The parameters need to change. The sections below tell you exactly how to change them.

16.3 Risk Factors

The phenotype-specific risk factors below are clinical pattern-recognition from QEEG observation. The trial data on phenotype-by-practice interaction doesn't yet exist. These are informed starting points.

Certain factors increase the risk of adverse effects. This is not a checklist for who "shouldn't" meditate; it's a list of reasons to go slowly, titrate carefully, and maintain access to professional support:

- **Childhood adversity or unresolved trauma.** Lindahl et al. (2017) documented trauma history as a practitioner-level factor influencing meditation-related difficulty. If you have a trauma history, body-based practices need titration, and a trauma-informed therapist should be part of your support structure.
- **Prolonged sitting and eyes-closed practice.** Lindahl et al. (2017) documented practice intensity, approach, and type as influencing factors in meditation-related challenges. In clinical observation, prolonged stillness and eyes-closed formats are the conditions that most reliably escalate Lifeguard scanning. If your Lifeguard is active, these are the exact conditions that escalate scanning. Go slowly. Keep eyes open. Keep sessions short.
- **Intensive retreat settings.** Multi-day silence retreats remove the social co-regulation that normally buffers difficult experiences. Alone, internal experiences can escalate beyond the person's capacity to regulate them.
- **Active psychiatric crisis.** Untreated psychosis, active suicidality, severe dissociation, or recent psychiatric hospitalization. These are not contraindications to *all* meditation, but they are strong indicators that solo practice without clinical supervision is not safe right now.
- **Psychosis history, severe anxiety, or sensory over-responsivity.** People with these profiles likely have reduced sensory gating: the P50 filter that suppresses redundant input runs weak or absent. For them, heavy body-scan or "notice every sensation" practice risks further opening the gate and amplifying distress. External-first practices, shorter durations, and eyes-open formats reduce this risk. If the Princess & the Pea chapter resonated strongly, this applies to you: your sensory gain is already high, and interoceptive amplification practices need careful titration.

- **Intense interoceptive focus without gradual titration.** "Do a 45-minute body scan" as a first practice is the meditation equivalent of putting 300 pounds on the bar for your first gym visit. The dose matters.
- **No teacher, guide, or support system.** Solo practice, and no one to check in with when things get difficult. The book you're reading provides structure, but it's not a substitute for a human who knows your history and can hold space when the practice opens something unexpected.

16.4 Practicing While Medicated

Read this first. I am a neuroscientist, not a prescriber. Nothing in this section is medical advice, and none of it is a reason to start, stop, or change a dose. It describes how meditation tends to interact with each drug class so you can have a better-informed conversation with the clinician who manages your prescriptions. Any change happens with them.

A significant number of you reading this book are on psychiatric medication: mood meds, stimulants, anti-anxiety drugs, beta-blockers, or some combination. That is not a problem. Medication isn't cheating, and it doesn't mean you're skipping the work. For many dysregulated brains, medication provides the floor of stability that makes training possible at all.

But medication changes your neurochemistry, and meditation works *with* your neurochemistry. So the two interact, sometimes helpfully, sometimes in ways that matter for your practice.

16.4.1 SSRIs and SNRIs

SSRIs (sertraline, escitalopram, fluoxetine) and SNRIs (venlafaxine, duloxetine) increase serotonin availability in the brain. They are the most commonly prescribed medications for anxiety and depression, and a large proportion of the people this book is written for are on them.

What changes for practice: SSRIs can alter interoceptive processing, your ability to detect and interpret subtle body signals (Burrows et al., 2022). Emotional blunting is a common clinical complaint: duller responses to both positive and negative outcomes.

If body scan practices feel muted, flat, or hard to connect with, use an external anchor instead. People on SSRIs report a wide range here, and it does not run one way: some describe emotional blunting, while one study comparing medicated and unmedicated depression actually found the SSRI group reporting body sensations as more intense (Burrows et al., 2022). So treat a flat body scan as information about today's practice.

What to do: If body-based practices feel numb or distant, lean toward external anchoring: visual, auditory, movement-based practices, where the signal arrives from outside the body. You can still build interoceptive capacity on an SSRI. How that capacity builds on an SSRI has not been studied directly, so treat your own pace as the only reliable guide. Titrate *up* in interoceptive practices as your system allows. Don't force body scans that feel like staring at a blank wall. Do not adjust your SSRI or SNRI dose based on anything in this book. Dose changes are clinical decisions made with your prescriber.

A note on taper: MBCT (Mindfulness-Based Cognitive Therapy) was originally designed as a relapse-prevention tool for people tapering off antidepressants (Segal, Teasdale, & Williams, 2002). An individual-patient-data meta-analysis pooling four RCTs found no significant difference in relapse risk between therapist-delivered sequential psychological interventions (including MBCT and preventive cognitive therapy) during antidepressant taper versus continued antidepressant monotherapy (Breedvelt et al., 2021). MBCT in those trials is an eight-week, therapist-delivered protocol. The book you are reading is not MBCT. If you and your prescriber are considering a taper, a therapist-delivered program is the evidence-based support structure. The practices in this book can complement that clinical work. They do not replace it.

Being medicated does not invalidate the training signal. The two approaches are complementary, not competing. Medication holds the floor. Meditation builds the capacity. Over time, as the capacity grows, you and your prescriber can decide whether the floor is still needed.

16.4.2 Stimulants

Here is a question worth sitting with before we get to the mechanics: if a medication makes meditation easier, is that good or bad?

The answer is "both, depending on what you're trying to build." Stimulants (methylphenidate, amphetamine salts, lisdexamfetamine) are the first-line treatment for ADHD. They directly affect the same attention networks that meditation trains. And they make those networks easier to use.

Practicing while medicated: Stimulants make meditation easier. Your sustained attention is better. Your mind wanders less. You can sit for longer. That feels like progress, and in a sense it is, because you're practicing. That is not borrowed progress, and there is no evidence that practicing unmedicated builds a truer skill. Research comparing family mindfulness training with methylphenidate in children with ADHD found each helped, on different timelines (Kosterman Zoller et al., 2025). It compared two separate programmes, so it cannot tell you which of your own sessions trains more. Practice while taking your medication as prescribed. Choose session timing for what is workable and for goals you have agreed with your prescriber.

What to do: Practice on your medication, especially in the early weeks when you're building the habit (Phase 1). A successful practice habit on stimulants is infinitely better than a failed practice attempt without them. As your practice matures (Phase 2 and beyond), consider experimenting with occasional sessions during your existing unmedicated windows: early morning before your first dose if that window is already part of your routine, or late afternoon as the medication wears off. Do not skip or delay doses to create new windows. This is about using time you already have. But this is an experiment, and nothing about it is required. If unmedicated practice is destabilizing, stay with medicated practice. You're still building circuits.

Timing matters: Short-acting stimulants create a distinct medicated window (typically 4–6 hours). Sessions inside and outside that window will feel different, and both count. Nothing in the evidence ranks one above the other, so practice at whatever times you can sustain, and settle the timing with your prescriber if it matters for your dosing.

16.4.3 Benzodiazepines

Benzodiazepines (alprazolam, clonazepam, lorazepam) are GABAergic anxiolytics: they reduce anxiety by enhancing the brain's primary inhibitory neurotransmitter. They work fast, they work well, and they create a problem for meditation training.

The signal problem: Meditation works in part by exposing you to manageable discomfort and teaching your nervous system that the discomfort passes. Benzodiazepines pharmacologically suppress the anxiety signal, which means the training stimulus, the arousal you're learning to regulate, may be absent or muted. There's also a deeper concern: postmortem research suggests that benzodiazepine co-treatment with antidepressants is associated with reduced hippocampal neurogenesis compared to antidepressant treatment alone (Boldrini et al., 2014). Whether this attenuates meditation-related brain changes hasn't been directly tested, but it's a plausible consideration worth discussing with your prescriber.

What to do: If you're on a stable benzodiazepine dose, practice anyway. The attentional training components (Return Counter, anchor focus, mind-wandering detection) still work regardless of your anxiety level. You're still building the concentration and attention-shifting circuits even if the emotional regulation component is pharmacologically buffered. The skills transfer.

A direct word about tapering: benzodiazepine withdrawal is medically dangerous and can be fatal without proper supervision. Do not adjust your benzodiazepine dose based on anything in this book. Taper schedules are set by prescribers for clinical reasons. If your prescriber has put you on a supervised taper schedule, meditation can be a useful skill during that period, as an adjunct to the medical taper, not a substitute for it and not a reason to taper faster. The regulation skills you have been building become part of your support structure as the pharmacological floor shifts. What you find out during a taper is how much you have built. That is useful information, but the medical scaffold comes first.

16.4.4 Beta-Blockers

Beta-blockers (propranolol, metoprolol) block sympathetic cardiac activity. They're prescribed for performance anxiety, hypertension, and sometimes PTSD-related hyperarousal. They directly affect heart rate variability.

The HRV interaction: If you're doing HRV biofeedback or breath-paced meditation (Chapter 14), beta-blockers will change your heart rate variability profile. Beta-blockers work by blocking cardiac sympathetic receptors, which shifts sympathovagal balance. In post-infarction patients, propranolol raised high-frequency HRV, the vagal index, and lowered the LF/HF ratio (Lampert et al., 2003). That trial did not test resonance breathing or HRV biofeedback, so treat what follows as metric interpretation rather than a predicted training effect: your numbers are being read through the medication, and your graphs may look different from an unmedicated baseline. The most likely reading is that the medication altered the *metric* rather than the training, though that has not been tested directly. One upside: beta-blockers may make breath-paced practices *more* comfortable for panic-prone individuals, because the cardiac spikes are muted.

What to do: If you're on a beta-blocker and practicing HRV biofeedback, tell your provider. They can adjust targets and interpretation. For non-HRV practices like breath focus, body scan, open monitoring, and movement meditation, there is no evidence that beta-blockers interfere with the training. Continue normally. Do not adjust your beta-blocker dose based on anything in this book. Dose changes are clinical decisions made with your prescriber.

16.4.5 Cannabis

A client asked once whether cannabis was "cheating" at meditation. It's not. But it's the wrong question.

Cannabis use before or during meditation is increasingly common. I'm not here to judge it. I am here to be honest about what it does mechanically, because "it makes meditation feel better" and "it makes meditation practice more effective" are two claims that don't always overlap.

THC affects the endocannabinoid system, which modulates attention, memory consolidation, and the default mode network. In subjective terms: things feel more present, more vivid, more "mindful." The internal narrator may quiet. Body sensations may amplify. The experience *feels* like deeper meditation.

The borrowed-state problem: The state cannabis produces overlaps with the states meditation builds, but the mechanism is different. Cannabis borrows the state from chemistry. Meditation builds it from repeated neural training. THC acutely impairs attention, working memory, and error monitoring, the exact skills meditation trains. Research on substance use and interoception (Verdejo-García et al., 2012) points to altered interoceptive processing in addiction: a blunted, less reliable read on internal bodily states. The cannabis-assisted session may feel profound, but the attentional skill, noticing wandering, redirecting, and sustaining focus, is not being trained at the same intensity, because the chemistry is doing the redirecting.

What to do: If cannabis is part of your life, keep it separate from your formal practice sessions, at least most of the time. Practice sober. Build the skill. The calm you build sober is the calm that's available at 3 AM when you can't sleep, in the meeting when your boss is triggering your Lifeguard, in the traffic jam when the Problem Child wants to lay on the horn. Borrowed states don't show up in those moments. Built states do.

If you occasionally practice with cannabis and find it opens something: a body connection, a sense of spaciousness, a relief from the narrator. Notice that. Use it as information about what's *possible* for your nervous system. Then go build it on your own.

16.4.6 Antipsychotics and Psychosis History

If you're taking an antipsychotic medication (aripiprazole, quetiapine, risperidone, olanzapine, or others), you likely have a clinical history that includes psychotic symptoms, severe mood instability, or a condition where reality-testing was compromised. Whether to practice at all depends on where you are. When you are clinically stable and your treating team agrees, meditation can be appropriate, and the format matters more here than for any other medication class. If psychotic symptoms are active or worsening, if reality-testing is shaky, or if you have been hospitalized recently, this is a stop-and-call condition. Contact your prescriber before starting or continuing, and let their guidance override anything on this page.

What to do: Stick to structured, external-anchor practices: breath counting, walking meditation, visual focus. Avoid open monitoring ("let whatever arises arise") and prolonged silence without structure. These open-ended formats can blur the boundary between internal experience and external reality in ways that are destabilizing for psychosis-vulnerable brains. Keep sessions short (three to five minutes). Keep eyes open. Practice in a familiar environment with predictable sensory input. If your prescriber has opinions about meditation practice, follow their guidance over this book's.

Do not adjust your antipsychotic dose based on anything in this book. These medications are managing conditions where discontinuation can be medically dangerous. The meditation practices here are adjuncts to your clinical care, not alternatives to it.

16.4.7 The Integration Principle

Medication and meditation are not competing approaches. They operate on different timescales and different mechanisms:

- **Medication** provides *immediate, borrowed regulation*: it changes your neurochemistry now, and the effect lasts as long as the medication lasts.
- **Meditation** provides *gradual, built regulation*: it changes your neural circuits over weeks and months, and the effect persists independently.

The ideal trajectory for many people: medication provides the stability floor while meditation builds the capacity. Over time, months to years, the built capacity may reduce the need for borrowed support. Or it may not. Some brains need both, permanently, and that is a perfectly legitimate outcome.

A note on the evidence: the research on medication-meditation interactions is still thin. Almost no controlled trials have studied the two together. But no major clinical guideline warns against mindfulness for medicated populations; MBSR and MBCT trials routinely allow concurrent medication, and benefit holds in those trials.

The only question that matters for your practice is: *Given the medication I'm on, what should I adjust?* The answers above are your starting point. When in doubt, practice at whatever intensity keeps you in the Green zone, on or off medication. The work is the work. The returns still count.

16.5 The Decision Framework

When practice feels wrong (not merely uncomfortable, but *wrong*), you have four options, in order:

16.5.1 1. Stop

The Stop Signal is a feature, not a failure. If you're in the Red zone (Chapter 1), stop immediately. Open your eyes. Feet on the floor, pressed down hard. Name five things you can see. Hold something cold if available. Ground yourself in the room, the present, the physical.

Stopping is a regulatory act. The pause between "this is getting worse" and "I'll push through" is the practice working. It's the same skill this book trains: noticing the moment before reactivity and choosing what comes next. That's what you're using when you stop a session that's escalating. You're regulating.

Then assess: one-time event (difficult session that resolved after grounding) or pattern (same escalation repeatedly)? One-time events are normal. Patterns mean the practice needs modification or the phenotype match needs reassessment.

If stopping consistently leaves you feeling better than continuing, that's your answer. The practice isn't right, for now, at this intensity, with this technique. Use that information.

16.5.2 2. Titrate

Most adverse effects respond to intensity reduction, not cessation. Shorten the practice. Open your eyes. Switch from body-based to visual anchoring. Move from seated to walking. Reduce the dose instead of eliminating it.

Find the intensity where you're solidly in the Green zone. Stay there until it's genuinely stable. Then edge forward slowly: one minute longer, one new body region in the scan, one session with eyes closed instead of open. Each step is a test with a clear answer: Green (proceed), Yellow (hold), Red (retreat).

16.5.3 3. Modify

Specific modifications for specific risks:

- **If eyes-closed triggers anxiety:** Practice with eyes open. Always. Indefinitely if needed. There is no requirement for eyes-closed meditation. The Lifeguard needs visual safety data. Provide it.

- **If body scan triggers flashbacks:** Scan the periphery only: hands, feet, face. Skip the torso entirely. Or switch to external anchoring: visual, auditory, tactile objects in the room. You can build interoceptive capacity gradually, one body region at a time, over months.
- **If stillness triggers panic:** Move. Walking meditation, standing practice, yoga, tai chi, gentle stretching. Stillness is not a prerequisite for meditation. Movement is a legitimate, complete practice.
- **If guided audio triggers reactivity:** Use unguided practice: timer only, no voice. The Bard's prosody circuit over-reads the instructor's tone. Remove the tone.
- **If interoception triggers dissociation:** Switch to exteroception. Listen for one sound. Look at one object. Touch something solid and notice its weight and temperature. External focus provides the grounding that internal focus cannot, because dissociation moves you *away* from the body. External anchoring brings you back to the room.
- **If breath focus triggers hyperventilation or panic:** Drop breath work entirely. Use body grounding instead: feet, hands, pressure, temperature. The breath will regulate naturally when the body settles. Don't try to control the breath when the breath is the trigger.

16.5.4 4. Seek Professional Support

Some experiences exceed what solo practice and self-help books can address. If any of the following are true, reach out to a therapist, psychiatrist, or trauma specialist:

- Adverse effects persist beyond the practice session: you feel worse *between* sessions, not just during them
- Flashbacks, dissociation, or depersonalization outside of practice
- Panic attacks occurring independent of meditation
- Significantly worse than before you started, across multiple sessions over multiple weeks
- Suicidal thoughts or self-harm urges have emerged or increased

This is not failure. Your nervous system is telling you that you need more support than solo practice provides right now. You may need co-regulation with a skilled professional before solo regulation is safe. That's the right call.

Resources:

- 988 Suicide and Crisis Lifeline (call or text 988)
- Cheetah House (cheetahhouse.org): support specifically for meditation-related difficulties
- Psychology Today therapist directory (filter by location, specialty, insurance)
- Full list in the Resources section (back matter)

16.6 The Safe Anchor List

When in doubt, return to these practices. They are the lowest-risk, highest-safety options in this book:

1. **The Permission Practice:** "I'm allowed to stop." (30 seconds). Safe for all phenotypes.
2. **Grounding: Five Things:** Name five things you can see. (30 seconds). Especially effective for the Lifeguard; use neutral, non-threatening objects.
3. **The Physiological Sigh:** Two quick inhales through the nose, one long exhale through the mouth. Three rounds. (15 seconds) (Balban et al., 2023). If breath focus triggers hyperventilation, skip this and use Grounding instead.
4. **The 90-Second Reset:** Body → Breath → Meaning. (90 seconds). If you feel floaty or dissociated, sit down first and press feet into the floor before starting.
5. **Walking Meditation:** Eyes open, movement, sensory engagement. (Any duration). Stabilizer initiation caveat: if you cannot initiate movement, start with one conscious step rather than a full walk.
6. **External Visual Anchoring:** Pick an object. Study it. Soften your gaze and let your peripheral vision widen. (Any duration). Pick a

neutral object: something without threat associations (Lifeguard) or body relevance (Princess).

These maintain external awareness, offer escape routes at every moment, and don't require intensive interoception. The physiological sigh works well in acute moments because it requires no counting and no cognitive load; your nervous system already knows this pattern. Low-risk, available in nearly every situation, and enough for most people most of the time.

16.7 Normalization Without Minimization

Most meditation guidance fails here: it either minimizes the risk or catastrophizes it. Both miss the mark. Hold these two things at once:

It's normal for meditation to feel uncomfortable sometimes. Boredom, restlessness, fleeting sadness, physical discomfort, a mind that wanders relentlessly: these are standard features of training. Discomfort is not automatically a problem; it's often the signal that you're at the edge of your current capacity, which is exactly where growth happens.

AND: destabilization is not normal discomfort. Panic, dissociation, flashbacks, or persistent worsening that doesn't resolve between sessions are signals that something needs to change: modify the practice, reduce the intensity, or get support.

The difference: Discomfort passes during or shortly after the session. Destabilization persists, escalates, or impairs function outside of practice.

If you're unsure, lean toward caution: modify, stop, try again tomorrow at lower intensity. There is no deadline. No shame in "not today."

You didn't break the practice. The practice found a circuit that needed attention. That's data, not failure.

16.8 A Vignette: The Marine Who Needed a Different Door

He came to the clinic two years after the VA group. He sat in the intake chair the way people sit when they have learned to make themselves invisible: upright, still, taking up less than his share of the space. He was a large man. The stillness was not relaxed.

"The VA gave me a worksheet," he said. He held it out, eyes forward. It was a breathing exercise with a diagram.

His history was three deployments, the last one ending with events he described as "operational," which is one way to close a door. He'd tried talk therapy, medication adjustments, two different apps, and what he called "the full energy-drink lifestyle." He was not, at this point, opposed to trying something. He was opposed to something trying to harm him, which the last group had done.

Week 3 of the VA MBSR group, during a body scan, the instructor said: "now bring your attention to your abdomen." The next thing he knew he was in a vehicle. Heart rate 140. Hands fully numb. The room was gone. For the next forty minutes he was present in body and absent in mind, dissociated somewhere between the VA conference room and a road in a country where the roads were wrong. He drove home on autopilot. He sat in his driveway for an hour before going inside.

He did not go back. This was the reasonable response to his nervous system's data.

We started differently.

No body scans. No eyes-closed. No guided audio, no voice telling him where to put his attention. No stillness. Week 1 was a twenty-minute walk outdoors, same route both days, eyes open. His only job was to name one thing per block that was *definitely* safe right now. Not probably safe. Definitely. He named: a yellow house. A mailbox. A truck he recognized from the previous session, still parked in the same spot. A woman walking a gray dog. His own hands, which he watched for the last two blocks. Six things. That was the session.

He asked why we weren't doing breathing exercises. I told him the Lifeguard can't hear the breath when it's convinced the room is dangerous. First you give the system safety data. Then you give it breathing. He looked at me for a moment.

"That makes sense," he said. We walked.

Week 3, he came in and nodded at the person at the front desk by name. This was new. He had not, in the first two weeks, acknowledged anyone in the waiting room.

We added Pendulation. I sat across the room while he sat near the window. The instruction was to find a place in the body that held tension, stay with it for three breaths, then find a place that felt neutral or settled, stay there for three breaths. Back and forth. He chose his hands as the settled place every session. He chose the stomach as the tense place every session. He never explained this and I did not ask. When the tense place was the stomach, three breaths was the ceiling.

The facilitator in the room breathed steadily nearby. She was not doing anything in particular. She was present. He borrowed her regulation naturally.

Week 6, he moved from the intake chair to the couch, unannounced. He spent five minutes looking at the window while his hands rested in his lap. Near the end of those five minutes, he watched a woman cross the parking lot below. He watched her for about thirty seconds.

"I wasn't scanning her," he said. "I was just watching."

He knew the difference. That was the shift.

Week 12, he closed his eyes for ninety seconds during Pendulation. Opened them, waited, closed them again. He did this three times. His hands were still. His shoulders were lower than they had been in Week 1.

He came in one morning and said, "Last time they just told me to breathe and close my eyes. Nobody asked if that was safe. It wasn't." He sat with that for a moment. "This time I got to decide when to close my eyes. That's the whole thing, right there."

His nervous system needed safety data before it could tolerate inward attention. The body scan that had sent him to the parking lot two years before would have worked if it had started with walking instead of sitting, eyes open instead of closed, peripheral vision instead of abdomen, sixty seconds instead of forty-five minutes. The sequence was the treatment. Most of what made the second attempt different was what was removed.

The entry point is always the person's choice. When it isn't, the nervous system votes with its feet, and the vote looks like failure.

16.9 Meditation and Sleep

The same system that needs the right door into practice needs the right door into sleep. Sleep is the most common complaint I hear from dysregulated brains.

The feedback loops that create meditation difficulty create sleep difficulty through the same mechanisms, and they compound each other. When sleep deprivation reduces prefrontal capacity, mindfulness practice gets harder. When mindfulness practice destabilizes a dysregulated nervous system, sleep gets harder. This section collects the sleep-relevant guidance from across this book into one findable place.

16.9.1 Phenotype-Specific Nighttime Practices

CEO rumination at night: The evaluation loop doesn't clock out when you get into bed. The Structured Worry Dump gives the CEO a formal endpoint: write the loop down. Every concern, every unfinished evaluation, every "what if." Write it in a notebook. Then close the notebook. Physically. The CEO's default is to keep evaluating until certainty arrives, and certainty never arrives. The notebook is a container. The closing is a release signal. In bed, let attention drift freely. That drifting is sleep onset.

Lifeguard scanning at night: The threat-detection system runs louder in the dark. Before bed, build a Safety Cache: name three true facts that mean you're safe right now. *The door is locked. No one is expected. I am in my home.* Then grounding: feet on the floor, pressed down. One long exhale. Feel the weight of the blanket, the temperature of the sheets, the mattress under your back. You're filling the Lifeguard's data stream with body-level safety signals rather than leaving it to scan a dark room. A dim nightlight is environmental regulation for a system that needs visual data to stand down.

Fog energy cycling: If you're a Fog phenotype, your circadian rhythm may be shifted. You crash in the afternoon, rally at midnight, and wonder why you can't fall asleep at a reasonable hour. Consistent wake time (not bedtime) is the strongest single intervention. Same alarm every morning, weekends included. Morning light within 30 minutes of waking. Sunlight does the job; a phone screen does not. The circadian clock anchors to the wake signal. Fix the anchor and the rest of the rhythm follows.

16.9.2 The Evidence-Based First Line

For chronic insomnia, the evidence-based first line is CBT-I (Cognitive Behavioral Therapy for Insomnia). Mindfulness-based interventions help too: added alongside CBT-I, they produce small-to-medium reductions in insomnia severity, though CBT-I remains the first-line treatment for sleep-specific outcomes (de Entrambasaguas et al., 2023). If your sleep problems are persistent, find a CBT-I provider. The phenotype-matched practices above work as adjuncts to CBT-I, not replacements for it.

16.9.3 Body Scan and Yoga Nidra as Sleep-Onset Facilitators

Body scans and Yoga Nidra practices downshift arousal and bridge into the drowsy transition toward sleep. In a lab trial, Yoga Nidra shortened sleep onset latency in adults with insomnia (Datta et al., 2021). These practices belong in the last 30 minutes before sleep. Save the focused attention practices from your phenotype chapter for earlier in the day. The distinction matters: body scans reduce arousal.

Focused attention engages executive circuits. At bedtime, you want the former.

16.9.4 Timing Your Practice

Standing meditation, fast noting, breath of fire, vigorous pranayama: these activate the nervous system. If you're doing these within an hour of bedtime and wondering why you can't sleep, the practice isn't the problem. The timing is. Move activating practices to morning or afternoon. Reserve the last hour before bed for body-based, low-arousal formats: body scan, Yoga Nidra, gentle breath awareness, or the Permission Practice from your Safe Anchor List.

16.9.5 Sleep Apnea

Sleep apnea is a separate category requiring medical evaluation. No meditation practice fixes obstructed breathing. If you snore loudly, wake gasping, or feel unrested despite adequate hours, talk to a sleep medicine physician before adjusting your practice. Untreated apnea undermines every regulation intervention in this book.

16.9.6 The Circadian Picture

This book gives you the practice layer. The full chronobiological picture (circadian timing, light exposure, zeitgebers, the two-process model) is in *Action Cadence* (Hill, Peak Brain Press).

16.10 Applying the safety signals

Whether the difficulty is from the practice itself, from medication interactions, or from sleep that won't settle, the same signals govern. Green / Yellow / Red and the Stop Signal are defined in Chapters 1 and 3. Here they apply when meditation destabilizes you or medications change how the signal shows up.

Trust the signals. They are your nervous system's quality control, and this book is built to respect them. When a signal says stop, stopping is always a valid response.

Titrate, stop, or switch format: the Return Counter still applies. A two-minute eyes-open walk that ends in Green trains the same gap as a twenty-minute sit that goes Red. One is usable data, the other is a warning.

You come back to this chapter too, even when you wish you didn't need it.

The safety signals are online. Carrying what you've built on the cushion into conversations, work, and the rest of your life is the job of Chapter 17, the integration field manual.

Ch 17: Mindfulness in Motion: Relationships, Work & Creativity

Read this when cushion practice is stable and you want the skills in your actual life.

The formal practice builds the capacity. This chapter is where you use it.

You've trained noticing, staying, and returning toward this moment: your phenotype pattern fires in real life and you catch it. In a conversation. In a meeting. In a creative block. In a fight with someone you love. In the three seconds between a trigger and the thing you're about to say.

This isn't a survey of "places you can be mindful." Cushion or conference room, you train the same gap. The body-breath-meaning stack from Chapters 2 and 3 is what holds it open long enough to matter, in three contexts that count: the people you're close to, the work you do, and the creative capacity that makes life worth regulating.

17.1 The Integration Template

Every real-life application runs the same five steps. The template is supporting structure. Learn the pattern once. Apply it everywhere. The template takes 15 to 30 seconds. Nobody around you will know you're doing it.

1. Trigger: What just happened? Identify it. Name it. Don't analyze it. "Partner raised voice." "Boss sent a vague email." "Creative block, twenty minutes in." "My child just screamed and I felt my whole body clench."

2. Body move: One physical action. Feet on floor, pressed down. Hands on desk, pressing. Stand up if you can. The body move takes attention out of the thought spiral and into the physical body. Two seconds.

3. Breath move: One breath technique. Extended exhale: in for 4, out for 6. Or one deliberate sigh. Or a box breath: 4 in, 4 hold, 4 out, 4 hold. The breath engages the vagal brake. Five seconds.

4. Meaning move: One reframe. Label the state: "Grumpy talking." Name the phenotype: "That's my Lifeguard." Give permission: "I'm allowed to feel this and still respond well." One sentence. Three seconds.

5. Return: You caught it. You came back. *Still here.* You just ran the five-step template in real time, in public, invisibly. The half-second you trained on the cushion just became fifteen seconds in a conversation. Same skill, different arena.

Total time: 15–30 seconds. Total external evidence: you paused slightly longer before responding. That's the visible integration. A wider gap before you answer. That's all anyone sees.

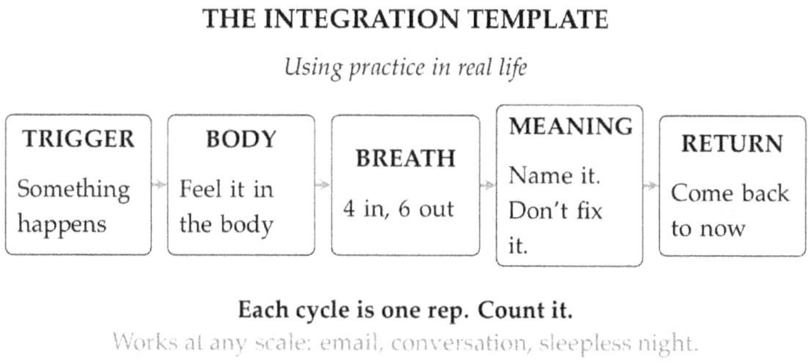

Figure 17.1: The Integration Template

17.2 Relationships: Co-Regulation Made Real

17.2.1 The 90-Second Repair

Trigger: Your partner raises their voice. Your Lifeguard activates: the tone is loud, the body tightens, the scanning system goes to high alert.

Or your Grumpy Old Man fires up withdrawal: "why do I even try." Or your Problem Child locks in: "you can't tell me what to do."

Body move: Feel both feet on the floor. Unclench your jaw. Don't move toward or away from the other person. Feel the ground. The ground is the one thing in this interaction that hasn't changed.

Breath move: One extended exhale. Slow. Through the mouth. If you can make it slightly audible, a sigh, even better. The sigh activates the vagal motor nucleus. Your nervous system starts braking before your mind has decided what to do.

Meaning move: "That's my [phenotype] talking. This person is not the threat. The activation is." Or, simpler: "My system is reacting. I don't have to react too." Or, simplest: "Is this now? Yes. Am I safe? Yes. Okay."

Return Counter: Count it (Chapter 3). You inserted a gap between the feeling and the behavior, where relationships either escalate or repair.

What you do next is up to you. But you're responding from a regulated state instead of a reactive one. The ninety seconds between trigger and response is where relationships change, in the space you just created, right there in the moment.

17.2.2 Scripts for Asking for Co-Regulation

Most mindfulness books mention co-regulation and then leave you to figure it out alone. The actual ask is simpler than the books make it sound. You're not requesting a therapeutic intervention. You're telling someone what helps.

- **To a partner:** "When I'm flooding, I don't need you to fix it. Sit near me. That's enough. If you want to put your hand on my shoulder, that helps. If you want to say 'I'm here,' that helps. Ten minutes of quiet proximity beats an hour of problem-solving."
- **To a friend:** "I'm running a three-minute practice twice a day. If you want to try it too, text me when you're done. Knowing someone else is doing it changes the consistency."

- **To a child:** "My brain is going fast right now. Want to do three breaths with me? In like we're smelling a flower, out like birthday candles." Kids co-regulate naturally. They also call you on it when you skip.
- **To a coworker:** "I do ten seconds of breathing before meetings. Stand, three breaths, sit. You'll see me do it. Feel free to ignore it or join in."

Co-regulation isn't a crutch. It's how mammalian nervous systems are designed to work. The Broken Hand Problem from Chapter 2 applies: if self-regulation is temporarily offline, borrow from a person while you rebuild the circuit.

17.2.3 Parallel Practice

The simplest co-regulation strategy: sit in the same room as another person and do separate practices. No coordination, no shared technique, no matching instructions. You do your thing. They do theirs, or they read, or they sit quietly. Proximity to a calm nervous system is itself regulatory.

Couples' version: "We practice at the same time, in the same room, but we don't have to do the same thing." This removes the coordination cost that kills most couples' practice attempts. Nobody has to agree on a technique, a duration, or a guided track. You share the space. That shared quiet is where the pause lives outside formal practice: two people practicing the pause in shared quiet.

17.3 Work: Micro-Practices for the Professional Brain

17.3.1 Pre-Meeting Centering (30 seconds)

Trigger: Five minutes before a high-stakes meeting, presentation, or call.

Body move: Stand up from your desk. Feel your feet. Shake your hands once, quickly, like flicking water off. The motor activation breaks the pre-event freeze.

Breath move: Three breaths. Fast if your Timekeeper is running hot; match the speed. Slow if your Grumpy is whispering "why bother"; extend the exhale, engage the brake.

Meaning move: "This is not a performance. There's no grade." Or: "I'm prepared enough. The rest is improvisation." Or, if the CEO is auditing: "I don't need to be perfect. I need to be present."

Return Counter: Count it. A proactive return (Chapter 3): you built the gap before the trigger arrived.

17.3.2 Between-Meeting Recovery (30 seconds)

Trigger: Meeting just ended. You're activated. Your Lifeguard is still scanning. Your Interpreter is replaying what you said. The next meeting starts in ten minutes.

Body move: Stand. Walk to the window or the door. Touch the wall or the window frame. The tactile contact is grounding data for a system still running in meeting-mode.

Breath move: One sigh. Let it be audible if you're alone; the vocalization engages the vagal brake more effectively than silent breathing.

Meaning move: "That meeting is over. This is now. The next meeting is later."

Return Counter: Add one. Between-meeting recovery is a return in the wild: the space between what just ended and what starts next.

> **If scheduling is the barrier:** If the problem is that you can never find the time, or your energy is wrong when the time arrives, that's a timing and rhythm problem. *Action Cadence* (Peak Brain Press) addresses scheduling, ultradian rhythms, and how to structure work around your brain's actual capacity curve. This book handles the practice. Cadence handles the calendar.

17.3.3 The Hyperfocus Exit Protocol

If you have a Timekeeper running fast or a Stabilizer that finally locked on. Hyperfocus is real.

The reframe that matters: hyperfocus *looks like* a meditative state. Single-pointed attention, sustained, fully absorbed. The attention system is working beautifully. The issue is the inability to *exit* the focus when you need to. That's a Supervisor problem (Chapter 4).

The protocol: Set a timer for your hyperfocus sessions. When it goes off, stand up. Three breaths. Feel your body. The chair has been holding you for two hours and you haven't noticed. Stretch. Look at something far away (your eyes have been at screen distance). The focal shift is regulatory. Then decide: continue the focus session, or switch to something else.

The choice is the practice. The timer is the mindfulness bell. And the act of standing up between focus sessions is the Supervisor practicing its exit skill. Here the gap is the exit: the beat between immersion and choice, where you decide to continue instead of being dragged.

17.3.4 Three Seconds in a Conference Room

She was mid-presentation when the senior VP interrupted with a question that felt like a challenge. Her Lifeguard started scanning the room for allies. Her CEO started evaluating whether her answer was good enough before she'd even opened her mouth. Feet on floor. One breath. *That's my pattern. The question is the question.* She answered from her prepared material instead of from her threat response. Nobody noticed the three-second pause. She did.

17.4 Creativity: The Regulated Flow State

17.4.1 Creative Block as Phenotype Collision

Creative block is rarely "no ideas." It's usually a phenotype collision: the generating system (approach, novelty, associative thinking) blocked by a regulating system (evaluation, dread, perfectionism).

The most common block constellation: the **CEO** evaluating every idea before it forms ("is this good enough?"), the **Grumpy Old Man** whispering "this won't be good enough anyway," and the **Interpreter** narrating the block itself ("I'm blocked. I'm stuck. I can't think of anything. This is terrible.").

The integration template, applied:

Trigger: Staring at the blank page, canvas, instrument, screen.

Body move: Stand up. Walk for sixty seconds. Let the body move while the mind is stuck. Movement activates the motor system, which often unsticks the cognitive system downstream.

Breath move: Three breaths, letting them fill the space the CEO was occupying.

Meaning move: "The first draft doesn't have to be good. It has to *exist*." Or: "I'm going to make something bad on purpose. The CEO can evaluate it later." Or, the nuclear option: "I give myself permission to produce garbage for the next ten minutes."

Return Counter: The block was wandering. Coming back to the page is the rep (Chapter 3).

17.4.2 The Wandering-Mind Advantage

Mind-wandering is *useful* for creativity. The default mode network, the same system that fuels Lifeguard scanning, CEO perseveration, and Interpreter narration, is also the primary engine of associative thinking, insight, and creative synthesis. The "aha" moments that seem to come from nowhere come from the DMN making connections while the focused attention system is offline.

One important difference between creative wandering and ruminative wandering is *awareness*. When you wander and don't know you're wandering: rumination. When you wander and know you're wandering, observing associations without judging, letting the mind connect dots without directing which dots: that's incubation.

Overlapping hardware. Awareness changes which mode you're in.

The skill is the same one you've been training: awareness of what the default mode is doing.

The creative practice: Set a timer for ten minutes. Alternate between focused attention on your creative problem (three minutes) and open monitoring (two minutes). In focused phases, work actively: write, sketch, compose, code. In open phases, let go of the problem entirely. Notice sounds. Feel the weight of your arms, the chair under you. Let the mind drift. The focused phase generates raw material. The open phase lets it cross-pollinate. The alternation is what trains it here.

17.5 The One-Breath Reset and the MVP

Call it the Minimum Viable Practice: the smallest thing that still counts as a rep. It is now your integration engine. One-Breath Return between tasks. One doorframe return. One temperature-check on the first sip of coffee. Zero dedicated time.

The formal sessions are where you train. The transitions are where you live.

If you did sixty micro-returns outside of formal practice each day, that is regulation at the scale of a normal Tuesday. Each micro-return is the gap practiced in the wild: a small pivot between the old pattern and a chosen response.

17.6 A Vignette: The Repair That Took Ninety Seconds

A couple, both dysregulated, both high-performing, both terrible at conflict, had been in therapy for six months. She was Lifeguard-dominant (threat-scanning, Chapter 7): during arguments, her scanning system went to high alert. He was Grumpy-dominant (effort-dread / withdrawal, Chapter 6): within two sentences of tension, he'd be emotionally offline. She'd escalate because his withdrawal looked like abandonment. He'd withdraw further because her escalation looked like attack.

Their couples therapist had taught them the 90-Second Repair. When one of them noticed the pattern starting (*I'm escalating* or *I'm withdrawing*), they'd call a pause. Ninety seconds. The escalating partner did Vagal Toning: 4-in, 6-out, three breaths, hand on chest. The withdrawing partner did Grounding: feet on floor, three things I can see, "Is this now?" Then they re-entered the conversation.

It didn't work the first time. Or the fifth. The Lifeguard didn't trust the pause. The Grumpy used it as an escape hatch. But by the third month, imperfectly, with about a 40% success rate, the ninety seconds had become a shared regulation tool. She'd say "I need the ninety." He'd nod. They'd both do their practice. When they came back, the conversation was different. The conflict hadn't resolved. Two nervous systems were closer to Green, and that changed what they could hear.

"We still fight," she said. "But we come back from it now. Sometimes in the same conversation. That didn't used to happen."

That's the repair available when you have a willing partner. Not everyone does.

17.7 When Co-Regulation Isn't Available

Not everyone has a willing partner, and some readers have no partner at all. Solo parents, people in unsupportive relationships, people whose primary dysregulation trigger *is* the person they live with. Co-regulation assumes a resource that isn't always there.

When it's not: **your own practice becomes the co-regulator**, with grounding sequence, vagal toning, Permission Practice. You borrow regulation from a practice instead of a person. Slower than a calm nervous system across the dinner table, but it works. The gap still opens. You built it. No one lends you what you've earned.

And: find *any* calm nervous system when you can. A friend on a walk. A therapist. A meditation group, even online. A dog. Dogs co-regulate beautifully, because their nervous systems mirror yours. Co-regulation doesn't require a romantic partner. It requires any regulated nervous system in proximity to yours.

You practiced in the middle of your life. In the real thing.

Keeping this for years, staying in it without burning out or turning practice into another performance, is the long game. That's Chapter 18.

Ch 18: The Long Game: Practice, Identity & the Mastery Loop

Read this at Month 3. Or Month 12. Or whenever you wonder if this is still worth doing.

A woman had been practicing for seven years when she came back to the clinic. She didn't come because something was wrong. She came because something had changed and she wanted to understand it.

"I stopped counting returns about a year ago," she said. "I just… practice now. I don't know if that's good or bad."

She'd started when she was overwhelmed, anxious, someone who had failed at three different apps and two retreats before walking through the door. The counting had been essential then: the scoreboard that let her prove something was happening when it didn't feel like anything was happening. But the counting had receded. It was still there if she needed it. She mostly didn't.

Her brain maps from Year 1 and Year 7 sat side by side on my desk. The cortical patterns had shifted, consistent with years of sustained practice.

What she was describing was the practice completing one of its jobs: the counting had done its work.

This is the last chapter. It's a map of what years five through ten look like, the two traps that take down experienced meditators, and the self-correction loop that keeps the whole system honest when life gets in the way.

The gap you've been widening, the returns you've been counting, the practice that still matches your brain when the story about you doesn't: that work continues. This chapter shows you how.

18.1 Designing a Practice That Lasts

Most practices don't fail because they stop working. They fail because life intervenes: a move, a crisis, a new job, a new baby, a pandemic. The practice drops.

When the crisis passes, the gap feels like failure. Three weeks becomes a month. A month becomes "I used to meditate."

This section builds a practice architecture that survives disruption. Not by being rigid. Rigidity breaks. By being designed for the interruptions, plateaus, and life phases that will try to kill it.

18.1.1 The Three Long-Term Phases (Repeating)

One way to picture the years ahead (just pacing): your practice will cycle through three phases, repeatedly, for the rest of your life:

Foundation. Rebuilding the basics. This happens after every lapse, every life transition, every period of stress that disrupted your routine. You go back to the 90-Second Reset. The 7-Day Start Sequence. The cascade match. The Permission Practice. You start small because starting small works, and because your nervous system needs to re-learn that practice is safe before it can go deep again.

No shame. This is the plan, not a failure of the plan. When you go back to Foundation, it's like a musician returning to scales after a month away from the instrument. It's not regression. It's maintenance.

Deepening. Longer sessions, harder practices, new channels, retreat exploration. This happens during stable periods, when your life provides enough structure and support that your practice can expand without destabilizing. You push into open monitoring. You try a half-day retreat. You sit with discomfort that would have triggered Yellow six months ago and now registers as barely Green. This is where the states-to-traits conversion accelerates.

Integration. The practice disappears into your life. The formal session continues, as it always does, but the real work happens between sessions. Micro-returns in conversations. Regulation applied in real time. Phenotype patterns caught in the wild. This is Chapter 17 embodied, Chapter 15's Phase 3 sustained.

These three phases cycle. Foundation → Deepening → Integration → (life disrupts) → Foundation → Deepening → Integration. Over and over. Each cycle builds on the last. The Foundation you rebuild in Year 3 is different from the Foundation you built in Week 1: it's faster, it's more refined, and it remembers what worked. You're not starting over. You're starting from a higher baseline each time.

18.1.2 When to Change Practices

Your practice should evolve. The practice that saved you in Month 1 may bore you in Month 6, limit you in Year 2, or feel wrong after a major life change. Here's how to tell the difference between healthy evolution and avoidance:

Outgrowth: The practice feels easy. Not just manageable: *easy*. You're not being challenged. Returns are rare because sustained attention holds effortlessly. The practice isn't producing growth anymore. You've succeeded at this level. You need a new weight.

Signal: You're bored. A deep, settled "I've gotten what I can from this" certainty. The Happy Little Kid's novelty-craving is a different signal.

Response: Switch to a more complex practice, a new channel, a longer duration, or open monitoring. Add one element of challenge. You've earned the progression.

Avoidance: The practice is hard, and you want to switch to something easier. This is the Grumpy Old Man, the Problem Child, or the CEO finding a creative way to dodge the training stimulus. The discomfort IS the work.

Signal: You want to change practices after a hard session. You're generating reasons why a different technique would be "better" or "more appropriate," but the reasons arrived right after the session that made you uncomfortable.

Response: Stay with it. Track whether the discomfort is productive (Green zone: challenging but manageable) or destabilizing (Yellow / Red: beyond your current capacity). Productive discomfort means stay. If discomfort is destabilizing, modify or retreat. The difference matters.

The test: Does the resistance come from *boredom* (outgrowth: change the practice) or *discomfort* (likely avoidance: stay with it, unless it's Yellow or Red)?

18.1.3 Seasonal Rhythms

Your practice will change with seasons, life phases, stress levels, and the general weather of your nervous system. This is expected, intelligent, and correct. A rigid practice that doesn't adapt to your life is a practice designed to break.

High-stress periods: Shorten sessions. Increase frequency. Lean on the 90-Second Reset and the One-Breath Return. Don't try to "practice through" a crisis with ambitious twenty-minute sits. That's heroic and counterproductive. When the house is on fire, you grab the extinguisher, not the remodeling plans.

Stable periods: Expand. Try longer sessions, retreat half-days, new techniques from Part II, practices you were curious about but weren't ready for. This is when Deepening happens. The stability is the container.

Transition periods (when life reorganizes around you): Go back to Foundation. Stabilize with the basics. Rebuild from the cascade match. The transition itself is consuming regulatory bandwidth; don't add more demand. Simplify until the new normal establishes itself.

Creative periods: Let the practice stay loose: open monitoring, walks without counting, journal before formal practice. Creative thought runs on cooperation between the default mode and executive control networks (Beaty et al., 2016), so the practice can shift toward open awareness without dropping focused work entirely.

18.1.4 The Plateau

At some point, usually between Month 3 and Month 6 of consistent practice, progress stalls. Returns don't increase. Sessions feel flat. The Return Counter shows the same number it showed three weeks ago. You wonder if you've hit a ceiling.

You haven't. You're deepening. Reviews of contemplative training describe rapid early gains, then slower consolidation as gains become trait-level (Cahn & Polich, 2006; Tang et al., 2015).

Early gains are rapid and obvious. Later gains are subtler and harder to see from the inside.

Less reactivity in a conversation: you didn't snap at your partner, but you don't know what didn't happen. A faster recovery from stress: the bad mood that used to last two hours lasted forty-five minutes, but you didn't time it. A longer gap between trigger and response, so long you don't notice it as a gap. At that point it feels like how you are now.

These gains are structural, trait-level.

They only become visible in retrospect, when you look back and realize the person who started this book wouldn't have handled Tuesday's meeting the same way.

When the plateau hits: Maintain consistency. Don't add intensity hoping to force a breakthrough. Don't switch practices compulsively. Sit with the flatness. The plateau is the foundation compacting under the weight of sustained practice. The next phase of growth builds on top of it. Plateaus are consolidation.

18.1.5 Three Cadences: Daily, Weekly, Retreat

Everything above is about the daily practice, the floor that changes your brain one return at a time. The daily practice is the engine, and nothing replaces it. But the sturdiest architecture I see in people who sustain practice for decades has three cadences:

Daily (the floor): Your matched practice, three to ten minutes, most days. This is where the reps accumulate and the trait-level changes compound. Habits built into daily life take a couple of months of repetition to stabilize, and the number of days varies enormously from person to person (Lally et al., 2009), which is the real reason the daily floor has to be small enough to survive a bad week.

Weekly (the social container): Once a week, sixty to ninety minutes, practicing with other people. A class, a sitting group, a sangha, a guided session on a screen, whatever you'll actually attend. It does work the cushion at home can't.

Retreat (the deep cadence): A few times a year, a longer block. This is steady, repetitive practice sustained across a day or several days: a half-day, a weekend, occasionally a longer intensive. It is where state shifts a ten-minute sit can't reach become available.

Most people who quit had only the first cadence, practiced alone, with nothing to hold it when it got hard.

18.1.6 The Weekly Cadence: Practicing With Others

The solo-app model of meditation makes practice a private thing, and private things are the easiest in the world to skip.

Sit alone and your Grumpy Old Man can end the session at minute ten with a perfectly reasonable excuse, and no one will ever know. Sit in a room where everyone else is still sitting for another ten minutes and the math changes. You stay because the social container holds you. The bodies around you do the regulating your own appraisal circuit couldn't manage today. This is co-regulation from Chapter 2, made structural: you borrow stability from a roomful of nervous systems instead of grinding it out of your own.

This is not just "the same practice, with company." Practicing in relationship appears to be a different lever with its own signature. In the largest training study to test it directly, a partnered, relational practice lowered the body's cortisol response to stress, while a solo attention practice of the same length did not (Engert et al., 2017). The same program found that months of partnered practice raised people's felt sense of social connection (Kok & Singer, 2017), and that relational and attentional training reshaped measurably different parts of the brain (Valk et al., 2017). Same rule as the anchors in Chapter 3: different door, different circuit, different regulation. This time the door is who's in the room.

The group sit doesn't end when everyone opens their eyes. The few minutes of quiet that often follow a group practice happen in a state most of us rarely enter on purpose: settled, less defended, less reactive, attention turned toward other people while the nervous system is still wide and calm. Processing your week from inside that state is a different experience than processing it from your usual reactivity. For the Lifeguard especially, whose scanning system stands down in trusted company, the after-quiet of a group sit is some of the most valuable regulation available.

How to use the weekly cadence:

- **You don't need a tradition.** A secular sitting group, a weekly class, a guided session on a screen with the camera on, a standing date with one friend who also practices: all of it counts. My read is that what carries it is other regulated nervous systems in the room.
- **Let the group hold the duration.** This is the point. If the group sits twenty minutes, let that carry you through the ten you would have quit at home. Borrowed structure is the feature. Your Stop Signal still travels with you. If the session triggers Yellow or Red, modify or stop, even when the room is still sitting.
- **If your Lifeguard runs loud, start with people you trust.** A small group or one practice partner before a room of strangers. Co-regulation needs safety to work.
- **Guided counts.** A teacher's voice working the language axis, a group body scan, partnered practice: none of these is lesser than solo silent sitting. They are different channels, and for many phenotypes they are easier to stay inside of.

The weekly cadence costs ninety minutes a week, and it solves the problem that kills more practices than boredom ever does: practicing alone, with nothing to hold you when the daily practice gets hard.

18.1.7 Retreat Practice

If retreat appeals to you, a dedicated period of extended practice, here's a graduated approach:

Half-day at home (4–6 hours): Alternating practice and rest. Three or four 30-minute practice sessions with 30-minute breaks (walking, eating, lying down). No screens. One day. At home. Alone or with one practice partner. The first time you do this, you'll be surprised how long six hours feels phone-free.

Full-day retreat (dawn to dusk): Same structure, extended. Alternating 30-minute sits and walking meditation. Meals eaten in silence. The longest single practice session you've done, plus 10%. One day that's entirely yours.

Weekend retreat: Two days. Same alternating structure. Add yoga or movement if your body needs it (most do after extended sitting). Consider doing this with a friend. Co-regulation during retreat is powerful.

Organized retreat: Only after you've done at least one solo half-day and know your phenotype's reactions to extended practice. Bring the Safe Anchor List from Chapter 16. Know your Green / Yellow / Red signals cold. Have an exit plan: know where your car is, know you can leave, know leaving is permitted.

Retreats are tools, not badges. Many people sustain lifelong practices without ever attending one. If retreat calls to you, answer. If it doesn't, the daily practice is complete.

18.2 The Identity Trap

Here's the first trap that sabotages experienced meditators, and it's insidious because it looks like success.

"I am a meditator."

Notice what happens when you shift from a verb ("I meditate") to a noun, "I am a meditator."

The practice becomes a role. The role becomes identity. And any lapse, any failure, any day you skip the cushion threatens not just your practice but your *self*. You're no longer someone who practices meditation. You're someone whose identity depends on practicing meditation. The practice has been colonized by the ego, which is exactly the thing meditation is supposed to help you notice.

"I am dysregulated" vs. "I am in a dysregulated state." The first is identity: permanent, defining, fatalistic. The second is a state: temporary, manageable, changeable. Your brain runs different patterns. AND those patterns are trainable. Both are true simultaneously. The phenotypes in this book are not who you are. They're patterns your brain runs: consistent, identifiable, and trainable. You are the one who notices the pattern and chooses what to do about it. The Stabilizer, Grumpy Old Man, Lifeguard, Princess, and Interpreter are circuits you run. That's a different relationship to your own brain.

The meditator identity trap: When "I meditate" becomes "I am a meditator," the practice calcifies. The role eclipses the training. You meditate to stay someone who meditates, not because the practice is serving you today. You sit twenty minutes because "meditators sit twenty minutes," not because your nervous system needs twenty minutes today. Shame after a skip is about a threatened self-concept.

The antidote: Hold the practice lightly. It's a tool. Tools get picked up and put down based on need. A carpenter doesn't identify as "a hammer person." They use the hammer when the job requires it and put it down when it doesn't. Your meditation practice is a hammer. A good hammer. Use it when it serves you. Put it down when it doesn't. Pick it back up tomorrow.

18.3 The Productivity Trap

The second trap: **turning meditation into another efficiency project.**

"How can I meditate more efficiently?" "What's the right session length for my brain type?" "Should I add a second session? What about a third?" "My Return Counter was lower today. What went wrong? How do I fix it?"

If you recognize this, hello, CEO. Your evaluation circuit just hijacked the practice.

The Productivity Trap turns meditation into performance. Streaks become anxiety triggers: you keep the app's "30-day streak" to avoid breaking the badge. Missed days read as failure. The Return Counter (built to replace shame with data) becomes another KPI dashboard. The practice you started to *reduce* stress is now a *source* of stress.

Brilliant work, CEO.

The test: If you're tracking your meditation streaks, scoring your sessions, comparing this week's returns to last week's, and feeling anxious about maintaining your practice schedule: the tool has become the weapon. You're using the practice against yourself.

The antidote: Periodically practice metric-free. No timer. No Return Counter. No tracking. No app. Sit for however long feels right. Do whatever practice calls to you. Stop when you're done. Don't record anything. This is "purposeless" practice: the radical act of doing something on instinct, every variable left alone.

Aim for purposeless practice at least once a week. More during high-stress periods. The CEO needs to learn that not everything requires scoring, and the practice needs to be reminded that it exists for regulation, not for achievement.

By now, many people have developed a two-word reflex, something they say silently when they catch a return. *Still here.* Or *still now.* Or something else entirely. If you haven't found yours yet, that's fine. If you have, you probably didn't realize it until just now. It's the thing that fires automatically in the gap between wandering and coming back. That pause, and whatever fills it, is the whole practice distilled.

Regulation means feeling without suppressing. Training is returning. Meditation can sit off the to-do list without generating guilt when you miss a day. That's the trap. Here's how you stay out of it.

18.4 The Mastery Loop: The Meta-Skill

Everything in this book has been building toward one ability. You catch yourself when the whole system drifts and gently correct course: wandering in a session, a slipping practice, a phenotype hijacking your life, an identity calcifying around the wrong story. The Mastery Loop is how you do that.

Notice → Normalize → Regulate → Reassign → Reflect

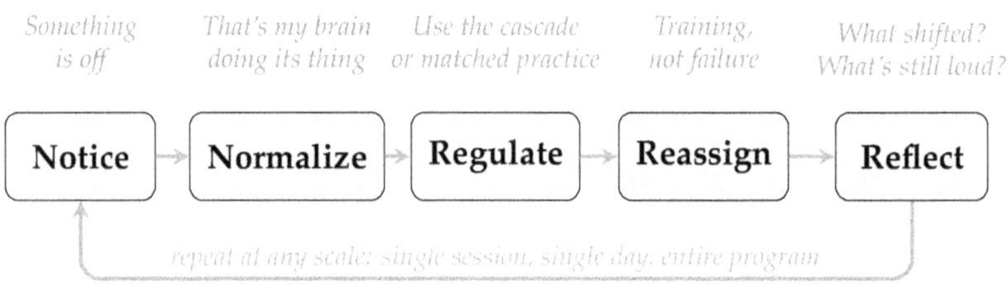

Figure 18.1: The Mastery Loop. The five-step cycle that turns practice into lasting change.

Here's a scenario I see every month:

Scenario: You've been avoiding your practice for three days. The cushion is in the corner. You know you should practice. You haven't. And now the guilt about not practicing is adding to the general dysregulation that not practicing was supposed to address. Classic.

Notice: "I've been avoiding my practice for three days." Not: "I'm lazy." Not: "I've failed." Just the observation. The fact. Three days, no practice. That's Skill 1: noticing.

Normalize: "That's what the Grumpy Old Man does with anything effortful: it appraises the cost as too high and shuts it down. Three days of avoidance is a circuit pattern, not a character flaw." Without this step, the noticing turns into self-criticism, which turns into more avoidance. Normalizing is not excusing. It's naming the mechanism so you can work with it instead of against it.

Regulate: "I'll do the 90-Second Reset. Right now. Feet on floor. Three breaths. One phrase: 'I'm allowed to start over.'" The smallest possible practice, right now.

Reassign: "My practice is about returning. This moment (picking up the book, doing the Reset after three days away) is a return. The biggest return in the whole Return Counter, and it happened after the longest gap."

Reflect: "What was the first domino? Was it stress at work? Poor sleep? A life event? What does that tell me about my nervous system right now? Do I need to go back to Foundation phase? Do I need to simplify my stack?"

The five steps work at any scale, including the advanced case where you watch yourself avoid the practice, name the pattern doing the avoiding, and return anyway:

- A wandering mind during a single session
- A three-day lapse
- A six-month drift after a life change
- A decade-long evolution of your relationship to your own brain

Notice. Normalize. Regulate. Reassign. Reflect. The loop doesn't end. It gets faster, quieter, and more automatic over time.

18.5 The Trajectory: What Sustained Practice Looks Like

Books don't usually tell you this part. Here's what the long game often looks like, based on clinical observation:

Year 1: The Foundation. You build the habit. You find your phenotype match. You learn the levers. Some months you practice daily. Some months you fall off and restart. The falling off is normal. The restarting is the skill. By the end of Year 1, you have a practice you trust. Reliably available. Your baseline has likely shifted. Many practitioners are detectably less reactive than they were twelve months ago, even when it doesn't feel dramatic from the inside. The gap appears. You catch the moment before the reaction, sometimes, rarely at first. But when you do, you recognize it. The thesis of this book, lived: your brain loses control in different places. Every time you come back, you train it to hold longer.

Year 2–3: The Deepening. The practice becomes less about "doing meditation" and more about how you respond to life. You notice the half second between stimulus and response, between the urge and the action, in situations that used to be automatic. For many people, the space widens. You start to feel it not as something you do but as something you have. You adjust your stack seasonally. Winter might need more vagal toning. Summer might need more grounding. Stressful quarters at work might need shorter, more frequent sessions. You become your own clinician: reading your state and prescribing the matched practice accordingly.

Year 5+: The Integration. Practice is no longer something you do. It's something you are. The returns happen on their own. The grounding is automatic. The Mastery Loop runs in the background. The gap is you, inherently accessible. The space between what happens and what you do about it is how you move through the world. You don't feel like "a meditator." You feel like yourself, with slightly better brakes, wider peripheral vision, and a longer fuse.

In the research literature, long-term meditators show something consistent with this: elevated gamma activity even at baseline and during sleep (Lutz et al., 2004; Ferrarelli et al., 2013), a trait-level shift that correlates with lifetime practice hours. Those studies tracked practitioners with tens of thousands of hours. Your trajectory will be different, and individual variation is large. When the system drifts (it will), you notice sooner and correct faster. Compound interest. Regulation deposited one return at a time.

You don't have to be old to get there. You have to practice. And return. And keep counting.

18.6 A Note on Retreats

Eventually, some of you will consider a meditation retreat: a weekend, a week, a ten-day silent intensive.

Retreats can deepen practice in ways daily sessions rarely match. Extended practice time allows state shifts that aren't available in ten-minute sits. Many experienced practitioners describe retreat as a turning point.

The length matters, and not in a straight line. A half-day of alternating sits and walks does something a ten-minute morning practice does not: by the third or fourth session in one day, the mind settles in a way it rarely reaches from a cold start. A weekend reaches further, and the shape is lopsided; the first day is mostly your backlog settling, and the depth tends to arrive on day two. A classic ten-day intensive is a different category again, and the research supports the pattern: a meta-analysis of traditional retreats found meaningful reductions in anxiety, depression, and stress (Khoury et al., 2017), and a three-month intensive measurably sharpened perception and sustained attention (MacLean et al., 2010).

Attentional skill in long-term practitioners scales with lifetime hours on the cushion (Brefczynski-Lewis et al., 2007). Past a certain cumulative volume, with stable enough attention to use it, retreat practice can reorganize how attention and perception orient to ordinary life, during the retreat and after. That deep reorganization is a niche pursuit, not the target of this book. This book is built for the floor: the daily practice that changes a dysregulated brain enough to make Tuesday easier. If the deeper end ever calls you, the door is real and so is the research. Most people get most of the benefit from the daily floor and the weekly group, and never need a ten-day sit to find it.

Retreats can also be destabilizing, especially for dysregulated brains. Read Chapter 16's risk factors before signing up. In particular:

- **If your Lifeguard is active:** Multi-day silence removes social co-regulation. Your scanning system will have nothing to work with.

Consider a retreat with a teacher who offers daily check-ins, not a pure "noble silence" format.

- **If you have trauma history:** Ensure the retreat is explicitly trauma-sensitive (Treleaven's framework). Ask the teacher directly how they handle adverse effects during intensive practice.
- **If you're in your first year of practice:** Wait. Build the foundation first. A retreat amplifies whatever you bring to it. Stable baseline deepens; shaky baseline can shake apart.

When you're ready, with Phase 2 practice solid, at least three months of consistent daily practice, and Safety Signals reliable, a retreat is worth exploring. Titrate: start with a day-long sit, then a weekend, then a multi-day retreat. The same progression principle applies.

18.7 Come Back to This Chapter When...

You won't need this chapter once. You'll need it repeatedly, at different scales, in different seasons. Bookmark it. Here's when to return:

- **You've lapsed or life has disrupted everything.** Reread the Mastery Loop. Don't judge the gap. Return to the 90-Second Reset and Phase 1 intensity. You haven't lost what you built.
- **Practice feels stale?** Return to the Decision Tree. Your loudest circuit may have changed.
- **Missed a week?** The 90-Second Reset. Right now. That's the restart.
- **"Is this still doing anything?"** Ask someone who's known you for five years. The changes are invisible from the inside and obvious from the outside.
- **What progress looks like from the inside at Year 2:** You start to notice what you *didn't* do: the reaction that didn't happen, the spiral that stopped at the top, the conversation that didn't require recovery afterward. The absence of the old pattern is the evidence.

Last supporting frame, then the throughline.

18.8 The Orchestra Metaphor (One Last Time)

You're the conductor. The phenotypes are the sections: strings, brass, woodwinds, percussion. Each section has its tendencies: the Grumpy cellos want to play slower, the Timekeeper percussion wants to rush, the Interpreter winds won't stop their solo, the Lifeguard brass keeps playing the alarm motif.

The conductor keeps every section employed, lets the orchestra play, and shapes the balance moment by moment: *noticing* what each section is doing, *accepting* the material they're producing, *directing* gently or firmly as needed.

Some days the orchestra sounds terrible, or the sections play at different tempos with brass and strings each running their own clock. That's a rehearsal. Other days the conductor puts down the baton and lets the orchestra play whatever it wants, and that's creativity.

And some days the conductor doesn't show up at all. The orchestra plays anyway, because that's what it does. When the conductor returns, the orchestra is still there. The music continues.

Different networks handle different jobs: motor circuits, arousal systems, attentional networks, emotional processing, evaluative loops. They interact, but they can fail independently and recover at different rates.

The regulation is distributed (five systems, twelve voices, each with its own timing), and no single practice controls all of it. But the conductor doesn't need to play every instrument. The conductor needs the gap: half a second between the sour note and the correction, between the impulse and the response, between the trigger and the choice. That space is what every practice in this book builds.

And when I forget, when the baton drops, when the Grumpy cellos take over, when the Lifeguard brass drowns everything out, I notice, normalize, and pick it back up. That's the long game this book has been building toward.

18.9 The Final Practice

We're going to end where we began.

Find your feet on the floor. Feel them. The ground pushing up. Your weight pressing down.

One breath in through your nose. Feel the air crossing your upper lip.

One breath out through your mouth. Feel the release in your chest.

Say silently: *I'm allowed to be here.*

Note that you returned. Count it.

You started this book with a 90-Second Reset and a Permission Practice, before cascade, before phenotypes, before you had reason to believe your meditation "failures" weren't failures. You already had the gap. You've widened it ever since.

You have the map (the Decision Tree, the cascade, the Three-Phase Model, the Mastery Loop), but maps aren't the territory. The territory is the half-second you keep reclaiming, the returns you keep counting, the phenotype-matched move you reach for when your old pattern loads first.

Use it messy, use it briefly: One-Breath Return in your car, bathroom, office, bed, kitchen. At 3 a.m. when the Lifeguard won't let you sleep. In the meeting where your CEO scores every word. Keep what fits; drop what doesn't. Return when you wander. Stop when you need to. Come back when you're ready. That's regulation, and the whole game is yours.

Your last practice: ___ returns. Your next practice: whenever you open this book again.

You've been counting returns since page one. That number is yours. You earned every one. You always came back; now you have a count for it.

Before You Go: Your Companion Kit

You read the book. Here is the part you can put to work this week.

There is a free **Half a Second More Companion Kit** that goes with these pages:

- The twelve **Practice Cards**, formatted to print and carry
- The **90-Second Reset** card for your wallet or your mirror
- The full **Symptom to Practice** quick-reference guide
- A short series of notes from me on making the practice stick

It is free. First name and email, nothing else, and you can leave any time.

Scan with your phone's camera

or visit **peakbrainpress.com/hasm-bonus**

Glossary

Alpha Peak Frequency (APF): Your brain's dominant alpha rhythm, measured in the EEG. In laboratory tasks, higher APF correlates with finer temporal resolution. Proposed basis of the Timekeeper phenotype (Chapter 10).

Anchor: The object of attention during meditation: breath, body sensation, mantra, or visual focus. Each return to the anchor is one noticed moment.

Arcuate Fasciculus: The white-matter fiber bundle connecting Wernicke's area (language comprehension) to Broca's area (language production). The "cable" in the Interpreter's language loop.

Bottom-Up Regulation: Regulation that flows from body to brain: movement, breathing, sensory grounding. Doesn't require cognitive effort. Preferred entry point for most dysregulated brains.

Cascade: See Regulation Cascade.

Co-Regulation: Borrowing regulation from another person's calm nervous system. Not weakness, but how nervous systems are designed to work.

Decision Tree: The book's one-page diagnostic: "If you feel X → start here." Located in Chapter 2.

Default Mode Network (DMN): The brain's background chatter system, active during mind-wandering, self-referential thinking, and mental time travel. The Interpreter's home territory and the Lifeguard's surveillance platform. Meditation practice is associated with reduced DMN overactivity.

Environmental Regulation: Changing the environment to support regulation: dim lights, quiet, weighted blanket, sensory sanctuary.

Four Channels: Four qualities of attention used in meditation: Single Point, Present Moment, Feeling Tone: Internal, Feeling Tone: External.

Green / Yellow / Red: Safety signal system. Green = keep going. Yellow = modify (adjust intensity). Red = stop and seek support.

Heart Rate Variability (HRV): The variation in time between heartbeats. Higher HRV indicates a stronger vagal brake and greater autonomic flexibility. Trainable through breath practices and HRV biofeedback.

Mastery Loop: Notice → Normalize → Regulate → Reassign → Reflect. The self-correcting framework for sustained practice (Chapter 18).

Minimum Viable Practice (MVP): A micro-practice attached to an existing behavior: noticing one thing, once, requiring zero dedicated time. A doorframe return, a phone-pickup breath, a first-sip temperature check. The practice for when even 90 seconds is too much.

Neurofeedback: Involuntary operant conditioning of brain activity using real-time EEG feedback. Trains circuits below conscious awareness. Complements meditation; does not replace it.

Permission Practice: "I'm allowed to stop." The book's foundational practice: training the nervous system to approach meditation without clenching.

Pendulation: A practice of oscillating attention between a tense body region and a safe one, typically in 3-second intervals. Used for the Lifeguard and trauma-sensitive brains. Builds interoceptive capacity gradually.

Phenotype: A pattern of brain activity that shapes how you experience the world. Twelve phenotypes in this book, each with matched meditation practices. Training profiles, not diagnoses. You'll shift between them depending on sleep, stress, and context.

The Twelve Phenotypes

Stabilizer (MOVE, Ch. 4): Can't initiate action. The "go" button is misfiring. Entry: Walking Meditation.

Supervisor (MOVE, Ch. 4): Can't inhibit impulse. The brake pedal is soft. Entry: Insight / Nonreactive Attention.

Fog (MOVE, Ch. 5): Defaults to low arousal. Falling asleep the moment external stimulation drops. Entry: Eyes-Open Standing Awareness.

Grumpy Old Man (MOOD, Ch. 6): Effort-dread. Right frontal withdrawal system pre-screens everything and rejects it. Entry: Vagal Toning.

Happy Little Kid (MOOD, Ch. 6): Flat approach. The system that should say "ooh, let's try this" is quiet. Often surfaces after burnout, illness, or chronic stress. Entry: borrowed approach (co-practice, Curiosity Meditation). *(Note: "I start everything and the next shiny thing pulls me away" is a Supervisor brake-leak (Ch. 4) or CEO novelty-capture (Ch. 7), not Happy Little Kid.)*

Problem Child (MOOD, Ch. 6): Anti-coercion circuit. Resists instruction, even self-instruction. Entry: Choice-Based Practice.

CEO (ORIENT, Ch. 7): Conflict-monitoring loop. Evaluates the meditation instead of doing it. Entry: Structured-to-Open Transition.

Lifeguard (ORIENT, Ch. 7): Threat-scanning system on high alert. Can't close eyes. Entry: Grounding: "Is This Now?"

Princess & the Pea (SENSE, Ch. 8): Sensory gain at maximum. Everything arrives at full volume. Entry: Sensory Sanctuary + Titrated Body Scan.

Bard (SENSE, Ch. 8): Right temporal prosody circuit over-reads emotional tone in every voice. Entry: Non-Verbal Practice.

Interpreter (SENSE, Ch. 9): Left language axis running a constant verbal loop. Internal narrator won't stop. Entry: Mantra Redirect.

Timekeeper (PROCESS, Ch. 10): Processing speed mismatch. Practice pace is wrong for the brain's alpha frequency. Entry: Rapid Noting or Self-Paced Concentration.

Regulation Cascade: MOVE → MOOD → ORIENT → SENSE → PROCESS. The book's core framework: a sequence of five regulation systems that fail in order. Start at the first broken step.

Respiratory Sinus Arrhythmia (RSA): The natural rise and fall of heart rate with breathing. Inhale = heart rate rises (vagal brake releases). Exhale = heart rate falls (vagal brake re-engages). Maximized at ~6 breaths per minute.

Return: Each time attention wanders and you bring it back to your anchor. The fundamental unit of meditation practice. The count is your engagement log, not a neural dose or an efficacy score. Count returns, not minutes.

Return Counter: The book's engagement log. Track returns per session instead of duration.

90-Second Reset Stack: The book's emergency regulation tool. Body lever (30 sec) → Breath lever (30 sec) → Meaning lever (30 sec). Customizable.

7-Day Start Sequence: Phase 1, Week 1. Your first week of cascade-matched practice. Introduced in Chapter 3.

Stop Signal: Permission to stop any practice at any time. A feature, not a failure.

Three-Phase Model: Stabilize (Weeks 1–3) → Train (Weeks 4–8) → Integrate (Week 9+). The program structure (Chapter 15).

Titration: Gradually increasing the intensity, duration, or complexity of a practice. The opposite of "push through." Find the Green zone, stabilize there, then edge forward one variable at a time.

Top-Down Regulation: Regulation that flows from brain to body: reframing, labeling, choosing attention targets. Requires the nervous system to be at least partially settled (bottom-up first).

Vagal Brake: The vagus nerve's mechanism for slowing heart rate. Releases on inhale, re-engages on exhale. The physiological basis of breath-based regulation.

Symptom → Practice Lookup

This is your return-to-it-in-crisis index. Every entry below maps a feeling to the circuit that's closing the gap and the practice that reopens it. If you need "what do I do RIGHT NOW," find what you're feeling in the left column, go to the chapter on the right.

Quick Reference: What You Feel → Where to Go

What You're Feeling	Cascade	Ch.	Practice
Can't make yourself start	**MOVE**	4	Micro-Session Activation (60 sec)
Frozen, can't move	**MOVE**	4	Walking Meditation (3 min)
Impulsive, can't stop	**MOVE**	4	Insight / Nonreactive Attention (3 min)
Falling asleep during meditation	**MOVE**	5	Eyes-Open Standing Awareness (3 min)
No energy, brain fog	**MOVE**	5	Tide-Honoring Micro-Sessions
Dread, "what's the point"	**MOOD**	6	Vagal Toning (3 min)
Flat affect, no spark, nothing pulls	**MOOD**	6	Curiosity Meditation / co-practice
Start everything, novelty pulls you away	**MOVE**	4	Supervisor brake-leak: Insight / Nonreactive Attention (3 min); if it doesn't fit, see Ch. 7 CEO
Oppositional, "you can't make me"	**MOOD**	6	Choice-Based Practice

What You're Feeling	Cascade	Ch.	Practice
Hypervigilant, scanning for threat	**ORIENT**	7	Grounding: "Is This Now?" (3 min)
Perfectionism loops	**ORIENT**	7	Structured-to-Open Transition (5 min)
Sensory overwhelm, body too loud	**SENSE**	8	Sensory Sanctuary + Titrated Body Scan
Overwhelmed by tone of voice	**SENSE**	8	Non-Verbal Practice (3 min)
Internal narrator won't stop	**SENSE**	9	Mantra Redirect (3 min)
Verbal rumination, worry loops	**SENSE**	9	Writing-to-Silence + Mantra
Everything too fast	**PROCESS**	10	Rapid Noting (3 min)
Everything too slow	**PROCESS**	10	Self-Paced Concentration (3 min)
Racing mind at night	**PROCESS**	10	Rapid noting, gradual deceleration
Anger, quick to snap	**MOOD**	6	Vagal Toning (4-in, 6-out) + Permission Practice
Rage, explosive or simmering	**MOOD**	6	Physiological Sigh (3 rounds), then Vagal Toning; see Ch. 16 if persistent
Dissociation, feeling unreal	**Safety**	16	Grounding: Five Things + external anchoring. Do not continue inward practice.
Numbness, can't feel anything	**MOOD**	6	Vagal Toning first; then gentle Feeling Tone (hands only). See Ch. 8 if somatic.
Procrastination, avoidance	**MOVE**	4	Micro-Session Activation (60 sec); for effort-dread, see Ch. 6 Grumpy

What You're Feeling	Cascade	Ch.	Practice
Trauma flashback during practice	**Safety**	16	Stop. Ground. Feet on floor. Five things you can see. Ch. 16 modification list.
Can't sleep (rumination)	**Sleep**	7	Closure Ritual + Structured Worry Dump
Can't sleep (scanning)	**Sleep**	7	Safety Cache + grounding in bed
Feeling worse after practice	**Safety**	16	Stop Signal + modify or stop
Panic during practice	**Safety**	16	Stop. Ground. Feet on floor.
Multiple phenotypes competing	**Stacks**	11	Loudest-circuit-first + Stack Builder
Don't know where to start	**All**	2	Start at MOVE. Walk.
Need a reset now	**Any**	All	90-Second Reset Stack

The Universal Emergency Kit

If nothing above fits, or you just need to get regulated right now:

1. **Feet on floor.** Press down. Feel the ground.
2. **Three breaths.** In for 4, out for 6.
3. **Say silently:** "I'm allowed to be here."

That's the 90-Second Reset. It works for most people, most of the time, and it's available anywhere. Start there.

Resources

Books

On Mindfulness and Meditation:

- *Altered Traits* by Daniel Goleman and Richard Davidson. A comprehensive, evidence-based popular science treatment of meditation research, written by the scientists who ran the studies.
- *The Mind Illuminated* by Culadasa (John Yates). The most detailed meditation instruction manual available. Dense but precise. Best for readers who want the deep model.
- *Mindfulness in Plain English* by Bhante Gunaratana. Clear, practical, tradition-grounded. Excellent introduction to vipassana without the jargon.

On Trauma-Sensitive Practice:

- *Trauma-Sensitive Mindfulness* by David Treleaven. Essential reading if your practice has triggered adverse effects, or if you work with trauma populations.
- *The Body Keeps the Score* by Bessel van der Kolk. The foundational text on embodied trauma and body-based healing.

On Neuroscience and Regulation:

- *Gifted & Tortured* by Andrew Hill and Jessica McCann (Peak Brain Press, 2026). The phenotype system this book is built on. Chapters 2–13 cover the twelve phenotypes in depth. Chapter 17 is the meditation chapter this book expands; Part III's Quick-Start Hierarchy maps to the Regulation Cascade in Chapter 2 here. Not a prerequisite, but a companion for readers who want the full brain-mapping framework.

Apps and Guided Practice

- **Insight Timer:** Free, vast library, timer-only option. Useful for unguided practice (set a timer, no voice). Recommended for the Bard and Interpreter phenotypes.
- **Waking Up (Sam Harris):** Theory-heavy, high-quality instruction. Good for the CEO phenotype who needs to understand the model before practicing it.
- **Headspace / Calm:** Accessible, well-designed, gamified. The variety and engagement features can help if your Supervisor brake leaks toward novelty (Ch. 4) or your CEO gets captured by new patterns (Ch. 7).
- **Consumer EEG headbands** (Muse, Emotiv, and others). Useful as meditation gauges and for gamification. See Chapter 14 for an honest assessment of what they can and can't do.

Finding a QEEG Provider

This book's phenotype system was built from quantitative EEG brain mapping. Using the book requires no equipment: the Decision Tree and chapter descriptions are designed to get you to the right practice without a scan. If you want your own brain map to confirm your match, here's how to find a provider:

- **BCIA** (bcia.org): Board Certification International Alliance. Look for practitioners with BCN (Board Certified in Neurofeedback) credentials. Their provider directory is the most reliable starting point.
- **ISNR** (isnr.org): International Society for Neuroregulation and Research. Conference and provider network. Members are typically clinicians who do QEEG as part of neurofeedback practice.
- **Ask for:** A full 19-channel QEEG with eyes-open and eyes-closed recordings, compared against a normative database. A "mini-Q" or single-channel recording is not sufficient for phenotype identification.

- **Expect:** A 60–90 minute recording session, followed by a report that maps your brain's activity by region and frequency band. A good provider will explain the results and connect them to your symptoms.
- **Cost:** Typically $300–800 for the assessment, depending on location and provider. Some providers include a feedback session in the price.

Crisis and Professional Support

- **988 Suicide and Crisis Lifeline:** Call or text 988 (U.S.)
- **Crisis Text Line:** Text HOME to 741741 (U.S.)
- **SAMHSA National Helpline:** 1-800-662-4357 (free, confidential, 24/7)
- **National Alliance for Eating Disorders Helpline:** 1-866-662-1235 (staffed by licensed therapists; referrals to treatment)
- **Psychology Today Therapist Directory** (psychologytoday.com): searchable by location, specialty, and insurance
- **Cheetah House** (cheetahhouse.org): support for meditation-related difficulties, founded by Willoughby Britton's research group

The Brain Map Picture

Each phenotype chapter in Part II describes what the pattern looks like on a QEEG brain map. For the full picture of what a brain map reveals, how quantitative EEG is recorded, what the numbers mean, and how the twelve phenotypes emerge from the data, see *The QEEG Field Guide* (Hill & Lomeli, Peak Brain Press). That book is the technical companion to this one: it covers the measurement. This book covers the training.

References Cited

What This Book Is Built On

This book is a clinical synthesis. The phenotype system was built from QEEG brain maps over twenty-five years. The practices came from clinical observation of what worked for which brains. The framework for thinking about adverse effects came largely from published research. But several published sources deserve explicit acknowledgment for shaping specific parts of the book's structure or vocabulary.

David Treleaven, *Trauma-Sensitive Mindfulness* (2018). Chapter 16's modification framework, the phenotype-specific risk factors for adverse effects, and the concept that meditation can be adapted rather than contraindicated for trauma histories are indebted to Treleaven's work. Treleaven made the field take adverse effects seriously a decade before the Lindahl data made them statistically undeniable. The "right door" framing in Chapter 16 is compatible with his framework, though arrived at from a different analytical direction.

Willoughby Britton and the Cheetah House research program. The adverse-effects taxonomy in Chapter 16 is built on the Lindahl et al. (2017) study that Britton led. Her research program at Brown University represents the field's most rigorous empirical work on what can go wrong in meditation, and Chapter 16 stands on it. The phenotype-specific risk framing in this book is intended as a complementary mechanism layer, not a replacement.

Tara Brach and Kristin Neff. The Permission Practice in Chapter 1 and the "you're not broken" framing throughout the book are consistent with, and draw on, the permission-giving and self-compassion traditions that Brach and Neff developed in accessible form. The Permission Practice's specific phrasing ("I'm allowed to stop at any time," "I'm allowed to do this imperfectly") evolved from clinical work, but the broader therapeutic move was pioneered by these authors.

Jill Bolte Taylor, *My Stroke of Insight* (2008). Taylor described what she called the 90-second rule: her account of how long a physiological emotional response runs if not re-triggered by thought. That observation informed the clinical logic behind the 90-Second Reset in Chapter 3. Ninety seconds is this book's design choice, built from Taylor's account and clinical experience. It is not an established neurochemical constant. The Reset's specific structure (Body Lever, Breath Lever, Meaning Lever) is this book's clinical development of that observation, not a direct adaptation.

The MBSR tradition (Jon Kabat-Zinn and colleagues). This book positions itself as addressing the gap between standard MBSR-style instruction and the dysregulated-brain population for whom it doesn't fit. That positioning depends on MBSR existing and working for the population it was designed for. The book's argument is with universalization of a good practice, not with the practice itself. Kabat-Zinn's work is the context this book argues within.

A Note on Evidence

This book uses three categories of evidence:

Peer-reviewed research: Specific studies cited by author, year, and key findings. These are drawn from the research literature and have been verified against original sources where possible.

Clinical observation: Patterns drawn from 25,000+ quantitative EEG brain maps at Peak Brain Institute. The phenotype-to-practice matching system is clinical synthesis, informed by but not identical to the peer-reviewed literature. Where I say "in my clinical experience," that's what I mean.

Where evidence is absent: Some claims in this book, particularly around phenotype-specific meditation matching, have not been tested in randomized controlled trials. I've tried to be transparent about where the data stops and clinical inference begins. The phrase "promising, not magic" appears more than once for a reason.

Chapter Notes

Chapter 2: Five Regulation Systems

Duncan (2010). The multiple-demand system of the primate brain. Menon (2011). Large-scale brain networks and the triple network model. Shamay-Tsoory et al. (2009). Double dissociation between emotional and cognitive empathy.

Chapter 3: Three Skills, Three Levers

Lally et al. (2009). How habits are formed: the 66-day median finding; the time to automaticity ranged widely across participants (18 to 254 days), which is why the daily floor is set low enough to survive a bad week. The "where this book aims" note draws on Khoury et al. (2017) for the evidence that extended retreat practice produces effects beyond what brief daily sessions reach; the full practice-architecture argument is developed in Chapter 18.

Chapter 4: Stabilizer / Supervisor

Lipszyc & Schachar (2010). Inhibitory control and the stop signal task: meta-analysis establishing stop-signal reaction time as a transdiagnostic marker.

Chapter 5: Fog

For SMR neurofeedback and thalamocortical circuit mechanisms: Sterman (1996), Sterman et al. (1969). For the theta/beta ratio discussion: the "multiple studies" claim references the TBR literature reviewed in Arns, Conners, & Kraemer (2013), who note that TBR's diagnostic specificity for ADHD has weakened under replication. The ratio remains a useful clinical heuristic when interpreted alongside the full QEEG. Lomas, Cartwright, Edginton, & Ridge (2015) documents experiential challenges in meditation practice, including practitioners wrestling with tiredness and forcing themselves to stay awake, relevant to the Fog pattern's drowsiness risk. Lomas, Ivtzan, & Fu (2015) is the separate EEG systematic review cited for the alpha and theta finding.

Chapter 6: Frontal Mood Axis

Davidson asymmetry framework: the approach/withdrawal model of frontal EEG asymmetry originates with Davidson (1992), which is the source cited in the chapter, and is elaborated in Davidson & Hugdahl (1995). Davidson et al. (2003), on brain and immune function after mindfulness training, is listed as background to that research program rather than as the source of a specific claim in this chapter.

Chapter 7: CEO / Lifeguard

Riesel, Goldhahn, & Kathmann (2017). Hyperactive performance monitoring (ERN) as a transdiagnostic marker relevant to the CEO's error-checking circuit.

Chapter 8: Princess & the Pea / Bard

Lindahl et al. (2017). Meditation-related challenges in Western Buddhists. Schlosser et al. (2019). Prevalence and predictors of unpleasant meditation-related experiences. P50 sensory gating: the Princess pattern's reduced sensory gating is consistent with P50 auditory gating literature. P50 is a pre-attentive ERP component measured at ~50 ms post-stimulus; reduced P50 suppression indexes failure to filter redundant sensory input. The P50 paradigm is reviewed in Cahn & Polich (2006) in the context of meditation ERP research. Clinical observation suggests that Princess-profile brains often show weak P50 suppression on QEEG, though this specific phenotype $\times$ P50 association has not been tested in a controlled trial.

Chapter 10: Timekeeper

Samaha & Postle (2015). Alpha-band oscillation speed and temporal resolution of visual perception. Ronconi et al. (2018). Alpha-band sensory entrainment and temporal windows. Rodriguez-Larios

& Alaerts (2019). Theta–alpha harmonic relationships and cognitive performance.

Chapter 12: States to Traits

HRV trait shift: the claim that meditation practice produces lasting increases in resting HRV is supported by meta-analytic evidence. Goessl, Curtiss, & Hofmann (2017) found moderate effects of HRV biofeedback training on stress and anxiety. Lehrer & Gevirtz (2014) review the mechanisms by which HRV biofeedback produces durable autonomic changes. Van Dam et al. (2018). Critical evaluation of mindfulness and meditation research. Desbordes et al. (2012). Mindful-attention training and amygdala response in non-meditative states. Brewer et al. (2011). Default mode network changes with meditation experience. (The long-term gamma findings, Lutz 2004, Ferrarelli 2013, and Braboszcz 2017, are detailed in the Chapter 13 notes.)

Chapter 13: Your Brain's Rhythms

Lutz et al. (2004). High-amplitude gamma synchrony in long-term meditators during compassion meditation; trait gamma elevation at baseline. Ferrarelli et al. (2013). Elevated parieto-occipital gamma during NREM sleep in experienced meditators. Braboszcz et al. (2017). Increased gamma across three meditation traditions (Vipassana, Himalayan Yoga, Isha Shoonya). Cahn et al. (2017). Meditation-state gamma oscillations and attentional modulation. Lisman & Jensen (2013). The theta-gamma neural code: foundational reference for theta-gamma coupling as a mechanism of working memory and information transfer. Sihn, Kim, & Kim (2024). Reduced infra-slow EEG activity and weaker coupling between infra-slow phase and alpha amplitude in experienced Vipassana meditators, predominantly left frontal; coupling with gamma showed no group difference. Zanesco et al. (2013). Executive control improvements following intensive meditation training. Skwara et al. (2022). Longitudinal reductions in resting EEG beta power with intensive meditation. Duan et al. (2019). Cortisol awakening response and resting frontal EEG asymmetry.

Kaul et al. (2010). Meditation acutely improves psychomotor vigilance and may decrease sleep need. Brand et al. (2012). Influence of mindfulness practice on cortisol and sleep in highly stressed humans. Torsvall & Åkerstedt (1987). Sleepiness on the job: Continuously measured EEG changes in train drivers (foundational reference for theta-band drowsiness signatures).

Chapter 14: Tech-Assisted Meditation

Johnson et al. (2013). Spectral dynamics and therapeutic implications of the theta/alpha crossover in alpha-theta neurofeedback. Johnson and colleagues analyzed 182 alpha-theta sessions and identified the multi-band configuration (theta, alpha, low beta) associated with therapeutic crossover episodes. The "80–90% of vagal traffic flows up" claim is sourced from Berthoud & Neuhuber (2000), who established through anatomical tracing that approximately 80% of vagal nerve fibers are afferent (body-to-brain).

Chapter 16: When Worse

Lindahl et al. (2017) and Schlosser et al. (2019) are listed under Chapter 8. Willoughby Britton's broader research program at Brown University's Contemplative Studies Program underpins the Lindahl typology. The phenotype-to-practice framework in this book functions as a candidate mechanism for predicting adverse event likelihood across the Lindahl taxonomy; a formal empirical test of that pairing has not been run. Boldrini et al. (2014) provides the postmortem data on hippocampal neurogenesis and benzodiazepine co-treatment cited in the benzodiazepine section. Breedvelt et al. (2021) is the individual-patient-data meta-analysis pooling four RCTs on sequential psychological interventions during antidepressant taper. Segal, Teasdale, & Williams (2002) is the foundational MBCT manual referenced in the SSRI taper section. Datta et al. (2021) is the Yoga Nidra sleep-onset latency trial. de Entrambasaguas et al. (2023) is the meta-analysis on mindfulness-based interventions as a component of CBT-I for chronic insomnia. Balban et al. (2023) is the cyclic-sighing / physiological sigh randomized trial that provides the research basis for item 3 on the Safe Anchor List.

Chapter 18: The Long Game

The weekly-tier argument draws on the ReSource Project, a large secular mental-training trial that compared training modules head to head. Engert et al. (2017) found that a partnered, relational practice (the "Affect" and "Perspective" dyads) reduced cortisol stress reactivity, whereas a solo attention-based module did not, the cleanest available evidence that relational practice is a distinct lever rather than solo practice with company present. Kok & Singer (2017) report increased perceived social connectedness following the dyadic practices over the nine-month program, and Valk et al. (2017) document differential cortical thickness change after socio-affective versus attention-cognitive training. The co-regulation framing connects to Coan et al. (2006), cited under Chapter 2. On the retreat tier: Khoury et al. (2017) is a systematic review and meta-analysis of 21 traditional-retreat studies (N=2,912), reporting moderate pre-post and controlled effect sizes (Hedge's g ≈ 0.45 to 0.49) maintained at follow-up; MacLean et al. (2010) is the Shamatha Project randomized waitlist-controlled study of a three-month intensive, showing improved perceptual discrimination and sustained attention. The lifetime-hours observation is from Brefczynski-Lewis et al. (2007), whose long-term practitioners averaged 19,000 to 44,000 hours and showed an inverted-U pattern of attention-network activation consistent with increasing neural efficiency at the highest practice volumes; the trait-gamma findings (Lutz et al., 2004; Ferrarelli et al., 2013) are detailed under Chapter 13. The claim that deep cumulative-hours reorganization is real but niche, and not this book's target, is stated as honest scope, not as a tested prediction of the phenotype framework.

Arns, M., Conners, C. K., & Kraemer, H. C. (2013). A decade of EEG theta/beta ratio research in ADHD: A meta-analysis. *Journal of Attention Disorders, 17*(5), 374–383. PMID: 23086616. https://doi.org/10.1177/1087054712460087

Baer, R., Crane, C., Miller, E., & Kuyken, W. (2019). Doing no harm in mindfulness-based programs: Conceptual issues and empirical findings. *Clinical Psychology Review, 71*, 101–114. PMID: 30638824. https://doi.org/10.1016/j.cpr.2019.01.001

Balban, M. Y., Neri, E., Kogon, M. M., Weed, L., Nouriani, B., Jo, B., Holl, G., Zeitzer, J. M., Spiegel, D., & Huberman, A. D. (2023). Brief structured respiration practices enhance mood and reduce physiological arousal. *Cell Reports Medicine, 4*(1), 100895. PMID: 36630953. https://doi.org/10.1016/j.xcrm.2022.100895

Basso, J. C., McHale, A., Ende, V., Oberlin, D. J., & Suzuki, W. A. (2019). Brief, daily meditation enhances attention, memory, mood, and emotional regulation in non-experienced meditators. *Behavioural Brain Research, 356*, 208–220. PMID: 30153464. https://doi.org/10.1016/j.bbr.2018.08.023

Beaty, R. E., Benedek, M., Silvia, P. J., & Schacter, D. L. (2016). Creative cognition and brain network dynamics. *Trends in Cognitive Sciences, 20*(2), 87–95. PMID: 26553223. https://doi.org/10.1016/j.tics.2015.10.004

Berthoud, H.-R., & Neuhuber, W. L. (2000). Functional and chemical anatomy of the afferent vagal system. *Autonomic Neuroscience, 85*(1–3), 1–17. PMID: 11189015. https://doi.org/10.1016/S1566-0702(00)00215-0

Bluschke, A., Schuster, J., Roessner, V., & Beste, C. (2018). Neurophysiological mechanisms of interval timing dissociate inattentive and combined ADHD subtypes. *Scientific Reports, 8*(1), 2033. PMID: 29391481. https://doi.org/10.1038/s41598-018-20484-0

Boldrini, M., Butt, T. H., Santiago, A. N., Tamir, H., Dwork, A. J., Rosoklija, G. B., Arango, V., Hen, R., & Mann, J. J. (2014). Benzodiazepines and the potential trophic effect of antidepressants on dentate gyrus cells in mood disorders. *The International Journal of Neuropsychopharmacology, 17*(12), 1923–1933. PMID: 24969726. https://doi.org/10.1017/S1461145714000844

Braboszcz, C., Cahn, B. R., Levy, J., Fernandez, M., & Delorme, A. (2017). Increased gamma brainwave amplitude compared to control in three different meditation traditions. *PLOS ONE, 12*(1), e0170647. https://doi.org/10.1371/journal.pone.0170647

Brand, S., Holsboer-Trachsler, E., Naranjo, J. R., & Schmidt, S. (2012). Influence of mindfulness practice on cortisol and sleep in long-term and short-term meditators. *Neuropsychobiology, 65*(3), 109–118. PMID: 22377965. https://doi.org/10.1159/000330362

Breedvelt, J. J. F., Warren, F. C., Segal, Z., Kuyken, W., & Bockting, C. L. (2021). Continuation of antidepressants vs sequential psychological interventions to prevent relapse in depression: An individual participant data meta-analysis. *JAMA Psychiatry, 78*(8), 868–875. PMID: 34009273. https://doi.org/10.1001/jamapsychiatry.2021.0823

Brefczynski-Lewis, J. A., Lutz, A., Schaefer, H. S., Levinson, D. B., & Davidson, R. J. (2007). Neural correlates of attentional expertise in long-term meditation practitioners. *Proceedings of the National Academy of Sciences, 104*(27), 11483–11488. PMID: 17596341. https://doi.org/10.1073/pnas.0606552104

Brewer, J. A., Worhunsky, P. D., Gray, J. R., Tang, Y.-Y., Weber, J., & Kober, H. (2011). Meditation experience is associated with differences in default mode network activity and connectivity. *PNAS, 108*(50), 20254–20259. PMID: 22114193. https://doi.org/10.1073/pnas.1112029108

Brown, L., Rando, A. A., Eichel, K., Van Dam, N. T., Celano, C. M., Huffman, J. C., & Morris, M. E. (2021). The effects of mindfulness and meditation on vagally mediated heart rate variability: A meta-analysis. *Psychosomatic Medicine, 83*(6), 631–640. PMID: 33395216. https://doi.org/10.1097/PSY.0000000000000900

Burrows, K., DeVille, D. C., Cosgrove, K. T., Kuplicki, R. T., Paulus, M. P., Aupperle, R., Khalsa, S. S., & Stewart, J. L. (2022). Impact of serotonergic medication on interoception in major depressive disorder. *Biological Psychology, 169*, 108286. PMID: 35149138. https://doi.org/10.1016/j.biopsycho.2022.108286

Cahn, B. R., & Polich, J. (2006). Meditation states and traits: EEG, ERP, and neuroimaging studies. *Psychological Bulletin, 132*(2), 180–211. PMID: 16536641. https://doi.org/10.1037/0033-2909.132.2.180

Cahn, B. R., & Polich, J. (2009). Meditation (Vipassana) and the P3a event-related brain potential. *International Journal of Psychophysiology, 72*(1), 51–60. PMID: 18845193. https://doi.org/10.1016/j.ijpsycho.2008.03.013

Cahn, B. R., Goodman, M. S., Peterson, C. T., Maturi, R., & Mills, P. J. (2017). Yoga, meditation and mind-body health: Increased BDNF, cortisol awakening response, and altered inflammatory marker expression after a 3-month yoga and meditation retreat. *Frontiers in Human Neuroscience, 11*, 315. PMID: 28694775. https://doi.org/10.3389/fnhum.2017.00315

Cearns, M., & Clark, S. R. (2023). The effects of dose, practice habits, and objects of focus on digital meditation effectiveness and adherence: Longitudinal study of 280,000 digital meditation sessions across 103 countries. *Journal of Medical Internet Research, 25*, e43358. PMID: 37725801. https://doi.org/10.2196/43358

Coan, J. A., Schaefer, H. S., & Davidson, R. J. (2006). Lending a hand: Social regulation of the neural response to threat. *Psychological Science, 17*(12), 1032–1039. PMID: 17201784. https://doi.org/10.1111/j.1467-9280.2006.01832.x

Datta, K., Tripathi, M., Verma, M., Masiwal, D., & Mallick, H. N. (2021). Yoga nidra practice shows improvement in sleep in patients with chronic insomnia: A randomized controlled trial. *The National Medical Journal of India, 34*(3), 143–150. PMID: 34825538. https://doi.org/10.25259/NMJI_63_19

Davidson, R. J. (1992). Anterior cerebral asymmetry and the nature of emotion. *Brain and Cognition, 20*(1), 125–151. PMID: 1389117. https://doi.org/10.1016/0278-2626(92)90065-T

Davidson, R. J., & Hugdahl, K. (Eds.). (1995). *Brain Asymmetry.* MIT Press.

Davidson, R. J., Kabat-Zinn, J., Schumacher, J., Rosenkranz, M., Muller, D., Santorelli, S. F., … & Sheridan, J. F. (2003). Alterations in brain and immune function produced by mindfulness meditation. *Psychosomatic Medicine, 65*(4), 564–570. PMID: 12883106. https://doi.org/10.1097/01.PSY.0000077505.67574.E3

de Entrambasaguas, M., Díaz-Silveira, C., Burgos-Julián, F. A., & Santed, M. A. (2023). Can mindfulness-based interventions improve outcomes in cognitive-behavioural therapy for chronic insomnia disorder in the general population? A systematic review and meta-analysis. *Clinical Psychology & Psychotherapy, 30*(5), 965–978. PMID: 37271575. https://doi.org/10.1002/cpp.2874

De Lissnyder, E., Koster, E. H. W., Derakshan, N., & De Raedt, R. (2010). The association between depressive symptoms and executive control impairments in response to emotional and non-emotional information. *Cognition and Emotion, 24*(2), 264–280.

Desbordes, G., Negi, L. T., Pace, T. W. W., Wallace, B. A., Raison, C. L., & Schwartz, E. L. (2012). Effects of mindful-attention and compassion meditation training on amygdala response to emotional stimuli in an ordinary, non-meditative state. *Frontiers in Human Neuroscience, 6*, 292. https://doi.org/10.3389/fnhum.2012.00292

Duan, H., Fang, H., Zhang, Y., Shi, X., & Zhang, L. (2019). Associations between cortisol awakening response and resting electroencephalograph asymmetry. *PeerJ, 7*, e7059. PMID: 31198648. https://doi.org/10.7717/peerj.7059

Duncan, J. (2010). The multiple-demand (MD) system of the primate brain: Mental programs for intelligent behaviour. *Trends in Cognitive Sciences, 14*(4), 172–179. https://doi.org/10.1016/j.tics.2010.01.004

Engert, V., Kok, B. E., Papassotiriou, I., Chrousos, G. P., & Singer, T. (2017). Specific reduction in cortisol stress reactivity after social but not attention-based mental training. *Science Advances, 3*(10), e1700495. https://doi.org/10.1126/sciadv.1700495

Farias, M., Maraldi, E., Wallenkampf, K. C., & Lucchetti, G. (2020). Adverse events in meditation practices and meditation-based therapies: A systematic review. *Acta Psychiatrica Scandinavica, 142*(5), 374–393. PMID: 32820538. https://doi.org/10.1111/acps.13225

Ferrarelli, F., Smith, R., Dentico, D., Riedner, B. A., Zennig, C., Benca, R. M., Lutz, A., Davidson, R. J., & Tononi, G. (2013). Experienced mindfulness meditators exhibit higher parietal-occipital EEG gamma activity during NREM sleep. *PLOS ONE, 8*(8), e73417. https://doi.org/10.1371/journal.pone.0073417

Fissler, M., Winnebeck, E., Schroeter, T. A., Gummersbach, M., Huntenburg, J. M., Gaertner, M., & Barnhofer, T. (2017). Brief training in mindfulness may normalize a blunted error-related negativity in chronically depressed patients. *Cognitive, Affective, & Behavioral Neuroscience, 17*(6), 1164–1175. PMID: 28975567. https://doi.org/10.3758/s13415-017-0540-x

Fox, K. C. R., Dixon, M. L., Nijeboer, S., Girn, M., Floman, J. L., Lifshitz, M., Ellamil, M., Sedlmeier, P., & Christoff, K. (2016). Functional neuroanatomy of meditation: A review and meta-analysis of 78 functional neuroimaging investigations. *Neuroscience & Biobehavioral Reviews, 65*, 208–228. PMID: 27032724. https://doi.org/10.1016/j.neubiorev.2016.03.021

Goessl, V. C., Curtiss, J. E., & Hofmann, S. G. (2017). The effect of heart rate variability biofeedback training on stress and anxiety: A meta-analysis. *Psychological Medicine, 47*(15), 2578–2586. PMID: 28478782. https://doi.org/10.1017/S0033291717001003

Goldberg, S. B., Lam, S. U., Britton, W. B., & Davidson, R. J. (2022). Prevalence of meditation-related adverse effects in a population-based sample in the United States. *Psychotherapy Research, 32*(3), 291–305. PMID: 34074221. https://doi.org/10.1080/10503307.2021.1933646

Goyal, M., Singh, S., Sibinga, E. M. S., Gould, N. F., Rowland-Seymour, A., Sharma, R., et al. (2014). Meditation programs for psychological stress and well-being: A systematic review and meta-analysis. *JAMA Internal Medicine, 174*(3), 357–368. PMID: 24395196. https://doi.org/10.1001/jamainternmed.2013.13018

Grandy, T. H., Werkle-Bergner, M., Chicherio, C., Schmiedek, F., Lövdén, M., & Lindenberger, U. (2013). Peak individual alpha frequency qualifies as a stable neurophysiological trait marker in healthy younger and older adults. *Psychophysiology, 50*(6), 570–582. PMID: 23551082. https://doi.org/10.1111/psyp.12043

Hasenkamp, W., Wilson-Mendenhall, C. D., Duncan, E., & Barsalou, L. W. (2012). Mind wandering and attention during focused meditation: A fine-grained temporal analysis of fluctuating cognitive states. *NeuroImage, 59*(1), 750–760. PMID: 21782031. https://doi.org/10.1016/j.neuroimage.2011.07.008

Hölzel, B. K., Carmody, J., Evans, K. C., Hoge, E. A., Dusek, J. A., Morgan, L., Pitman, R. K., & Lazar, S. W. (2010). Stress reduction correlates with structural changes in the amygdala. *Social Cognitive and Affective Neuroscience, 5*(1), 11–17. PMID: 19776221. https://doi.org/10.1093/scan/nsp034

Hölzel, B. K., Carmody, J., Vangel, M., Congleton, C., Yerramsetti, S. M., Gard, T., & Lazar, S. W. (2011). Mindfulness practice leads to increases in regional brain gray matter density. *Psychiatry Research: Neuroimaging, 191*(1), 36–43. PMID: 21071182. https://doi.org/10.1016/j.pscychresns.2010.08.006

Ingendoh, R. M., Posny, E. S., & Heine, A. (2023). Binaural beats to entrain the brain? A systematic review of the effects of binaural beat stimulation on brain oscillatory activity, and the implications for psychological research and intervention. *PLOS ONE, 18*(5), e0286023. PMID: 37205669. https://doi.org/10.1371/journal.pone.0286023

Johnson, M. L., Bodenhamer-Davis, E., Bailey, L. J., & Gates, M. S. (2013). Spectral dynamics and therapeutic implications of the theta/alpha crossover in alpha-theta neurofeedback. *Journal of Neurotherapy, 17*(1), 3–34. https://doi.org/10.1080/10874208.2013.758968

Johnstone, J., Gunkelman, J., & Lunt, J. (2005). Clinical database development: Characterization of EEG phenotypes. *Clinical EEG and Neuroscience, 36*(2), 99–107. PMID: 15999905. https://doi.org/10.1177/155005940503600209

Kaul, P., Passafiume, J., Sargent, C. R., & O'Hara, B. F. (2010). Meditation acutely improves psychomotor vigilance, and may decrease sleep need. *Behavioral and Brain Functions, 6*, 47. PMID: 20670413. https://doi.org/10.1186/1744-9081-6-47

Khoury, B., Knäuper, B., Schlosser, M., Carrière, K., & Chiesa, A. (2017). Effectiveness of traditional meditation retreats: A systematic review and meta-analysis. *Journal of Psychosomatic Research, 92*, 16–25. PMID: 27998508. https://doi.org/10.1016/j.jpsychores.2016.11.006

Kirk, U., & Axelsen, J. L. (2020). Heart rate variability is enhanced during mindfulness practice: A randomized controlled trial involving a 10-day online-based mindfulness intervention. *PLOS ONE, 15*(12), e0243488. PMID: 33332403. https://doi.org/10.1371/journal.pone.0243488

Kleeva, K., Ninenko, I., & Lebedev, M. A. (2024). Resting-state EEG recorded with gel-based vs. consumer dry electrodes: Spectral characteristics and across-device correlations. *Frontiers in Neuroscience, 18*, 1326139. https://doi.org/10.3389/fnins.2024.1326139

Klein, R. M. (2000). Inhibition of return. *Trends in Cognitive Sciences, 4*(4), 138–147. https://doi.org/10.1016/S1364-6613(00)01452-2

Koenigs, M., & Grafman, J. (2009). The functional neuroanatomy of depression: Distinct roles for ventromedial and dorsolateral prefrontal cortex. *Behavioural Brain Research, 201*(2), 239–243. PMID: 19428640. https://doi.org/10.1016/j.bbr.2009.03.004

Kok, B. E., & Singer, T. (2017). Effects of contemplative dyads on engagement and perceived social connectedness over 9 months of mental training: A randomized clinical trial. *JAMA Psychiatry, 74*(2), 126–134. PMID: 28030741. https://doi.org/10.1001/jamapsychiatry.2016.3360

Kosterman Zoller, B., Bögels, S. M., Meppelink, R., & de Bruin, E. I. (2025). Methylphenidate or family mindfulness? Effects on internalizing, externalizing and social problems in children with attention deficit hyperactivity disorder. *Children, 12*(6), 681. PMID: 40564639. https://doi.org/10.3390/children12060681

Kral, T. R. A., Davis, K., Korponay, C., Hirshberg, M. J., Hoel, R., Tello, L. Y., Goldman, R. I., Rosenkranz, M. A., Lutz, A., & Davidson, R. J. (2022). Absence of structural brain changes from mindfulness-based stress reduction: Two combined randomized controlled trials. *Science Advances, 8*(20), eabk3316. PMID: 35594344. https://doi.org/10.1126/sciadv.abk3316

Lake, J. I., LaBar, K. S., & Meck, W. H. (2016). Emotional modulation of interval timing and time perception. *Neuroscience & Biobehavioral Reviews, 64*, 403–420. PMID: 26972824. https://doi.org/10.1016/j.neubiorev.2016.03.003

Lally, P., van Jaarsveld, C. H. M., Potts, H. W. W., & Wardle, J. (2009). How are habits formed: Modelling habit formation in the real world. *European Journal of Social Psychology, 40*(6), 998–1009. https://doi.org/10.1002/ejsp.674

Lampert, R., Ickovics, J. R., Viscoli, C. J., Horwitz, R. I., & Lee, F. A. (2003). Effects of propranolol on recovery of heart rate variability following acute myocardial infarction and relation to outcome in the Beta-Blocker Heart Attack Trial. *The American Journal of Cardiology, 91*(2), 137–142. PMID: 12521623. https://doi.org/10.1016/S0002-9149(02)03098-9

Lehrer, P. M., & Gevirtz, R. (2014). Heart rate variability biofeedback: How and why does it work? *Frontiers in Psychology, 5*, 756. PMID: 25101026. https://doi.org/10.3389/fpsyg.2014.00756

Lieberman, M. D., Eisenberger, N. I., Crockett, M. J., Tom, S. M., Pfeifer, J. H., & Way, B. M. (2007). Putting feelings into words: Affect labeling disrupts amygdala activity in response to affective stimuli. *Psychological Science, 18*(5), 421–428. PMID: 17576282. https://doi.org/10.1111/j.1467-9280.2007.01916.x

Lin, Y., Eckerle, W. D., Peng, L. W., & Moser, J. S. (2019). On variation in mindfulness training: A multimodal study of brief open monitoring meditation on error monitoring. *Brain Sciences, 9*(9), 226. PMID: 31500201. https://doi.org/10.3390/brainsci9090226

Lindahl, J. R., Fisher, N. E., Cooper, D. J., Rosen, R. K., & Britton, W. B. (2017). The varieties of contemplative experience: A mixed-methods study of meditation-related challenges in Western Buddhists. *PLOS ONE, 12*(5), e0176239. https://doi.org/10.1371/journal.pone.0176239

Lipszyc, J., & Schachar, R. (2010). Inhibitory control and psychopathology: A meta-analysis of studies using the stop signal task. *Journal of the International Neuropsychological Society, 16*(6), 1064–1076. PMID: 20719043. https://doi.org/10.1017/S1355617710000895

Lisman, J. E., & Jensen, O. (2013). The theta-gamma neural code. *Neuron, 77*(6), 1002–1016. PMID: 23522038. https://doi.org/10.1016/j.neuron.2013.03.007

Logemann-Molnár, Z., Veres-Székely, A., Demetrovics, Z., & Logemann, H. N. A. (2024). Mindfulness and inhibitory control: Insights from the stop signal task with neutral and reward-associated stimuli. *PLOS ONE, 19*(5), e0303384. PMID: 38776292. https://doi.org/10.1371/journal.pone.0303384

Lomas, T., Cartwright, T., Edginton, T., & Ridge, D. (2015). A qualitative analysis of experiential challenges associated with meditation practice. *Mindfulness, 6*(4), 848–860. https://doi.org/10.1007/s12671-014-0329-8

Lomas, T., Ivtzan, I., & Fu, C. H. Y. (2015). A systematic review of the neurophysiology of mindfulness on EEG oscillations. *Neuroscience & Biobehavioral Reviews, 57*, 401–410. PMID: 26441373. https://doi.org/10.1016/j.neubiorev.2015.09.018

Lutz, A., Greischar, L. L., Rawlings, N. B., Ricard, M., & Davidson, R. J. (2004). Long-term meditators self-induce high-amplitude gamma synchrony during mental practice. *Proceedings of the National Academy of Sciences, 101*(46), 16369-16373. https://doi.org/10.1073/pnas.0407401101

Lutz, A., Slagter, H. A., Dunne, J. D., & Davidson, R. J. (2008). Attention regulation and monitoring in meditation. *Trends in Cognitive Sciences, 12*(4), 163–169. PMID: 18329323. https://doi.org/10.1016/j.tics.2008.01.005

MacLean, K. A., Ferrer, E., Aichele, S. R., Bridwell, D. A., Zanesco, A. P., Jacobs, T. L., et al. (2010). Intensive meditation training improves perceptual discrimination and sustained attention. *Psychological Science, 21*(6), 829–839. PMID: 20483826. https://doi.org/10.1177/0956797610371339

Menon, V. (2011). Large-scale brain networks and psychopathology: A unifying triple network model. *Trends in Cognitive Sciences, 15*(10), 483–494. https://doi.org/10.1016/j.tics.2011.08.003

Mierau, A., Klimesch, W., & Lefebvre, J. (2017). State-dependent alpha peak frequency shifts: Experimental evidence, potential mechanisms and functional implications. *Neuroscience, 360*, 146–154. PMID: 28739525. https://doi.org/10.1016/j.neuroscience.2017.07.037

Nicholson, A. A., Ros, T., Densmore, M., Frewen, P. A., Neufeld, R. W. J., Théberge, J., Jetly, R., & Lanius, R. A. (2020). A randomized, controlled trial of alpha-rhythm EEG neurofeedback in posttraumatic stress disorder: A preliminary investigation showing evidence of decreased PTSD symptoms and restored default mode and salience network connectivity using fMRI. *NeuroImage: Clinical, 28*, 102490. PMID: 33395981. https://doi.org/10.1016/j.nicl.2020.102490

Norris, C. J., Creem, D., Hendler, R., & Kober, H. (2018). Brief mindfulness meditation improves attention in novices: Evidence from ERPs and moderation by neuroticism. *Frontiers in Human Neuroscience, 12*, 315. PMID: 30127731. https://doi.org/10.3389/fnhum.2018.00315

Ortner, C. N. M., Kilner, S. J., & Zelazo, P. D. (2007). Mindfulness meditation and reduced emotional interference on a cognitive task. *Motivation and Emotion, 31*(4), 271–283. https://doi.org/10.1007/s11031-007-9076-7

Posner, M. I., & Cohen, Y. (1984). Components of visual orienting. In H. Bouma & D. G. Bouwhuis (Eds.), *Attention and Performance X* (pp. 531–556). Erlbaum.

Riesel, A., Goldhahn, S., & Kathmann, N. (2017). Hyperactive performance monitoring as a transdiagnostic marker: Results from health anxiety in comparison to obsessive-compulsive disorder. *Neuropsychologia, 96*, 1–8. PMID: 28041946. https://doi.org/10.1016/j.neuropsychologia.2016.12.029

Rodriguez-Larios, J., & Alaerts, K. (2019). Tracking transient changes in the neural frequency architecture: Harmonic relationships between theta and alpha peaks facilitate cognitive performance. *Journal of Neuroscience, 39*(32), 6291–6298. PMID: 31175211. https://doi.org/10.1523/JNEUROSCI.2919-18.2019

Ronconi, L., Busch, N. A., & Melcher, D. (2018). Alpha-band sensory entrainment alters the duration of temporal windows in visual perception. *Scientific Reports, 8*, 11810. https://doi.org/10.1038/s41598-018-29671-5

Saggar, M., King, B. G., Zanesco, A. P., MacLean, K. A., Aichele, S. R., Jacobs, T. L., Bridwell, D. A., Shaver, P. R., Rosenberg, E. L., Sahdra, B. K., Ferrer, E., Tang, A. C., Mangun, G. R., Wallace, B. A., Miikkulainen, R., & Saron, C. D. (2012). Intensive training induces longitudinal changes in meditation state-related EEG oscillatory activity. *Frontiers in Human Neuroscience, 6*, 256. PMID: 22973218. https://doi.org/10.3389/fnhum.2012.00256

Samaha, J., & Postle, B. R. (2015). The speed of alpha-band oscillations predicts the temporal resolution of visual perception. *Current Biology, 25*(22), 2985–2990. https://doi.org/10.1016/j.cub.2015.10.007

Schlosser, M., Sparby, T., Vörös, S., Jones, R., & Marchant, N. L. (2019). Unpleasant meditation-related experiences in regular meditators: Prevalence, predictors, and conceptual considerations. *PLOS ONE, 14*(5), e0216643. https://doi.org/10.1371/journal.pone.0216643

Segal, Z. V., Williams, J. M. G., & Teasdale, J. D. (2002). *Mindfulness-Based Cognitive Therapy for Depression: A New Approach to Preventing Relapse.* Guilford Press.

Shamay-Tsoory, S. G., Aharon-Peretz, J., & Perry, D. (2009). Two systems for empathy: A double dissociation between emotional and cognitive empathy in inferior frontal gyrus versus ventromedial prefrontal lesions. *Brain, 132*(3), 617–627. https://doi.org/10.1093/brain/awn279

Sihn, D., Kim, J., & Kim, S.-P. (2024). Meditation-type specific reduction in infra-slow activity of electroencephalogram. *Biomedical Engineering Letters, 14*(4), 823–831. https://doi.org/10.1007/s13534-024-00377-0

Skwara, A. C., King, B. G., Zanesco, A. P., & Saron, C. D. (2022). Shifting baselines: Longitudinal reductions in EEG beta band power characterize resting brain activity with intensive meditation. *Mindfulness, 13*(10), 2488–2506. https://doi.org/10.1007/s12671-022-01974-9

Slagter, H. A., Lutz, A., Greischar, L. L., Francis, A. D., Nieuwenhuis, S., Davis, J. M., & Davidson, R. J. (2007). Mental training affects distribution of limited brain resources. *PLoS Biology, 5*(6), e138. PMID: 17488185.

Sterman, M. B., Wyrwicka, W., & Howe, R. (1969). Behavioral and neurophysiological studies of the sensorimotor rhythm in the cat. *Electroencephalography and Clinical Neurophysiology, 27*(6), 678–689. PMID: 4187331. https://doi.org/10.1016/0013-4694(69)91281-4

Sterman, M. B. (1996). Physiological origins and functional correlates of EEG rhythmic activities: Implications for self-regulation. *Biofeedback and Self-Regulation, 21*(1), 3–33. https://doi.org/10.1007/BF02214147

Tang, Y.-Y., Lu, Q., Geng, X., Stein, E. A., Yang, Y., & Posner, M. I. (2010). Short-term meditation induces white matter changes in the anterior cingulate. *PNAS, 107*(35), 15649–15652. PMID: 20713717. https://doi.org/10.1073/pnas.1011043107

Tang, Y.-Y., Hölzel, B. K., & Posner, M. I. (2015). The neuroscience of mindfulness meditation. *Nature Reviews Neuroscience, 16*(4), 213–225. https://doi.org/10.1038/nrn3916

Taren, A. A., Gianaros, P. J., Greco, C. M., Lindsay, E. K., Fairgrieve, A., Brown, K. W., … & Creswell, J. D. (2015). Mindfulness meditation training alters stress-related amygdala resting state functional connectivity: A randomized controlled trial. *Social Cognitive and Affective Neuroscience, 10*(12), 1758–1768. PMID: 26048176. https://doi.org/10.1093/scan/nsv066

Teper, R., & Inzlicht, M. (2013). Meditation, mindfulness and executive control: The importance of emotional acceptance and brain-based performance monitoring. *Social Cognitive and Affective Neuroscience, 8*(1), 85–92. PMID: 22507824.

Torsvall, L., & Åkerstedt, T. (1987). Sleepiness on the job: Continuously measured EEG changes in train drivers. *Electroencephalography and Clinical Neurophysiology, 66*(6), 502–511. PMID: 2438115. https://doi.org/10.1016/0013-4694(87)90096-4

Treleaven, D. A. (2018). *Trauma-Sensitive Mindfulness: Practices for Safe and Transformative Healing.* W. W. Norton.

Treves, I. N., Greene, K. D., Bajwa, Z., Wool, E., Kim, N., Bauer, C. C. C., Bloom, P. A., Pagliaccio, D., Zhang, J., Whitfield-Gabrieli, S., & Auerbach, R. P. (2024). Mindfulness-based neurofeedback: A systematic review of EEG and fMRI studies. *Imaging Neuroscience, 2*, 1–28. https://doi.org/10.1162/imag_a_00396

Valk, S. L., Bernhardt, B. C., Trautwein, F.-M., Böckler, A., Kanske, P., Guizard, N., et al. (2017). Structural plasticity of the social brain: Differential change after socio-affective and cognitive mental training. *Science Advances, 3*(10), e1700489. https://doi.org/10.1126/sciadv.1700489

Van Dam, N. T., van Vugt, M. K., Vago, D. R., Schmalzl, L., Saron, C. D., Olendzki, A., et al. (2018). Mind the hype: A critical evaluation and prescriptive agenda for research on mindfulness and meditation. *Perspectives on Psychological Science, 13*(1), 36–61. PMID: 29016274. https://doi.org/10.1177/1745691617709589

van der Kolk, B. A., Hodgdon, H., Gapen, M., Musicaro, R., Suvak, M. K., Hamlin, E., & Spinazzola, J. (2016). A randomized controlled study of neurofeedback for chronic PTSD. *PLOS ONE, 11*(12), e0166752. https://doi.org/10.1371/journal.pone.0166752

Verdejo-García, A., Clark, L., & Dunn, B. D. (2012). The role of interoception in addiction: A critical review. *Neuroscience & Biobehavioral Reviews, 36*(8), 1857–1869. PMID: 22659642. https://doi.org/10.1016/j.neubiorev.2012.05.007

Zanesco, A. P., King, B. G., MacLean, K. A., & Saron, C. D. (2013). Executive control and felt concentrative engagement following intensive meditation training. *Frontiers in Human Neuroscience, 7*, 566. PMID: 24065902. https://doi.org/10.3389/fnhum.2013.00566

Zanesco, A. P., King, B. G., MacLean, K. A., & Saron, C. D. (2018). Cognitive aging and long-term maintenance of attentional improvements following meditation training. *Journal of Cognitive Enhancement, 2*(3), 259–275. https://doi.org/10.1007/s41465-018-0068-1

Zylowska, L., Ackerman, D. L., Yang, M. H., Futrell, J. L., Horton, N. L., Hale, T. S., Pataki, C., & Smalley, S. L. (2008). Mindfulness meditation training in adults and adolescents with ADHD: A feasibility study. *Journal of Attention Disorders, 11*(6), 737–746. PMID: 18025249. https://doi.org/10.1177/1087054707308502

What This Framework Predicts

Chapters 1 and 12 name three nested claims the book is making. This section states what a trial would need to measure to test them.

The central claim is a matching claim: for a brain with a given dominant phenotype, the matched-chapter practice beats an unmatched one or a standard breath-and-sit protocol. It decomposes into three sub-claims with different evidentiary standards.

Claim 1: Engineering claim (strongest). Routing a meditation-failure patient to a phenotype-matched practice via the Decision Tree produces better subjective fit, faster habit formation, and lower early dropout than a default protocol. This is an adherence claim, not an efficacy claim: it asks only that the path to a working habit be shorter and less painful, not that twelve-month outcomes differ. Test it with a two-arm randomized study, Decision Tree routing versus standard MBSR-style assignment in a phenotype-screened population, primary outcome session-completion rate at eight weeks, about 120 per arm.

Claim 2: Harm-reduction claim (moderate evidence). For some phenotypes, especially the Lifeguard and Princess, standard unmatched practice (eyes-closed, prolonged sitting, full-body scan) produces adverse events at higher rates than matched alternatives. The literature supports adverse events at the population level (Farias et al., 2020; Lindahl et al., 2017; Schlosser et al., 2019); the phenotype-specific attribution is clinical inference. Test it by adding a phenotype-by-practice interaction term and pre-specified adverse-event reporting to the design above, predicting more Yellow and Red events for Lifeguards in the unmatched arm.

Claim 3: Efficacy claim (weakest, not yet tested). Matched practice produces larger or more durable regulation gains, measured at twelve months on resting HRV, attention metrics, and dysregulation symptom scales. Test it with a three-arm trial (matched, mismatched, MBSR control; about 80 per arm, QEEG-screened, six-month follow-up), with adherence pre-specified as a mediator, since Claim 1 predicts any efficacy edge runs through adherence rather than a direct mechanism.

The book bets most confidently on Claim 1, diverges most sharply from standard advice on Claim 2, and states Claim 3 plainly so a future trial knows what would refute it.

Where PMID numbers are provided, citations can be verified at pubmed.ncbi.nlm.nih.gov. For studies without PMID, search by author, year, and journal title.

What you're feeling → where to go

Triage card (17 rows). Full reference: Symptom → Practice Lookup, back matter.

What You're Feeling	Practice	Ch.
Can't make yourself start	Walk 10 mindful steps	**4**
Impulsive, can't stop	Insight / Nonreactive Attention	**4**
Falling asleep, foggy	Eyes-Open Standing Awareness	**5**
Dread, "what's the point"	Vagal Toning (4-in, 6-out)	**6**
Flat, no spark, nothing pulls	Curiosity Meditation	**6**
"Don't tell me what to do"	Choice-Based Practice	**6**
Scanning for threat	Grounding: "Is this now?"	**7**
"Am I doing this right?"	Structured-to-Open Transition	**7**
Sensory overwhelm	Sensory Sanctuary	**8**
Tone of voice feels threatening	Non-Verbal Practice	**8**
Narrator won't stop	Mantra Redirect	**9**
Everything too fast	Rapid Noting	**10**
Everything too slow	Self-Paced Concentration	**10**
Multiple patterns competing	Loudest-first rule	**11**
Feeling worse after practice	Stop Signal + modify or stop	**16**
Can't sleep	Structured Worry Dump	**7**
Don't know where to start	Start walking	**4**

If nothing fits, do this:

Feet on floor. In for 4, out for 6. *"I'm allowed to be here."*

You came back. That's enough.

About the Author

Andrew Hill, PhD, is a cognitive neuroscientist and the founder of Peak Brain Institute in Los Angeles, with offices in St. Louis and West Palm Beach. He holds a PhD in Cognitive Neuroscience from UCLA, where he also lectured in the Department of Psychology.

He started reading brain maps in 2000, first in clinical settings before graduate school, then running research subjects through EEG protocols at UCLA, then building his own practice. For his doctoral research he developed a double-blind sham neurofeedback protocol, showing that real neurofeedback produces measurable brain responses that sham controls do not.

Twenty-five years of clinical practice and more than 25,000 brain maps have given him a front-row seat to the ways different brains succeed and fail at self-regulation, and the specific meditation practices that work for each. What he cares about most isn't using a brain map as a diagnostic label. It's teaching people to read their own patterns, connect them to their experience, and understand what is actually trainable and why.

He hosts the *Head First* podcast and has been a guest on more than 100 podcasts discussing attention, regulation, meditation, and the neuroscience of performance. He is a member of the International Society for Neuroregulation and Research (ISNR).

He lives in Los Angeles with too many screens, not enough sleep, and a brain that still benefits from 20 minutes of eyes-closed practice most mornings.

Also from Peak Brain Press

Half a Second More is part of the Peak Brain Press portfolio:

- *Gifted & Tortured*

- *Neurofeedback Explained* (with Madeleine McCann)
- *The QEEG Field Guide* (with Jonathon Lomeli)
- *Your Brain on Drugs*
- *Your Brain on Trauma*
- *The Dynamic Brain*
- *Borrowed Peace*

Peak Brain Institute: peakbraininstitute.com

Head First podcast: available wherever you listen

One Last Thing

If any of this helped, take the free **Companion Kit** with you: the twelve printable Practice Cards, the 90-Second Reset, and the full Symptom to Practice guide.

Scan with your phone's camera

or visit **peakbrainpress.com/hasm-bonus**

Your mind will wander. Come back. Count the return.